Exploring Glasgow

Exploring
Glasgow

The Architectural Guide

Robin Ward

BIRLINN

First published in 2017 by Birlinn Limited

West Newington House, 10 Newington Road, Edinburgh EH9 1QS

www.birlinn.co.uk

ISBN 978 1 78027 454 6

British Library Cataloguing-in-Publication Data

A catalogue record for this book is available from the British Library

Designed and typeset in Minion and Myriad by Robin Ward

Printed and bound in Latvia by PNB Print Ltd

Title page: *Rococo plasterwork, St. Andrew's in the Square*

Contents

City Chambers, marble staircase

Introduction

IN THE EARLY 1980s I met Lord Provost Michael Kelly in the City
Chambers. My publisher then, Richard Drew, was promoting a book,
The Spirit of Glasgow, which I was writing and illustrating with photographs. At the time Glasgow was not thought worth the bother. Drew
was keen to show we knew it was.

Kelly said the book was a great idea, until he saw the photos. He liked
those of Kelvingrove Park, the Art Galleries . . . but when I showed him
a sunset shot of cranes at Fairfield shipyard, Govan and said it might
be the cover picture for the book he was shocked. 'Cranes? Shipyards?
Sunset? And it's red. Red Clydeside! That's not the image we want.' My
reaction was to put the picturesque Victorian skyline of Park Towers
on the cover but to make the inside more moody than it had been. The
book was not for tourists, most of whom headed for Edinburgh or the
Highlands, but for Glaswegians. It showed an illustrious Victorian city
with architecture to match trapped in faded grandeur, shipyards and all.

Kelly was a big-city mayor on a mission and he was right. Glasgow's
slide from being a world-beating industrial centre to irrelevance seemed
terminal. Shipbuilding, and nostalgia for it, was not a way out. The
city's economy had to change and the reputation as a depressed, violent
post-industrial slum with it. The sun would rise over a new Glasgow, a
confident city of culture reconciled with its past, which is what has happened and is the city *Exploring Glasgow* is about.

Around 1900 Glasgow had over one million people. Boosters called it 'The Second City of the Empire', a city-state of civic and commercial enterprise with arts and industries second to none. International exhibitions at Kelvingrove Park in 1888 and 1901, and the Scottish National Exhibition of 1911, showed it at the height of its power. This was still evident in 1938 at the Empire Exhibition in Bellahouston Park, but in the 1950s imperial markets were lost. The mercantile *palazzi* in the Victorian city centre stood like ghosts from glory days. Shipyards and factories closed. Postwar public housing replaced 19th-century tenement slums. Planners 'decanted' people to peripheral housing schemes and new towns. The population was reduced to 600,000 (the city region is around two million). Industrial decline and unemployment turned many of those Utopian schemes from hope to despair. The old tenements, typically four-storeys with common stairs (called closes), each block integrated with the street but enclosing an inner courtyard, gave the city its characteristic, coherent urban form and sense of community. Those which remain have been refurbished. New housing, the best by architects for housing associations, reworks the tenement typology.

It was 50 years before another expo was held. The 1988 Glasgow Garden Festival on repurposed docklands altered perceptions and encouraged investment. The post-industrial revival began in 1983 when the Burrell Collection opened in a purpose-built gallery in Pollok Park. It had what's now called 'the Bilbao effect', after the down-at-heel Basque city became trendy when a Guggenheim museum opened in 1997. The Burrell put Glasgow on the cultural tourist trail, a novelty which Glaswegians, whose humour is tuned to the absurd, would previously have thought a joke. In 1990, Glasgow was the first city in the UK to host Doors Open Day, part of European Heritage Days. The awards of European City of Culture 1990 and UK City of Architecture & Design 1999, and hosting the UEFA Champions League Final 2002, continued an upward trend that led to the city being chosen to host the 2014 Commonwealth Games.

Glasgow made the shift from rust belt to recovery by smart marketing. It has a solid cultural foundation—Victorian architecture, art galleries, theatres, music—and a can-do attitude. It is outward-looking but with a feisty sense of place. A home-grown architect, Charles Rennie Mackintosh, promoted by the tourist board and marketing bureau, became a pin-up of the revival. His unique style of Art Nouveau was perfect to compete in the image-is-everything league of cities hungry for urban regeneration. The popular narrative that he was an unsung genius was a bonus. He worked for Honeyman & Keppie, an established practice, studied at Glasgow School of Art and designed its new building (1897–1909), a masterpiece now famed worldwide. In 1900 he became a celebrity among the avant-garde at the Vienna Secession where he exhibited. Back home he had a handful of clients who appreciated his maverick talent, but the Glasgow Style which he led went out of vogue. In 1914 he left Honeyman & Keppie and ended up in the South of France, painting watercolours. His legacy was generally ignored outside academe until the Charles Rennie Mackintosh Society was formed in 1973 to rescue it from obscurity. He is now as well known to Glaswegians and visitors as Gaudí is in Barcelona.

Glasgow's other star architect was Alexander 'Greek' Thomson. His buildings took the 19th-century Greek Revival out of its comfort zone, were structurally advanced and decorated exotically. Like Mackintosh most of his work is in Glasgow. Admiration of him among peers was unqualified but his work has since been overshadowed by Mackintosh despite efforts by devotees to save it from neglect. Photographs portray him as a formidable Victorian. Mackintosh was a dreamer and looks young, raffish and bohemian.

In *fin-de-siècle* Glasgow, wealth and the desire of its creators to display it supported a design community of artists, sculptors and architects whose outlook was both Scottish and cosmopolitan. The architect whose work best expresses the city's buccaneering capitalism was John James (J.J.) Burnet. He joined his father's practice in 1882, studied at the École des Beaux-Arts, Paris and travelled in France and Italy. In Glasgow he made his mark with a blustery but sophisticated baroque style which incorporated modern structural techniques after he visited North America in 1896. Any list of top ten buildings in the city would have to feature his Clyde Navigation Trust Building, along with Thomson's St. Vincent Street Church and Mackintosh's Glasgow School of Art. For seven others? Readers of this book can judge.

GLASGOW has a dense downtown grid but sprawls out from it on both banks of the River Clyde. *Exploring Glasgow*'s ten chapters, structured as tours around the city, reveal a representative variety of buildings, old and new. The routes are focussed on the accessibility of the city centre, inner city neighbourhoods, arterial roads and the river. They are organised for walking, cycling and public transit—the subway, urban rail and bus routes. Many entries are a short walk from stations, which are marked on maps. Entries are numbered and keyed to the maps; the area covered by each tour is shown on a map of the metropolitan area.

'Look up', people say of Glasgow because there are many fascinating buildings. Not all could be included here. In the city there are over 1800 buildings listed by Historic Environment Scotland as having architectural and historical interest. *Exploring Glasgow* is a portable guide so some hard choices had to be made. I don't expect every reader to agree with all of them and confess to including personal favourites among the 485 entries citywide. These are featured for their design excellence, heritage and cultural interest, engineering, eco-friendliness; or because they reveal urban trends or social and political histories. All have been visited and photographed. The selection is restricted to those which are public, i.e., those which can be entered, or viewed and photographed from the street. Each entry features the building's name, the street it is on, the architect(s) where known and the date of completion. Start dates of construction are noted where projects have taken more than a few years to complete. Some entries feature more than one building, highlighted in the text. The names cited for historic buildings are mostly the original ones; current names are given for contemporary buildings or where there has been significant adaptive reuse. Design awards are too numerous for all to be mentioned here. Some buildings certified BREEAM (Building Research Establishment Environmental Assessment Methodology), meaning 'green', eco-friendly are featured. The use of technical terms has been kept to a minimum; for a glossary of architectural terms, *www.lookingatbuildings.org.uk* is recommended. There is a short selection of source material. Entries are indexed, not by page but by the entry numbers under which they can be found.

GLASGOW SCHOOL OF ART was where I caught the architecture bug, as a first year student in a studio above the Library. I graduated in graphic design but it was Mackintosh's building that stayed with me. I was also fortunate to meet Lesley Duncan, then Saturday features editor at *The Herald*, who encouraged me to write and illustrate with sketches a weekly architectural column for the paper. This book would not have happened without those formative experiences. I thank my wife Porta and publisher Hugh Andrew, editorial manager Andrew Simmons and their colleagues at Birlinn. Thanks also to architects and other professionals who responded to my research enquiries, and to the people of Glasgow. The best way to get to know them and the city is on the streets, for which this guide is intended.

—Robin Ward 2017

Riverside Museum

1

Govan to Glasgow Green

IN FAIRFIELD HERITAGE CENTRE is a painting, *The Fairfield Fleet*, showing warships built by the Fairfield Shipbuilding and Engineering Company of Govan steaming in fantasy formation in 1907. The painting promoted the firm at a time when shipbuilding on the River Clyde was cresting a wave. At the industry's peak in 1913 Clydeside yards built around 20 percent of the world's tonnage.

'The Clyde made Glasgow and Glasgow made the Clyde' the saying goes. It refers to the city's enterprising merchants and inventive engineers and their project, begun in the 18th century, to create a 20-mile channel deep enough for ocean-going ships to reach the city. Enormous docks were excavated and lined with stone. Slipways where big ships could be built and launched were laid. Coal and iron ore mined in the West of Scotland supplied Glasgow's foundries and shipyards with raw materials. Production at Fairfields included liners for Canadian Pacific and Cunard, warships and even a steam-yacht for Tsar Alexander II of Russia. The yard was the largest among 16 which lined the river from Yorkhill to Dalmuir and around the same number downstream as far as Greenock. They included Alexander Stephen, Barclay & Curle, Beardmore, John Brown, Fergusons, Scotts and Lithgows.

The names sound tough, the work was and so were the tens of thousands of men who did it. A network of skilled trades—iron founders, steel workers, boiler makers, carpenters and many others—supplied the

yards and depended on them. Almost all of that is now history. The loss
of empire, shifting patterns of global trade, foreign competition and
squabbles between management and labour were the reefs on which the
shipbuilders foundered. By the 1980s most yards had closed leaving rust-
ing debris in a post-industrial landscape of epic desolation.

Now there is a new fleet on the Clyde. Its ships are architectural
icons launched to stimulate urban renewal. The first was the Scottish
Exhibition and Conference Centre (SECC), a sprawl of sheds and a high-
rise hotel, built in the mid 1980s on Queen's Dock which was filled
with rubble as a foundation for it. In the late 1990s the Bilbao effect—
the flashy architectural gesture of regeneration—had civic boosters
climbing aboard to revitalise the river, its economy and image abroad.
Masterplans were commissioned and 'starchitects' courted for iconic designs—the Clyde Auditorium, Riverside Museum and the Hydro.
Waterfront walkways have been extended but their fragmented hin-
terlands are a long-term challenge, despite efforts by the multi-agency
Clyde Waterfront strategic partnership (2003–2014). As architect David
Chipperfield said of his BBC Scotland Headquarters, the building was
an attempt to bring a sense of place to a zone which looked 'as if it might
blow away with the first gust of wind.'

The wind-blown community of Govan has no need for new icons—it
has old ones, a collection of ancient carved stones in the parish church.
Govan is one of the oldest Christian settlements in Scotland, a seat of
the royal court of Strathclyde during the Viking period (a ceremonial
mound called Doomster Hill survived into the 19th century). The community was home to farmers, salmon fishers, ferrymen and weavers
centred around the church and a row of cottages at Govan Ferry before
shipbuilding shifted the economy in the mid 19th century. When Govan
gained burgh status in 1864 the population was around 9,000 people; by
1912, when it was annexed by Glasgow, that figure was nearly 100,000.

Govan area's population now is just over 30,000.

Despite depopulation and deprivation since the 1960s Govan has retained its identity and pride in its industry. The forest of cranes at Fairfields has been clear-cut but the yard (with Yarrows across the river) remains open, operated by BAE Systems which fabricates Royal Navy warships in huge, climate controlled sheds. Shipbuilding is no longer the biggest employer; that status belongs to Queen Elizabeth Hospital opened in 2015. The office building at Fairfields has been converted as a business and heritage centre. Housing association dwellings fill gap sites and tenements have been refurbished. Govan Cross became a conservation area in 2008 and there is a heritage trail.

Regeneration has rebranded the Clyde. Glasgow Harbour is not for ships, only a name on a masterplan for the redevelopment of derelict docklands west of the SECC. The BBC Scotland building is part of a media village called Pacific Quay, site of the 1988 Glasgow Garden Festival. The name has no historical significance—ships sailed from the quay to the Caribbean and North America, not to the Pacific rim. Understandably the previous name, Plantation, was erased, slavery on sugar and cotton plantations which supplied the city's mills with raw materials not being a marketable memory. Atlantic Quay is the tag of the International Financial Services District, a zone conspicuous in its lack of diversity. The common name is Broomielaw, where engineer Henry Bell on his steamboat *Comet* arrived in 1812 from Port Glasgow, pioneering steam navigation on the Clyde. Broomielaw became the departure point for subsequent services on the river and the west coast.

Atlantic Quay at least evokes Glasgow's trading traditions, as do the remaining industrial structures and heritage buildings along the river. These range from the colossal Finnieston Crane to Merchants Steeple (at the upper reach of navigation near Glasgow Green) from where the city's early 19th-century traders could watch their ships come in.

1

Fairfield Shipyard Offices
1048 Govan Road

Honeyman & Keppie architects 1891;
ADF Architects, Page\Park Architects,
Tom Sneddon Architect 2014

Fairfields was Govan's most famous
industrial enterprise, a paragon of
Clydebuilt quality, the largest shipyard
on the river. It evolved from Randolph,
Elder & Co., a marine engineering
partnership forged in 1854. The Govan
yard opened in 1864 on the site of
Fairfield Farm. In 1886 it was named
Fairfield Shipbuilding and Engineering
by new owner William Pearce, and this
Italianate office was commissioned.

Carved figures *(James Pittendrigh
Macgillivray sculptor)* of an engineer
and a shipwright each stand on a ship's
prow flanking the entrance, where
mermaids languish below a sea god on
the keystone. Neptune is on the frieze
above. The engineer and shipwright

are similar to the figures on the Govan
coat of arms and symbolise its motto,
Nihil sine labore (Nothing without
work). The east tower overlooks the
gate where hundreds of men hurried
out, like a football crowd, when the
yard's siren sounded the end of their
shifts.

Solidarity steered the work-in which
saved the yard from closure in 1971.
That spirit started the campaign to
save the building after it was vacated
by BAE Systems in 2001. In 2009 owner
Clydeport sold it to Govan Workspace,
which was raising funds to rehabilitate
it as leasable office space and as a heritage centre now open.

A palatial lobby led to managers'
offices and a boardroom; skylit upstairs
spaces were drawing offices where the
thousands of plans for every ship were
produced. These historic interiors have
been kept and the building is again at
the heart of the community.

2

John Elder Monument
Elder Park
Joseph Edgar Boehm sculptor 1888
On a granite pedestal, the bronze
figure of engineer and shipbuilder John
Elder with a compound steam engine,
his invention. More efficient than
conventional engines it gave shipbuilders on the Clyde a competitive edge.
Inscriptions on the pedestal testify to
his fame—'He effected a revolution
in engineering second only to that of
James Watt'—and 'efforts to promote
the welfare of the working classes [and]
services to the community among
whom he lived.' The monument was
erected by public subscription.

Elder Park was laid out by architect
John Honeyman. Also here is a statue
*(Archibald Macfarlane Shannan sculp-
tor 1906)* of John Elder's widow Isabella
who inherited his shipyard after he
died in 1869. In 1883 she bought for
the people of Govan farmland to create
the park, opened in 1885 in memory
of him.

3

Elder Park Library
228 Langlands Road
J. J. (John James) Burnet 1903

Another gift to Govan from Isabella
Elder, opened officially by Scottish-
American steel baron and patron of
public libraries Andrew Carnegie. The
style is Beaux-Arts. The colonnaded
curving porch and a dome bring civic
presence to the single-storey structure;
the rear elevation has twin chateauesque pavilions. A sculpted rendering
of Govan's coat of arms greets citizens
at the entrance, which leads to an interior with fine plasterwork and a plaque
recording Isabella Elder's generosity.

4

The Italian Portico
Elder Park
A classical ruin like an 18th-century
garden folly, with curving stairs, Ionic
columns and pediment. These were the
entrance to Linthouse Mansion (1791),

bought by shipbuilder Alexander Stephen in 1869 and used as his shipyard office. It was demolished in 1920 and the portico relocated to the park. Stephen had built a new office (1914) which still stands, refurbished (1996) by Govan Workspace, on Linthouse Road. The nearby cottage (c.1850), once part of Fairfield Farm, was Elder Park superintendent's house.

5

Pershal Trust Community Hall
Aboukir Street
Elder & Cannon Architects 2013

A brick-faced box for charity which helps the socially excluded be part of the community. The recessed entrance is braced with cross, a subtle piece of Christian symbolism. *Pershal* is Gaelic for 'precious'. The box is elegant but robust, in a tough setting near the old Fairfield shipyard. Facing it is **Trafalgar Court**, twin infill blocks for Linthouse Housing Association (*DO Architecture 2011*). Contemporary style scaled to fit the local tenement context.

6

Ronald McDonald House
1345 Govan Road
Keppie Design 2015
A 'home from home' for families of kids being treated at the Royal Hospital

for Sick Children on Queen Elizabeth Hospital campus. The architecture is soothing, vernacular outside but without nostalgia. Interiors are smooth-finished and bright. A colonnade connects the accommodation block with communal areas, all arranged as a courtyard cluster shielded from Govan Road. Gabled elevations were chosen to evoke the Alexander Stephen shipbuilding workshops previously across the road.

7

Queen Elizabeth University Hospital
1345 Govan Road
IBI Group, Brookfield Multiplex 2011–2015

Several buildings suckle round this mother ship built for NHS Greater Glasgow and Clyde. The 14-storey block has a full height, top-lit atrium as its social hub and four wings (one with a rooftop helipad) at the corners.

Barcode cladding, usually a cliché, seems appropriate here given statistics which cite 1,000-plus single rooms en suite, 30 operating theatres and a staff of thousands. The campus replaced Southern General and three other aging city hospitals. It was Scotland's biggest construction contract at the time and the largest critical care complex in Europe. Rated BREEAM Excellent.

On the east side of the campus is the Southern General's **Old Administration Building** (*James Thomson c. 1870*), originally Govan Parish Poorhouse, when parish boards provided welfare.

8
Queen Elizabeth University Hospital Parkade
1345 Govan Road
Hypostyle Architects 2011

A multilevel concrete car park (one of three here) whose design rethinks the usually banal typology. Stair towers are glazed, lit like beacons at night. Vehicle access drums are prominent. Louvred cladding in larch, mesh screens and sandstone walls soften the drums and parking deck structure. Outside is a brightly-coloured bike shelter, one of five **Pavilions and Shelters** (*ZM Architecture, Jephson Robb artist c. 2016*) on

the campus. They are part of the hospital's innovative Art and Therapeutic design programme.

9
Imaging Centre of Excellence (ICE)
Langlands Drive
BMJ Architects 2017

A Glasgow University clinical and neuroscience research facility, part of Queen Elizabeth University Hospital campus. The building is a glazed box dressed with vertical steel mesh to limit solar gain—reflected in the glass the mesh looks like origami. Inside is an ultra-high resolution 7 Tesla MRI scanner weighing more than 17 tonnes, one of the world's most advanced and the first of its type in Scotland.

10
Luma Building
510 Shieldhall Road
Cornelius Armour 1938; Cornelius McClymont Architects 1995
Former Luma Light Bulb Factory, built as a joint venture by the Stockholm-based Luma Company and the Scottish Cooperative Wholesale Society (SCWS). The building is now flats, initiated by Linthouse Housing Association. The structure, steel-framed with concrete floor slabs, was extended to the east;

the west end acquired porthole windows. A trio of two-storey blocks was
added at the rear. The Bauhaus-style
lantern was the bulb testing deck, first
illuminated for the Empire Exhibition
at Bellahouston Park. The factory is all
that remains of the SCWS Shieldhall
industrial complex.

11
William Quarrier Scottish Epilepsy Centre
20 St. Kenneth Drive
Anderson Bell + Christie 2013

The charity needed a quiet location
close to the Institute of Neurological
Sciences at Queen Elizabeth Hospital
for this care centre for adults aged 16
and over with epilepsy. The site was

formerly Elder Park Primary School
(1898), declared surplus by the city,
sold and demolished. Its boundary
walls, railings and trees were retained.

The centre's stone-clad main block
has a butterfly roof to prevent solar
gain. Laminated timber struts—'a
playful nod to the type of colonnade
associated with civic buildings'—animate the front elevation. They are not
as structural as they look but help keep
the roof stable in gusting winds.

There is a soaring coloured glass
window *(Paula Thompson artist)* at the
entrance. Its vertical pattern symbolises electrodes used in EEG scanning of
epilepsy patients, who have rooms in a
bright, low-rise extension timber-faced
around a landscaped inner courtyard.

12
Taransay Street Tenement Project
ASSIST Architects 1975
ASSIST emerged in 1972 from
Strathclyde University's Department
of Architecture. The architects set
up shop in the community. That was
radical and so was the plan. Two city
blocks of late 19th-century tenements,
bounded by Govan Road and Elder,
Howat and Taransay streets, were
saved from demolition and upgraded,
with floor plans reconfigured to

improve livability. That had never been done before. It challenged city planners' tear-down culture and established a template for community-based housing associations. Govan Housing Association, registered in 1971, was the first of its kind in Scotland.

13
Park View
Golspie Street
DO Architecture 2012

Colourful pods jazz up this Govan Housing Association project, an upbeat take on the old tenement tune. The new walk-ups filled gap sites on Golspie and Shaw streets, and fit the scale and rhythm of the block's tenements. The back court with parking is landscaped and accessed through a pend, a traditional feature. The palette on the pods was chosen to reflect colours of old closes and shopfronts. Also here, at Shaw Street and Govan Road, is a typically muscular corner-turreted tenement *(Frank Burnet & Boston 1900)*.

Pavement art *(The Govan Timeline; Kate Robinson artist 2013)* shows Fairfield's gate and shipbuilders heading home. It is overlooked by the former

Hill's Trust Primary School, Italianate *(James Thomson 1874)*, bought from the city in 2016 for office use by Elderpark Housing Association.

14
Lyceum Cinema
908 Govan Road
McNair & Elder 1938

Streamline moderne supersize cinema like a cruise ship floated ashore. Art Deco vertical fins sail round the curving corner, across a wave of glass-block windows. The 2,600-seat auditorium was reconfigured in 1974 with a small screen and a bingo hall. The venue closed in 2006. A photo mural across the front shows it as built, to replace a music hall and picture palace of the same name destroyed by fire.

Glasgow was 'cinema city' with more movie theatres per head of population than any other metropolis in Europe. There were several in Govan. This was the best, the last built and is the only one left.

Across the road is the Romanesque style **St. Anthony's Church** *(John Honeyman 1879)*. Behind it is **Six Harmony Row** (1981), a former school rehabilitated for startups by Govan Workspace.

15

Govan Old Parish Church
866 Govan Road

Robert Rowand Anderson 1888

Govan's war memorial, shaped like a mercat cross, stands by the kirk gate which opens to a graveyard with stone markers from the 16th to 19th centuries. Some have carvings of skulls and crossbones, others cherubs; respectively *memento mori* and hopeful symbols of ascent to heaven. Some have the names or emblems of trades—baker, blacksmith, printer, weaver—while others display the heraldry and architectural pretensions of the gentry who owned local estates.

Older still are the **Govan Stones**, 31 burial markers, including Viking 'hog-backs', displayed in the church, now a museum for them. The stones date from the 9th- to 11th-century kingdom of Strathclyde. The most elaborate is the Govan Sarcophagus, buried in the churchyard during the Reformation and found by gravediggers in 1855. It is thought to be royal or related to St. Constantine who founded a monastery here in the 6th century.

After Strathclyde became part of the Scottish crown the administration of Govan was transferred to Glasgow Cathedral. The present Govan Old Church replaced a Georgian building of 1826. The style is Gothic Revival. Sketches show a steeple planned but not built. The interior feels mystical, not only due to the Govan Stones but also to stained glass commissioned by the minister, Rev. John MacLeod, who sought to beautify Presbyterian churches. The chancel (windows by Charles E. Kemp c. 1898), is barrel-vaulted like an upturned boat hull. A later MacLeod of the parish is better known. During the hard times in the 1930s Rev. George MacLeod founded the Iona Community and employed out of work Govanites to rebuild the 12th-century Iona Abbey.

16

The Black Man
Govan Road at Burleigh Street

Edward Onslow Ford sculptor 1894

Bronze figure, nicknamed 'the black man', representing shipbuilder William Pearce. He stands on a granite plinth,

unrolling a blueprint of one of his ships. Behind him is the Scots Baronial style **Cardell Temperance Hall** (1894), ironically now Brechin's Bar. On its north side is an eroded heraldic plaque and on the south cornice a carving of a legendary rat-catching cat.

17

Pearce Institute
840 Govan Road
Robert Rowand Anderson 1906

Working men's club in the style of a Scottish Renaissance palace, endowed for the people of Govan by the widow of William Pearce, owner of Fairfield shipyard. Her ghost is said to walk on the corbelled balcony below the clock. The façade is a fantasy of carved stone, crow steps, an oriel window, and a Dutch gable billowing like a sail. The finial is a ship made by metalworkers at Fairfields. An Italianate belvedere, or 'captain's lookout', with a cupola and weathervane sits on the roof.

The 'PI' was 'dry' and non-sectarian, with a board of parish trustees to apply Victorian values of self-education and improvement. It sails on, refurbished and reopened (2003) after a campaign to save it from permanent closure. In-

scribed inside are the founding words of 1903: 'This is a house of friendship. This is a house of service. For families. For lonely folk. For the people of Govan. For the strangers of the world. Welcome.'

18

Aitken Memorial Fountain
Govan Cross
Cruikshanks & Co., Denny Iron Works, Sun Foundry (design) 1884

A cast iron curiosity erected to honour Dr. John Aitken, Medical Officer for the Burgh of Govan, who devoted his life to helping the poor. The fountain's canopy is crowned with a fish-scale patterned dome above the burgh coat of arms, alligators (a symbol of apothecaries) and Masonic symbols. Under the canopy is a cherub-like child on an urn from which drinking water flowed. The memorial was restored in 2011.

The Gothic Revival church here was **St. Mary's United Free Church** (*Robert Baldie 1873*). The plaza, and that at the revamped subway station, are part of the Govan Cross Townscape Heritage

Initiative. Public art may include a statue of Mary Barbour, leader of the 1915 rent strike. A maquette was unveiled in 2016.

19
Bank of Scotland
Govan Road at Water Row
James Salmon (junior) and John Gaff Gillespie 1900

Glasgow Style, built for the British Linen Bank which had the corner unit on the ground floor. Eye-catching entrance with a stone ship propelled by wind gods blowing shell trumpets *(Francis Derwent Wood sculptor).* There are columns with Art Nouveau capitals, wide eaves and a spider crown (a reference to crown steeples). Flats here, for white-collar tenants, had higher ceilings and more space than those in shipyard workers' tenements.

Next door is the French Renaissance style former YMCA *(William Tennant 1897).* Also, a good piece of infill on a tight site in the lane, **10 Pearce Street** *(Austin-Smith: Lord 2010)*, for Bield Housing Association.

Water Row leads to the old Govan Ferry slip, used by workers when the river was lined on both sides with wharves and shipyards. The 18th-century Ferry Inn and a few weavers' cottages survived into the 20th-century, when they were torn down for expansion of the Harland and Wolff shipyard whose slipway alignments are replicated along the waterfront walkway upriver.

20
Govan Gateway
Govan Road at Broomloan Road
Collective Architecture 2011

A Govan Housing Association development anchored by and deferential to the **Savings Bank of Glasgow** *(Eric A. Sutherland 1904).* The Beaux-Arts bank boasts lion and unicorn heraldry, paired Corinthian columns and a corner turret, actually a washhouse (the flat roof was the drying area).

The 'gateway' block of flats on Govan Road is angled for views of the bank and replicates its scale, as does the second block which curves toward the town centre. A crescent of two-storey flats and townhouses is set back from the main road. Good stuff, with a variety of built forms and sensitive response to site.

21
Broomloan Subway Depot
Robert Street
1896

When the Glasgow District Subway opened in 1896 it was one of only three in the world, after those in London and Budapest. It was the world's only cable-hauled subway, 1.2 metre gauge in narrow tunnels. Glasgow Corporation took it over in 1923 and electrified the trains in 1935. They were still in service in the 1970s when the subway was closed for a three-year modernisation. Two of the old subway cars are now at **Riverside Museum** (see 27).

The route is a 10.5 kilometre circle line in two parallel tubes with 15 stations—'Round the City in Half an Hour', early publicity posters said. Govan Cross was accessed through the ground floor of a tenement, an expedient which avoided demolitions in the densely populated districts the subway served; Kelvinhall (Partick Cross) is still like that.

The depot is the only point where the trains surface. The brick exterior of the old workshops can be seen on Broomloan Road. The transverse section of the roof was built high for a crane which lifted the cars direct from the tunnels. They now enter and exit

the depot on an incline. A 21st-century upgrade to the subway by Strathclyde Partnership for Transport (SPT) includes driverless trains.

22
Orkney Street Enterprise Centre
18 Orkney Street
John Burnet 1866; Wylie Shanks Architects 2009

Former burgh hall, police and fire station converted for startups, part of the Central Govan Action Plan. The neoclassical façade, entrance hall with Corinthian columns and grand stair-case, and the brick jail in the backyard are well preserved. The jail, a typical atrium with cells off galleried walk-ways, is now offices with one cell left as it was. The tenement directly south (1898) had flats for firefighters.

At 580 Govan Road is the **Govan Press Building** *(Frank Stirrat 1890)*, originally a newspaper office featuring on the façade carved heads of publishers John and Jane Cossar and print and literary celebrities Gutenberg, Caxton, Burns and Scott. No proofreader— Gutenberg is misspelled with a double 'T'. He and his gang look across to **Govan Graving Docks** (1869–1898) built by the Clyde Navigation Trust.

The ship repair complex closed in 1988. A maritime heritage centre, park and housing have been variously proposed for this historic site.

23
Govan Burgh Halls
401 Govan Road
  Robert Sandilands 1901; AHR
  Architects 2009
A gallus civic chateau with pavilions

and cupolas galore and a Renaissance dome above the council chamber. The porch on Govan Road has the burgh coat of arms and portrait medallions of a provost and a bailie. An extension included a concert hall. Its façade has the words 'music' and 'drama' and a frieze (*Archibald Macfarlane Shannan sculptor*) with bagpipe-playing *putti*. The building has been rehabilitated as a creative centre, Film City Glasgow.

24
Glasgow Harbour
Castlebank Street
  Masterplan: Kohn Pedersen Fox 2000.
  Residential phases: east RMJM; centre
  Cooper Cromar; west Gordon Murray
  + Alan Dunlop Architects 2005–2015
A docklands redevelopment between the Scottish Exhibition and Conference Centre (SECC) and the Clyde Tunnel. It

follows a masterplan that set guidelines for high density neighbourhoods, some commercial, with parkland and water-front promenades. **Riverside Museum** (see 27) is the cultural component.

The residential zone is on the site of Meadowside Granary whose four giant silos (1914–1968) were said to have been the largest brick-built complex in Europe. Imaginative adaptive reuse—think acres of floor space repurposed as a multilevel urban farm—was not considered. The granary was an industrial icon which the regeneration boosters preferred to bury . . . and buried it was, its millions of bricks pulverised as aggregate for new developments.

The granary brought a real sense of place to the waterfront. The new buildings resurrected its linear form and scale but strayed off-course from the masterplan which recommended mainly courtyard blocks, the tenement urbanism long established in Glasgow.

A crucial aspect promoted was connectivity to the walkable streets of the West End, but the Clydeside Expressway was and remains a formidable barrier. The masterplan acknowledged that problem but failed to resolve it. Had real place making been intended instead of a quick fix the only solution—as has been achieved in some North American cities—would have been to remove or bury the expressway.

The style of Glasgow Harbour is a rebooted modernism. The real deal is four blocks north of the expressway (see next entry).

25
Crathie Court
57 Laurel Street
Ronald Bradbury, Archibald George Jury, Glasgow Corporation 1949–1952
Horizontal composition of multi-storey deck access flats, punctuated vertically with stair towers. Porthole windows add a nautical touch. Style, prewar Euro modernism. The building, originally for single women, was Glasgow's first experiment in high-rise housing. The project won a 1952 Saltire Award for the best apartment block in Scotland.

26
Partick Burgh Hall
9 Burgh Hall Street
William Leiper 1872
French Renaissance style *hôtel de ville* built for the Burgh of Partick. Like Govan Burgh Halls it symbolised local pride, until Partick was annexed by Glasgow in 1912 as Govan was that

year. Baroque bell tower slightly askew
and cast iron cresting on a Parisian
roof; relief panels of Justice, Miseri-
cordia (Mercy) and Truth *(William
Mossman sculptor)* on the façade.
An upgrade *(ZM Architecture 2004)*
included a linear atrium and elevator
shaft inserted cleverly, contrasting
with heritage features and stonework.

The building overlooks **West of
Scotland Cricket Club** (1862; clubhouse later but traditional). The first
Scotland v England football international was played here in 1872 (a
draw 0–0). Across Dumbarton Road,
at Anderson and Gullane streets, is
the Italianate **Partick Marine Police
Station** *(Charles Wilson 1853)* whose
officers patrolled the docks. Old jail
in situ similar to the one on Orkney
Street (see 22) but derelict.

27

Riverside Museum
100 Pointhouse Place
*Zaha Hadid Architects, Buro
Happold engineers, Gross Max
landscape design 2011*
City council wanted a starchitect and
iconic building to house the contents
of the former Museum of Transport
(see 308 and 421) and got them after an
international competition. The result is
a showy shed packed with exhibits. The
steel structure is clad with zinc panels
which shimmer in the sun and turn
battleship grey in the Glasgow rain.
The metals and the sectional sawtooth
evoke workshops of industry, and the
twist on the plan fluidity. The site, at
the confluence of the rivers Kelvin
and Clyde, was the shipyard of A.& J.
Inglis, builders in 1947 of famous pad-
dle steamer *Waverley*.

Exhibits are revealed as a sequence of
surprises in a column-free promenade
which culminates in a luminous hall

facing the Clyde. The roof is supported by a dense canopy of computer modelled steelwork, impressive during construction but now concealed. A cathedral window frames the tall ship *Glenlee* (1896), built at Port Glasgow, restored by the Clyde Maritime Trust.

The hall is dominated by a Glasgow-built steam locomotive, the museum's biggest exhibit, repatriated from South Africa. Among the other 3,000-plus objects are trams, subway cars, and shops on a heritage street. Shipbuilders' models previously in glass cases are animated on a 'ship conveyor' as if on a celestial voyage. But there is more than the ghosts of ships and the steam engines that built an empire. There are words of the people of Clydeside and the stories they tell.

28

Queen's Dock Pumping Station
Stobcross Road

John Carrick, City Architect 1877
A Tuscan campanile built to hide a water accumulator for hydraulics which powered cranes and a swing bridge at Queen's Dock. The Clyde Navigation Trust anchor and Glasgow's bird, tree,

bell and fish symbols adorn the pediment of the adjoining pump house. Site preparation for adaptive reuse as **The Clydeside Distillery** and visitor centre *(Hypostyle Architects)* began in 2016.

29

Bell's Bridge
BMJ Architects, Crouch & Hogg engineers 1988

Retro-futurism, Glasgow Garden Festival style. The steel bridge, cable-stayed from a sci-fi pylon, is the festival's only surviving structure. The butterfly canopied deck pivots through 90 degrees to allow ships to pass, a rare event. Downstream, a pedestrian and cycle bridge between Riverside Museum and Govan is planned.

30

Glasgow Science Centre
Pacific Quay

Building Design Partnership (BDP), Fairhurst & Partners engineers 2001
Two pods and a pinnacle built on Prince's Dock which was filled in for the Glasgow Garden Festival. One pod is an IMAX cinema; the other, the Science Mall with exhibit and activity space glazed to the riverside. Their titanium-clad shells delivered the iconic look of regeneration. The pinnacle is

the **Glasgow Tower** *(Richard Horden architect, Buro Happold engineers),* intended for St. Enoch Square having won a competition in 1992.

It is Scotland's tallest freestanding structure (127 metres). A viewing pod climbs the pylon which was designed ingeniously to rotate in the wind, through 360 degrees on its vertical axis. Finned outriggers reduce turbulence and sway. Technical glitches closed the aerodynamic attraction periodically. It opened again in 2014.

31

BBC Scotland Headquarters
Pacific Quay
  David Chipperfield Architects; Faber Maunsell, Jane Wernick Associates engineers 2004–2007

The BBC moved from Queen Margaret Drive (see 371) to this digital media flagship following a design competition. The reinforced concrete container has a double-skin glass wrap with natural ventilation in its void and operable windows on the inner surface. The transparency maximises light and views. Open and inclusive is also how the BBC wanted to appear to be here.

The core of the building is a galleried, linear atrium with stepped terraces for

circulation. The space was designed for serendipity, as if in an Italian hill town, to invite conversation and collaboration. Soundproof studios are integrated within the terraces. Interior design was by Graven Images. Keppie Design completed the project. Public art *(Toby Patterson)* brightens the plaza. Another media flagship on Pacific Quay is **STV Studios** *(Parr Architects 2006).*

32

Prince's Dock Pumping Station
Pacific Quay
  J. J. Burnet 1894

A Clyde Navigation Trust pump house and power plant swaggering with a Florentine tower and gabled machinery hall, converted to offices c. 2005, The

hall extends to Govan Road. Panels representing the 'Four Winds', like engravings on antique maritime charts, decorate the truncated chimney.

33
Clyde Auditorium
Exhibition Way
  Foster + Partners, Arup engineers
  1997
Queen's Dock was filled with rubble from demolished buildings to provide a site for the **Scottish Exhibition & Conference Centre** *(James Parr & Partners 1985)*. Its halls were assembled quickly, followed by an American style, mirror-glass high-rise hotel *(Cobban & Lironi 1989)*. They were part of city council's strategy to remake Glasgow as a visitor attraction. Hosting conventions was one of the tactics.

  The 3,000-seat aluminium-clad, steel-framed Clyde Auditorium was commissioned to raise the SECC's profile in a competitive market, increase capacity and improve the quality of the centre's design. The foyer is cavernous, glazed for daylight and views. The prow-shaped entrance and overlapping roofscape were said by the architects to evoke maritime heritage, upturned boats perhaps. Glaswegians took one look and branded it 'the Armadillo'.

34
The Hydro (SSE Hydro)
Exhibition Way
  Foster + Partners, Arup engineers
  2013
Glows like a paper lantern, an illusion created by translucent panels which

can be animated with projected images
and many colours. The south-facing
panels are fritted to resist solar gain;
inside, natural and mechanical ventilation is programmed to reduce energy
costs. A green mound covers the entrance and service areas. The roof is a
steel lattice web which rises from steel
struts around a bowl-shaped, 12,000-
seat arena. The typology dates from
the Roman Empire but the structural
vitality recalls Victorian engineering
admired by high-tech architects like
Norman Foster.

The Hydro won the Supreme Award
2013 from Glasgow Institute of Architects (GIA). In 2015 it was rated the
world's second busiest live entertain-
ment venue, after the O2 in London.

35
The Finnieston Crane
Stobcross Quay

Cowans, Sheldon & Co. (tower),
Cleveland Bridge & Engineering Co.
(cantilever) 1931

This mighty hammerhead crane built
for the Clyde Navigation Trust could
hoist a Glasgow-made steam locomotive as if it were a matchstick and lower
it gently onto a ship. The lifting arm is
a giant cantilever with counterweights
below the operator's cab.

Originally it was called the Stobcross
Crane, from the quay it stands on.
There were several like it on the river;
the oldest is the Titan Crane *(Arrol*
& Co. 1907) at Clydebank. Finnieston
Crane is maintained by Clydeport as
a monument to Glasgow's industrial
heritage.

36

Glasgow Harbour Tunnel Rotundas

Simpson & Wilson engineers

1890–1895

Twin rotundas, North and South, were the entry points for the Harbour Tunnel (a bridge would have been a barrier for big ships on the then busy river). Each rotunda covered a shaft to three cast iron tube tunnels, one for pedestrians, two for vehicles. Steel ring beams on cast iron columns show where the entrances were. Hydraulic lifts for vehicles were supplied by Otis of New York; pedestrians used stairs.

The vehicle tunnels were closed in the 1940s and later filled in. The pedestrian tunnel stayed open until 1980. Access is now restricted to service a water main. The North Rotunda is an eatery; the South one, long derelict, was reha-bilitated (*GD Lodge Architects 2016*) for Malin Group marine engineering.

The Harbour Tunnel was a model for the Elbe Tunnel (1911) in Hamburg which is still in use.

37

Clyde Arc

Finnieston Street and Govan Road

Halcrow Group engineers 2006

Dubbed the 'Squinty Bridge' because of its skewed alignment, necessary to

secure suitable anchor points. The road deck is suspended from and crossed diagonally by a steel bowstring arch, diamond-shaped in section. The angled surfaces and cables catch the light, animating the unconventional design. The span, by the old Harbour Tunnel, connects the West End and the SECC to the regeneration zone at Pacific Quay.

38

Lancefield Quay

Broomielaw

Thomson, McCrea & Sanders 1990

A conversion of a 1930s Clyde Naviga-tion Trust transit shed. Four levels were created for flats after the top half of the building was peeled off to reveal an upper floor slab which was retained along with the gables at each end. The brick elevation on the landward side has old pediments and ventilation roundels above doors to residents' parking. On the riverfront elevation apartments appear between and above the riveted posts and beams of the original structure. One of the first projects marketed as 'contemporary waterfront living'.

39
Kingston Bridge
W. A. Fairhurst & Partners engineers
1967–1970
A 10-lane motorway bridge, one of Europe's busiest, cantilevered from each side of the river. There are two prestressed concrete box-girder decks carrying the M8 across the Clyde. The sides are clad with aggregate panels.

No beauty but impressive. Built high to allow ships to pass, which they once did all the way to Broomielaw.

40
Scottish Co-operative Wholesale Society (SCWS)
95 Morrison Street
Bruce & Hay 1897
The architects denied recycling their competition design for the City Chambers (see 104) but the SCWS HQ looks the part. Its Second Empire roof brought Parisian grandeur to Morrison Street and Kingston Dock (1867; closed 1966 and filled in). The pediment has a tableau with figures of Justice, Commerce and the Four Continents *(James Alexander Ewing sculptor)*. The dome had a cast concrete figure, Light and Life (also by Ewing), which became unstable and was removed in 1994. In 2016, a fibreglass replica was commissioned, gilded and installed *(Bill*

Ritchie of Atelier Ten; Kenny Mackay sculptor, Scott Telfer gilder).

The SCWS was a trading and retail empire established in 1868. The buildings in the shadow of the great HQ were part of a warehouse complex that covered several city blocks with eclectic architecture. The HQ's neighbour *(James Ferrigan 1919)* on Morrison Street is Beaux-Arts; on Dalintober Street is a medley of gables and crow steps (1887); on Carnoustie Street a Jacobean façade (1893) with a plaque and the Co-op motif of a handshake and the guiding word *Unitas*. Since the 1980s the complex has been repurposed as flats and offices.

41
Glasgow City Mission
20 Crimea Street
Elder & Cannon Architects 2010
This Christian charity, founded by David Nasmith in 1826 to relieve poverty and homelessness, was the world's first city mission. Latterly it was on the waterfront at McAlpine Street until the site became part of the Financial Services District masterplan. A land swap was agreed which enabled this new headquarters.

The straight-up elevations are steel-framed. Brick cladding and varied fenestration add texture and shadow play. There is a roof garden, defined by a colonnade which brings full height to the street corner. The building is tough but inclusive, maximises available daylight and gives those who use its drop-in facilities dignity.

42
Tobacco Warehouse
41–45 James Watt Street
John Baird (1) 1854

A brooding hulk of industrial classicism originally single storey, heightened with a pediment raised c. 1870. The pediment and eroded lion and unicorn heraldry (see 49) distinguish it from additional floors constructed in 1911. Opposite are neoclassical warehouse façades *(John Stephen 1848, 1863)*, retained for a new development. James Watt had a villa here, hence the name of the street previously Delftfield Lane where a pottery (1748) produced Dutch-style delftware for which Glasgow was known.

43

One Atlantic Quay

Broomielaw at Robertson Street

Building Design Partnership 1990

Between Robertson and York streets is phase one of the Financial Services District (masterplan by BDP). The area was previously packed with tobacco warehouses and flour and grain mills built close to waterfront where stands

the former **Clyde Navigation Trust Building** (see next entry), a reminder of that earlier era of commerce.

One Atlantic Quay is scaled and articulated to pay homage to the Clyde Trust edifice, with columns and curved bays turning the corner above a recessed entrance. It greets the old building with a high-tech, anodised aluminium handshake and steps back respectfully.

44

Clydeport Headquarters

16 Robertson Street at Broomielaw

J. J. Burnet 1883–1886; 1906–1908

Of Glasgow's *fin-de-siècle* power and confidence there is no better architectural rival to the City Chambers (see 104) than this baroque spectacle, like

a great ship, decks loaded with Beaux-Arts stonework. It was built as the headquarters of the Clyde Navigation Trust. The trust administered shipping and docks on the river and kept it dredged for ocean-going vessels to reach the city.

A grand staircase connects a tiled hallway to opulent meeting rooms on the top floor. The *pièce de résistance* is a circular boardroom from where the trustees could observe the river they ruled. There is stained glass *(Stephen Adam)*. The façade is awash with classical features and sculpture *(John Mossman, Albert Hemstock Hodge)*. Neptune crowns the pediment; there are figures of Henry Bell, Telford and Watt. Classical groups—*Ceres leading a Bull* and *Amphitrite with Seahorses*—

symbolising land and sea flank the Beaux-Arts dome added in 1905. Glasgow's high tide began to ebb after 1914. The Robertson Street façade, to have been symmetrical, was not completed.

45
Radisson Blu
301 Argyle Street
Gordon Murray + Alan Dunlop Architects 2003

The marketing catch-phrase 'Glasgow, Scotland with Style' could apply to this hotel which jumps out of the bland hospitality box. A lightweight copper screen creates a canopy and a sense that urban life flows into the building. A pod of premium rooms cantilevered through the screen bridges a linear atrium. Standard rooms are stacked behind side elevations less extrovert than Argyle Street's canted copper.

The metal evokes industrial heritage and challenged planners' preference for stone cladding. The form contested vigorously the city's street grid discipline. The façade of an Edwardian commercial building was retained on Robertson Street.

46
Hielanman's Umbrella
Argyle Street
James Miller architect, Donald A. Matheson engineer 1899–1906

Cast iron and glass façades illuminate Central Station from this immense bridge built when the Caledonian Railway enlarged the terminus. Shops and an entrance to the Central low level station (1896) are under the bridge. It got its nickname because folk from the Highlands who worked in the city used the sheltered space on Argyle Street as a rendezvous. (See also 48 and 222.)

47
The Iron Building
36 Jamaica Street
John Baird (1) 1856

'Form follows function'—before the phrase was associated with the Modern Movement—fits this innovative design. It was built for A. Gardner & Son, Cabinet Makers & Upholsterers who needed large floor areas and natural light. The structural system was patented by ironfounder Robert McConnel. Floors are timber on wrought iron beams supported on cast iron columns,

and were served by a birdcage elevator, the first in the city, made by Otis, New York. Modular façades were prefabricated in cast iron to Baird's design which called for minimum metal and maximum plate glass—technology used for the Crystal Palace at the Great Exhibition of 1851. Gardner's building was the first to exploit it for commercial premises.

Similar buildings exist in America, pioneered in New York at the time. Few anywhere match the subtlety of Baird's pen which resisted unnecessary decoration. The style is Italianate with the rhythm of Venice on three levels of arched, thinly mullioned windows layered in classical proportions, fringed with a delicate cornice.

Gardner's was refurbished c. 2000 as a bar and restaurant. Other heritage iron fronts on Jamaica Street were demolished in the 1990s—a disgrace, especially as what's in their place is worse, not better. Another *(McConnel and James Thomson 1863)* survives beside the Hielanman's Umbrella, and there is the Ca' d'Oro (see 220).

At 42 Jamaica Street is a tough commercial tenement *(Clarke & Bell 1897)* built for publican Philip MacSorley who opened a bar on the ground floor. It was decorated lavishly. Its gin palace

windows with etched glass and Glasgow Style woodwork remain in place.

48
Central Station Bridges
Blyth & Cunningham engineers 1878; Matheson & Barry engineers 1899–1906

The first Caledonian Railway Bridge had four tracks on a wrought iron deck supported on rusticated granite piers. The second bridge added nine tracks on massive steel lattice girders. The deck of older bridge was dismantled in 1967 leaving its piers in the river where they look like relics of a drowned civilization. That effect was accented with a typographic artwork, *All Greatness Stands Firm in The Storm (Ian Hamilton Finlay artist 1999)*, with letters carved in Greek and English on the granite.

49
Customs House
298 Clyde Street
John Taylor 1840

A façade with fluted Doric columns, boasting the British lion and unicorn royal coat of arms on the parapet (the

lion English, the unicorn Scottish).
The architect was a customs official.
The muscular dignity of the Greek Revival style was favoured by the agency,
whose officers collected duties on
imports and exports at the harbour.

50

Carlton Place Suspension Bridge

Alexander Kirkland architect
George Martin engineer 1853

A suspension bridge with wrought iron
chains threaded through stone pylons
rendered as ancient triumphal arches.
It was initially not a triumph of construction—the south tower fractured
when the chains were fitted. The bridge
was re-engineered and reconstructed.

It connects the city with **Carlton
Place** *(Peter Nicholson 1802–1818)*, two
terraces built for James and David
Laurie after whom Laurieston district

was named. Laurieston House (the
eastern one and the first built) has an
outstanding Georgian interior.

On Clyde Street is the zinc-clad,
Saltire Society Award-winning **Icon**
(Elder & Cannon 2004), 12 storeys of
flats with each unit given a river view.

51

St. Andrew's Cathedral
172 Clyde Street

*James Gillespie Graham 1816; Pugin
& Pugin 1889–1892; Page\Park
Architects 2011*

St. Andrew appears on the façade of
this Gothic Revival church, the earliest
example of the style in Glasgow. It was
granted cathedral status in 1889. Many
worshippers then were migrant workers from the Highlands and Ireland
who settled in the city.

The fan-vaulted interior has been
beautifully restored and artworks
commissioned. The most striking is
a painting *(Peter Howson artist)* of

the martyrdom at Glasgow Cross in 1615 of Jesuit priest John Ogilvie. The Italian cloister contains a memorial *(Giulia Chiarini designer 2011)* to the Scots-Italians who perished when the *Arandora Star*, taking them to internment in Canada, was torpedoed and sunk by a U-boat in 1940.

52
Carrick Quay
100 Clyde Street
Davis Duncan Partnership 1989

A block of flats in nautical gear, with steel masts and timber decking on the brick elevation. Developed by The Burrell Company, it was the first to revive this part of the riverfront. The name refers to the tall ship *Carrick*, an old tea clipper berthed here until 1991.

Carrick Quay overlooks **Stockwell Street (Victoria) Bridge** *(James Walker engineer 1854)*. It replaced a 14th-century bridge which linked Bridgegate (Briggait) and Gorbals village. 'Briggait', *gait* in old Scots, did not refer to a gate but means 'the way to the bridge'.

On the south bank is the Kafkaesque **Glasgow Sheriff Court** *(Keppie Hen-*

derson & Partners 1981–1986) isolated on an arid plaza, detached from the riverfront setting. Residual classicism in its colonnade; lavish use of stone and exotic wood inside but ultimately chilling. Solar panels on the roof, however, were the most extensive array in Scotland when installed in 2008.

53
Glasgow Central Mosque
Gorbals Street
Coleman Ballantine Partnership 1984

The first purpose-built mosque and Islamic centre in the city. Composed with traditional elements: a minaret, an arcaded courtyard, arched entrance, domed prayer hall, and a garden for contemplation. The prayer hall faces a path to a gate on Gorbals Street but access is at Mosque Avenue by the railway arches off Ballater Street.

54
Merchants Steeple
Bridgegate (Briggait)
c. 1665

The campanile is a Gothic relic of the medieval city. Aloft shines a finial of a sailing ship, the emblem of Merchants House founded 1605 to promote trade and lobby for members' interests and help their families in hard times. After

the merchants moved out of the old town the building was demolished in 1818 except for the tower. Tenements were built around it, then torn down for the Fish Market.

55
Briggait Fish Market
64–76 Clyde Street
Clarke & Bell 1873

A French Second Empire *bouillabaisse* garnished with sculpted seahorses and portrait medallions above iron gates set in triumphal arches. The other façade, on Briggait, is Italianate with roundels of Neptune and cartouches displaying fish and the city's coat of arms. Market hall inside.

56
The Briggait
141 Bridgegate
Clarke & Bell 1873; Alexander Beith McDonald, City Engineer 1903; ASSIST Architects 1986; Nicoll Russell Studios 2009

A luminous Victorian iron and glass market hall, originally Briggait Fish Market. Two smaller halls are in the same style. After the fish traders flitted to an out-of-town facility in 1977 city council's intent to demolish the building was seen off by an adaptive reuse of the galleried main hall, inspired by the conversion of Covent Garden in London. Timing and location were against the progressive project which failed.

The building was reopened recently by Wasps Trust and Wasps Studios as an arts centre. The interventions in the 1980s were contemporary and avoided pastiche, a principle followed during the recent rehab.

57
St. Enoch Viaduct
Clyde Street
William Melville engineer 1899

The City of Glasgow Union Railway
was the first to cross the Clyde, here in
1870. The present bridge was built by
the Glasgow & South Western Railway.
Its cast iron parapet, crenellated turrets
and towers with dummy gargoyles
were in tune with Gothic style of the
company's St. Enoch Station Hotel.

58
**City of Glasgow College, Riverside
Campus**
21 Thistle Street
*Reiach & Hall Architects, Michael
Laird Architects, Arup engineers,
rankinfraser landscape architecture
2015*
Built for City of Glasgow College (see
114). The riverside site was previously

the College of Nautical Studies (1962).
Its Marine Skills Centre (*BDP 2010*) and
boat landing have been retained.

The new campus has two towers,
respectively teaching and student digs.
Modular bronze and glass curtain
walling evokes Glasgow's 19th-century
cast iron façades (see 47). There is an
engineering workshop big enough for
a marine turbine. The teaching block
is hollowed out with a multistorey atrium, above a concrete colonnade where
a walkway engages the campus with
the river. This landscaped interface is
elegant, better than anything at Pacific
Quay or the SECC. The campus made
the Royal Institute of British Architects
(RIBA) Stirling Prize shortlist 2016.

59
Justiciary Court
212 Saltmarket
*William Stark 1809–1814; Clarke
& Bell 1845, with J. H. Craigie 1913*
Greek Revival with Doric columns
supporting a frowning pediment. The
style was typical of any building of
the time required to project authority,
here to humble prisoners and reassure
citizens that justice would be served.

The edifice, facing Jocelyn Gate (see
next entry), housed the municipal
offices, a wood-panelled courtroom
and 122 prison cells. It was remodelled
after city council moved to the City
and County Buildings (see 86) and in
1910–1913 when a second courtroom
was built. Behind the old building is
the **High Court of Justiciary** (*TPS
Architecture 1998*) with a postmodern
rotunda at its entrance.

60

McLennan Arch

Glasgow Green

Robert & James Adam 1796; John Carrick, City Architect 1894

This grand arch with relief panels of classical mythology—Apollo and The Three Graces—was the central feature on the façade of the Assembly Rooms on Ingram Street, demolished c.1892 for an extension to George Square's Post Office. The arch was named for the bailie who funded its relocation to the north side of Glasgow Green. In

1991 it was dismantled and moved to Saltmarket where it dignifies the main entrance to the park.

The plaza was re-paved and landscaped as part of a 1990s renewal of the Green, which introduced formal French *allées* with topiary. An inscription on the paving notes the site as Jocelyn Gate, previously Jocelyn (or Jail) Square where, until 1865, public executions were staged. Jocelyn was the bishop of Glasgow Cathedral (see 123). He initiated the annual Glasgow Fair, originally held where the McLennan Arch now stands.

Glasgow Green was granted by James II to Bishop William Turnbull in 1450 as a commons. It was landscaped by unemployed weavers and others on poor relief, following a plan of 1813 by James Cleland, Superintendent of Public Works. Over the centuries it has been used for grazing cattle and sheep, bleaching cloth, political protests, sports and concerts. In the winter of 1745–1746 it was briefly Bonnie Prince Charlie's Jacobite army camp. Today the annual World Pipe Band Championships are held here.

On the park side of the arch is a drinking fountain (1881) built by temperance reformers to praise Lord Provost and publisher William Collins who campaigned against 'the demon drink'. In the distance is an obelisk, the Nelson Monument (1806), among several architectural curiosities on the Green. These are featured in Tour 4, *The East End*.

Former Union Bank, Ingram Street

2

The Merchant City

ON THE SIDE WALL of the British Linen Bank, built in 1895 on High Street, is a plaque with a bas-relief illustration of the building previously on the site. It was a two-storey and attic tenement with crow-stepped gables, like many others on High Street before the Victorians swept them away. Also lost—in an act of vandalism not surpassed until the destruction of tenement communities in the 1960s—was the Old College on the east side of High Street, the site of Glasgow University from 1460 to 1870. Its 17th-century Scottish Renaissance campus buildings were demolished after the college principals sold the land in 1864 to the City of Glasgow Union Railway and moved to the West End.

In the Middle Ages, High Street was the route between the bishop's settlement at Glasgow Cathedral and a salmon fishing village on the Clyde. In the 13th century a wooden bridge was built, the first across the river. Mercat or Market (now Glasgow) Cross, was the centre of the town. The Union of the Crowns in 1603 boosted trade. Glasgow became a royal burgh in 1611. Its merchant and trades guilds were represented on the town council which was based at the Tolbooth, of which the steeple built in 1627 survives. Most dwellings were wood and thatch and burned in the great fires of 1652 and 1677. The council decreed they be rebuilt externally with slate and stone.

In 1668 the council bought land on the Clyde estuary and built Port Glasgow. The river was later made navigable to the city centre. Until the Union of the Parliaments in 1707, foreign trade had been with the Continent, Ireland and England. The Union gave Scots access to English colonies in America. Glasgow was well placed on the west coast for transatlantic voyages. Sugar, tobacco and cotton were imported, processed in the city's mills and exported for profit. In 1772, to encourage and manage growth, the council bought land west of the Old College. A map drawn by 'land surveyor of Glasgow' James Barrie, published in 1780, shows an embryonic street grid and George Square.

The tobacco lords lived in Palladian villas and met at the Tontine Coffee House, by the Tolbooth on Trongate where, on a pavement laid for their exclusive use, they 'strutted about every day as the rulers of the destinies of Glasgow'. Their wealth was legendary until the American War of Independence hit them hard. They made it, like traders in Bristol, Liverpool and London, from slavery on plantations in the West Indies and America. This is evident in street names: Virginia, Jamaica, Buchanan, the latter after one of the tobacco lords. Sugar and cotton mill owners were also implicated, and other citizens owned slaves, buying a few or more, advertised in newspapers like stocks and shares.

After the British parliament voted to abolish the trade in 1807 the government compensated not the slaves but their owners. The money helped fuel the Industrial Revolution and Glasgow's boom in real estate, manufacturing and heavy industry. Palatial buildings appeared, among them the Union Bank and the Royal Exchange. The westward shift of commercial and civic power following Barrie's plan was decisive. Council relocated to the upcoming area in 1845. The college principals followed the trend. Thomas Annan photographed the Old College before it was torn down, and recorded High Street's slums for the City Improvement Trust before they were cleared. The squalor was one reason why the university principals moved out. They also judged the college too costly to restore and that it would not accommodate increasing enrolment. The old town was sidelined. The Glasgow Improvement Act was drafted in 1866 to help revive it, inspired by slum clearance and redevelopment seen by a civic delegation to Haussmann's Paris. 'Greek' Thomson, among local architects consulted, produced a visionary plan—grid-iron blocks of tenements with arcade-like, glass-roofed linear courtyards. Unfortunately this salubrious urban environment was not created; instead, conventional tenements were constructed in baronial style.

The district had a garment trade and the city's fruit and vegetable markets. But it remained a backwater, known only to those who made a living there or came for concerts at City Halls. In the 1980s artists moved in, attracted by big empty spaces in warehouses and low rents. The market halls, vacated in 1969, were converted for live music and shopping. Tron Kirk became a theatre and the City Halls complex was refurbished. The area became The Merchant City, a tag for council's strategy for a lively and diverse quarter. Loft-style living was promoted. The Tontine Building on Trongate is now a hub for start-ups, and there is an International Technology & Renewable Energy Zone.

This is the familiar trajectory of inner city regeneration, and gentrification: artists colonise cheap spaces and make a tired district trendy; coffee shops open, hipsters like the vibe and the lofts developers soon provide. Property values and rents rise; the artists and low-income residents are forced out. What was cool becomes conventional. The Merchant City still has that funky feel developers can never deliver, but it is on the cusp of change. A development plan, the 'Candleriggs Quarter', proposes more than 1200 units of accommodation—variously apartments, student digs and a boutique hotel—plus retail and a public plaza on vacant land between Candleriggs and Hutcheson Street. Renderings show the quarter's built forms to be unsympathetic to the historically incremental nature of development and human scale which give the Merchant City its special character.

61

Tolbooth Steeple

Glasgow Cross

John Boyd mason, Master of Works
1627

The steeple is the only remaining part of the 17th-century Tolbooth (or Town House), a five-storey Jacobean-style civic castle which contained council chambers, a courthouse and jail. It was rebuilt with a Gothic façade (1737) and renovated (1814) to attract commercial tenants after the city sold it and moved to the Justiciary Court (see 59).

The Tolbooth was demolished in 1921 following a plan by the City Improvement Trust to redevelop Glasgow Cross as a gateway to the city centre and to ease congestion. The steeple was to be moved stone by stone to the east side of cross. The First World War intervened. It stayed in place, isolated by traffic. Its stonework shows where the Tolbooth was severed. It once had spikes on which the heads of executed criminals were impaled. Original carvings are above the windows and a spiral stair leads to bells cast in 1881 at Gorbals Brass and Bell Foundry. The crown spire is one of only three from the middle ages in Scotland (the others are at Edinburgh and Aberdeen).

62

Mercat Building

Glasgow Cross

Andrew Graham Henderson 1931

A Beaux-Arts block with a cavernous

Ionic columned west front and façades with allegorical figures carved in situ. Facing Glasgow Cross are Painting and Sculpture *(Benno Schotz)*; on Gallowgate, Industry and Shipbuilding *(Archibald Dawson)*; on London Road, Science and Literature *(Alexander Proudfoot)*. The building was one of a trio on the improvement plan (see previous entry). The other built was the former **Bank of Scotland** (1927), with a concave façade on the west side of High Street. The third was not constructed; two blocks of flats (c. 2005) are where it would have been.

In front of the Mercat Building is the **Mercat Cross**, a unicorn on its column. The site was a medieval street market. Traditionally, official proclamations would have been posted on the walls of the structure or announced from its platform, but not here—this is a replica *(Edith Burnet Hughes architect, Margaret Findlay sculptor 1930)*; the original was removed in 1659. The designer, a niece of J. J. Burnet, was the first female architect in Scotland.

63
Tolbooth Bar
11 Saltmarket, Glasgow Cross
1906
Historic Irish bar, originally called

James Coggan's Coat of Arms, reflecting the area's immigrant demographic. The fish and chip shop next door, **Val d'Oro** on London Road, is Italian, said to be the oldest (1875) in town. Vintage fascia and interior, 1950s.

64
The Modern Institute
14–20 Osborne Street
RMJM 2010

A 19th-century washhouse derelict for 30 years cleaned up as exhibition space for contemporary art. The sandstone exterior and sliding door were retained and a picture window inserted to give passersby a glimpse inside. The roof was refurbished, for natural light to illuminate the minimalist long gallery.

65
Trongate 103
103 Trongate and King Street
John McKissack & Son 1902; Elder & Cannon Architects 2009
City Improvement Trust warehouse with a collage of contemporary arts

spaces inside. The adaptive reuse over six levels rationalised circulation and maximised natural light to galleries and studios. Original columns, beams and brick walls were exposed. Among the occupants are the long-established Transmission Gallery artists' co-op, Glasgow Print Studio and Street Level Photoworks.

At King and Osborne streets is **Wasps South Block** *(NORD Architecture 2012),* a low-cost, high-quality refurbishment with artists' studios and creative economy enterprises in a former textile warehouse unaltered outside. The project won the Royal Incorporation of Architects in Scotland (RIAS) Andrew Doolan Award for Best Building in Scotland 2013.

66

Britannia Music Hall

117 Trongate

Gildard & Macfarlane 1857
Pairs of *putti* hold cartouches with Glasgow's heraldry on the Venetian façade of this music hall, the oldest surviving in the world. It was famed for its 'dancing girls' when Trongate was 'one-eighth of a mile of iniquity',

according to the press. In 1906 show-man A.E. Pickard took over and renamed it the Panopticon, Greek for 'see everything'—and punters did, from freak shows, snake charmers and waxworks to a zoo promoted as Noah's Ark and the stage debut of Stan Laurel.

In 1938 the auditorium, by then a cinema but still with the original balcony, starry ceiling and proscenium arch, was boarded over and forgotten. The Britannia Panopticon Music Hall Trust, formed in 1997, is conserving it for future pleasure.

67

City of Glasgow Bank

60 Trongate

John Thomas Rochead 1855
Shortbread tin baronial built by the

City of Glasgow Bank, rehabilitated as an apartment hotel *(Holmes Partnership c. 2003)*. Rochead went on to design the Wallace Monument (1869), Stirling. The bank went belly-up in 1878, a crash unequalled in notoriety until the Royal Bank of Scotland was bailed out by the British government 130 years later. The City of Glasgow Bank's directors, manager and secretary were arrested, tried and convicted of fraud.

68
Tron Steeple
63 Trongate

Tower c. 1592; Steeple 1630–1636
The collegiate Church of St. Mary and St. Anne was founded here in 1484. During the Reformation the church was stripped of papal furnishings and decorations. It became known as the Tron Kirk because it was near the public weigh beam, or *tron*. The weigh scale was used to tax goods, fees being paid at the Tolbooth. The Gothic steeple is a scaled-down clone of the one at Glasgow Cathedral.

In 1793 the steeple and tower survived a fire caused by members of the Hellfire Club, a bunch of boozed-up anarchic toffs. A new kirk *(Robert & James Adam)* opened in 1794. When Trongate was widened the Tudor arch at the base of the tower was cut out for pedestrians *(John Carrick, City Architect 1855)*. On the west side of the tower is a contemporary sculpture of St. Mungo *(Sharmanka Kinetic Theatre 2002)*, designed to be animated hourly. The baroque screen *(J. J. Burnet 1899)* at Chisholm Street masked an air shaft

to extract smoke from steam trains in the Caledonian Railway tunnel (now the electrified Central low level line) below Argyle Street. The bronze cherub in the niche was added in 1997.

The Adam church was closed in 1946. Its shell is now the core of the **Tron Theatre** complex *(McGurn, Logan & Duncan 1982; RMJM 1998)*. Above the backstage loading bay on Parnie Street is a bronze skull complementing the cherub; both are symbols of dramatic arts *(Kenny Hunter artist)*. The skull is a memory of the old kirk's graveyard. Corpses were unearthed by the Caley's tunnel builders in 1899 and a skull and bones were found during excavations in 1997. No surprise that paranormal activity has been detected inside.

69

Tontine Building

20 Trongate

Thomson & Sandilands 1904

Many warehouses in the city were mixed-use with showrooms, offices and storage for wholesale or retail merchants. Some were gigantic, like this one with a baroque corner tower. It was built by the City Improvement Trust and named after the Tontine Hotel (c. 1840), a three-storey palazzo where merchants met until the Royal Exchange (see 96) opened. The hotel was destroyed by fire in 1911. Its famous Tontine Heads survived (see 121).

The city-owned Tontine Building was renovated in 2016 as a hub for business innovation and start-ups, part of the Glasgow City Region City Deal (2014) to promote economic development.

70

Empire Sign

34 Trongate, 62–64 Bell Street

1997

Wrought iron gates (if open) allow access to Tontine Lane, punched through the Tontine Building and a Victorian block on Bell Street. The inner courtyard is a moody void like a scene from

Hollywood noir, with an enigmatic, wrong-way-round neon artwork, *Empire (Douglas Gordon artist)*. Also here is the classic sign from the Mitre Bar, once in Brunswick Lane where *Empire* was first displayed. The bar's interior is preserved at Riverside Museum.

71

Bell Street Stables

142 Bell Street

A. W. Wheatley city engineer 1898

Sandstone-clad, iron-framed brick structure built for the Corporation Cleansing Department staff and their horses. Carts were parked on the cobbled courtyard accessed through a pend; the horses were stabled in stalls on the upper levels reached on ramps.

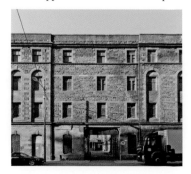

Adaptive reuse *(Collective Architecture 2017)* for Glasgow Housing Association (GHA).

72
Bell Street Warehouse
105–169 Bell Street
  1883; James Cunning, Young
  & Partners 1988

Bonded whisky was secured by the Glasgow & South Western Railway behind these colossal rusticated stone walls. The building, now flats, was the largest of several warehouses constructed around the rail yards on the east side of High Street. The gables on the north façade housed pulleys to haul goods to and from the storage levels.

73
Café Gandolfi
64 Albion Street
  Glasgow Corporation c.1905; 1979
Photographer Iain Mackenzie opened this bistro in the former Corporation Cheese Market office and named it after camera maker Louis Gandolfi. The startup was a gamble. The neighbourhood was faded, far from trendy, but the building had character—high ceiling, wood floors and panelling

and natural light. Organically styled furniture *(Tim Stead)* and fluid stained glass, *A Flock of Fishes (John K. Clark),* spice up the space. The main entrance to the market was on Walls Street (archways and façade in situ).

74
Babbity Bowster
16–18 Blackfriars Street
  Robert Adam 1790; Nicholas
  Groves-Raines 1985
A classical façade attributed to Adam, part of a grander plan not built. The building was a roofless wreck before rehabilitation as a boutique hotel, bar and restaurant. Like the Gandolfi, it put the upcoming Merchant City on the map. The hotel's name is from an 18th-century Scottish fertility dance.

75
Albion Buildings
60 Ingram Street
c. 1875

A richly decorated Italianate warehouse with Venetian windows and
Corinthian pilasters on the central bay.
Planning permission was granted in
1982 for 23 flats, the first residential
rehab in the Merchant City.

76
British Linen Bank
215 High Street
William Forrest Salmon 1895
Cherubs scamper around the window,
a statue broods on the gable, a stained-
glass ship sails through the oculus
above the door, the dome on the cupola

is thought to have once covered a well.
The puzzling façade hides riveted steel
beams and concrete floors. Some wood
panelling remains inside, and the
bank's walk-in vault.

Above the banking hall are flats
accessed from Nicholas Street, where
there is a mews house, shop unit and
a clothes-drying deck—dense shared
spaces, as the medieval High Street
was. A plaque designed by architect
Salmon shows the crow-stepped building the bank replaced. It was the home
of poet Thomas Campbell, the son of
a tobacco merchant, whose statue is
in George Square. Nicholas Street is
one of the few left from the medieval
townscape. It was named after Pope
Nicholas v whose Papal Bull of 1451
founded Glasgow University.

Behind the Linen Bank is the communal **Greyfriars Garden** *(ERZ Studio
2012)*, one of several 'stalled spaces' (see
also 145). Its fence was designed *(ZM
Architecture)* as a timeline, from the
present day back to the 13th-century.

77
High Street Tenements
235–283 High Street
*Frank Burnet, Boston & Carruthers
1903*
Terrific townscape with two rows
of Scots Baronial crow-step gabled,
turreted tenements curving up to
Cathedral Square. Commissioned by
the City Improvement Trust following
a design competition.

Directly southeast is **Collegelands**
*(Page\Park Architects, Ian White
Associates landscape design 2012)*, the

The land between here and High Street was the site of Greyfriars monastery, destroyed during the Reformation. Foundation work for the TIC had to overcome soggy subsoil attributed to ground water where the monastery's well was.

name recalling the Old College. The 17th-century college was replaced by High Street Goods Station. The station's boundary wall on Duke Street was retained in the Collegelands mixed-use redevelopment.

79
Daily Express Building
195 Albion Street
Owen Williams architect & engineer
1936; 3D Reid Architects 2005

78
Technology & Innovation Centre
(TIC), Strathclyde University
99 George Street
Building Design Partnership,
Struer engineers 2015

Originally modernist offices and a printing plant with glass and Vitrolite panels on a reinforced concrete frame. The fusion of engineering and architecture glowed like a beacon of progress and the free press. It was one of a trio built for the paper: the others are in London and Manchester.

A steel-framed wedge cutting into the Merchant City. Landscaping gives it a setting rather than just a street, and a view of the Daily Express landmark (see next entry). The energy-efficient TIC and adjacent **Inovo Building** *(BDP 2014)*, rated BREEAM Excellent, inaugurated the International Technology & Renewable Energy Zone.

The *Scottish Daily Express* was published here until 1974. In 1980 the open-plan floors were retrofitted with information technology for *The Herald,* which stayed for 20 years. Change of use to loft-style living required ceramic enamelled double glazing to replicate the old elevations and improve thermal performance.

80
Ramshorn Kirk
98 Ingram Street
Thomas Rickman 1826

Architect Rickman's self-taught medievalism, all lancets, parapets and pinnacles, is the personality here. There are carved faces in medieval style on hood mouldings around traceried windows. Stained glass is Victorian, much of it commissioned by the families of local worthies. James Cleland, Superintendent of Public Works, altered the plans to include a crypt which raised the height of the structure.

Ramshorn Kirk is early Gothic Revival. It replaced St. David's Parish Church (1724) which stood on the bishop's Ramshorn grazing land. Outside are engraved granite slabs *(Kate Robinson artist 2008)* which recall the position of the parish graveyard before Ingram Street (formerly a track called Cow Loan), was widened and Ramshorn Kirk built. The cemetery, extended behind the kirk, attracted 'resurrectionists' who dug up bodies

and sold them for anatomical study at the Old College, prompting families to fit iron cages around the lairs to deter the body snatchers.

The Church of Scotland sold Ramshorn Kirk in 1983 to Strathclyde University. Its founder John Anderson of Anderson's Institution (1796) rests in the crypt. Outside the church is a plaque to recall John A. Macdonald, the first prime minister of Canada, who was born (1815) in Ramshorn Parish.

81
City Halls and Old Fruitmarket
90–98 Candleriggs
Various architects 1817–1907; 1968; 2003–2006

Behind a Renaissance façade *(John Carrick, City Architect 1886)* is the oldest purpose-built performance space in the city: the 1,000-seat **Grand Hall** *(George Murray 1841)*. Its classic, shoebox shape provides excellent acoustics for concerts and oratory, on the former site of a market, the Bazaar *(James Cleland 1817)*. Less formal is the repurposed **Old Fruitmarket** *(John Carrick 1853)*, cast iron, like The Briggait (see 56).

In 1968 the Grand Hall became the home of the Scottish National Orchestra (SNO) after fire destroyed St. Andrew's Halls (see 294). It was upgraded during a three-year conservation and refurbishment *(Glasgow City Council, Arup engineers)* completed in 2006 which preserved its ambience and improved the acoustic range. The coffered ceiling was opened up for reflectors to better distribute sound,

and windows blacked out since 1968 were uncovered. The BBC Scottish Symphony Orchestra and Scottish Chamber Orchestra are based at City Halls. Also here is the **Scottish Music Centre**, behind a cast iron front (1856) on Candleriggs.

82
Merchant Square
Candleriggs, Bell and Albion streets
John Carrick, City Architect 1886;
Alexander Beith McDonald, City
Engineer 1907; Graven Images 1999

An Italianate façade curving from Bell Street into Candleriggs. On the gable is a stone basket with cornucopia symbolising the fruit and vegetable market once here. Traders moved to an out-of-town facility in 1969. The iron and glass market hall was rebranded Merchant Square, with bars, restaurants and events space in the covered courtyard.

The Renaissance-style Edwardian addition, by A. B. McDonald, turns the corner to Albion Street. McDonald had been assistant to John Carrick and, as City Engineer and Surveyor, headed a team of in-house architects. Their work is commonly attributed to him.

83
Candleriggs Warehouse
79 Candleriggs
Hamilton & Forbes 1932

Several American-style warehouses were built in the district between the wars, this one with characteristic classical proportions articulated by pilasters and cast iron window panels rising to a cornice. The elevations are interrupted by a corner tower, muted Art Deco with two stylised eagles, perhaps American-influenced but eagles are also native to the mountains and glens of Scotland.

84
Ingram Square
Candleriggs, Wilson, Brunswick and
Ingram streets
1984–1987

85
J. & W. Campbell Warehouse
Ingram Square
Robert William Billings 1856

Ingram Square covers a complete city
block of Scots Baronial, French Renaissance and American commercial style
buildings (see previous entry). It was a
pioneering mixed-use regeneration, the
vision of architects/developers Andrew
Doolan and Andrew Burrell. Elder &
Cannon Architects implemented the
14-building project which was significantly residential.

Heritage buildings (or their façades)
were retained. The back court was
infilled with new construction in and
around a redundant factory, and communal space provided. A postmodern
infill at Brunswick and Wilson streets
recalls the Victorian tradition in Glasgow of flamboyant corners. Added to a
mid-block gap site is **Brunswick Hotel**
(1996), also by Elder & Cannon, with a
pre-patinated copper bunnet on its top
floor suite.

Billings had a good eye, could draw
and write, was a conservationist and
penned illustrated books about the
antiquities of England and Scotland.
His work became as much an influence
on the baronial revival in the 19th
century as the writings of Walter Scott.
His buildings are slightly mad.

The Campbells were wholesale textile
and clothing merchants who started
trading in a Saltmarket tenement in
1817. They wanted billboard architecture (the new building featured in their
advertising). Billings gave them Dutch
gables, crow steps and a precarious,
saddleback corner turret.

Ingram Square has a later effort by
him, **100 Brunswick Street** (1859), its
façade quasi-gothic, spooky, inventive.
The unique doorway has an octagonal
upper light flanked by thistle carvings.
Was he a dilettante or genius? Who
cares? His buildings are a delight.

86

Old Sheriff Court

Wilson at Brunswick Street

Clarke & Bell 1844; Parr Architects,
Arup engineers, TGP *landscape design*
2002–2006

Built as the City and County Buildings and Sheriff Court, for civic offices
relocated in 1845 from the Justiciary
Court (see 59). Greek Revival portico
on Wilson Street and, on Hutcheson
Street, a Corinthian colonnade originally the front of Merchants House.
There are classical elevations all round
(the Ingram Street part added in 1871).
Very fine friezes *(Walter Buchan sculp-*
tor): *Trial by Jury* on Wilson Street; on
Merchants House *Maritime Trade.*

In 1863 the merchants moved to
George Square; councillors too when
the City Chambers opened in 1888. The
old building was reconfigured to enlarge the courts. Vacated by the 1980s
it was rehabilitated as flats, and for the
Scottish Youth Theatre whose entrance
is a pod in a Parisian-style passage
punched through the block.

The streets were hard-landscaped
to blur the conventional separation
of traffic and people. On Hutcheson

Street there is a monument, the Letter
of Guildry Pillar *(Doug Cocker artist*
2005), marking the 400th year of the
document which regulated craft and
trade guilds.

87

Hutchesons' Hall

158 Ingram Street

David Hamilton 1805; John Baird (II)
1876; Pollock Hammond Partnership
2014

A wedding cake owned by the National
Trust for Scotland since 1984. Built
for Hutchesons' charitable trust which
evolved from a hostel (Hutchesons'
Hospital) for elderly tradesmen and a
school for orphans founded by brothers George and Thomas Hutcheson.
Sculptures of them *(James Colquhoun*
c. 1650) are the oldest such artworks
in the city. They stand in niches on
the façade to where they were moved
after the hospital, on High Street, was
demolished in 1795. Victorian interiors
(John Baird) restored, now a café bar
and brasserie.

88

The Italian Centre

Ingram and John streets

Page\Park Architects 1988–1992

Boutique mall around a courtyard with heritage buildings rehabilitated. The urban design was inspired by the *palazzi* of the Renaissance, its public art and civic spaces. A statue, *Italia*, looks down Glassford Street while atop the John Street façade is *Mercury (Alexander Stoddart sculptor)*. The courtyard has a water feature and sculptures: free-standing *(Shona Kinloch)* and wall-mounted *(Jack Sloan)*. Fans of postmodernism will spot quotes from Scarpa and Graves.

89

Savings Bank of Glasgow

177 Ingram Street

John Burnet 1866; J.J. Burnet 1900

A domed banking hall with lavish sculptural work *(George Frampton, William Shirreffs)* applied to baroque façades. The ensemble above the entrance has miniature Atlantes supporting a split pediment, maidens symbolising Agriculture and Trade, barley sugar columns, St. Mungo and the city's heraldry. The bank's original headquarters by Burnet senior looms

above with a top floor colonnade added by J.J., his son. The bank, founded in 1836 to encourage the poor to save, was based initially at Hutchesons' Hall (see 87).

90

The Corinthian

191 Ingram Street

David Hamilton 1842; John Burnet 1878; G1 Group, Graven Images 1999, 2010

Originally this was the site of Virginia

Mansion, property of tobacco merchant George Buchanan. Glasgow Ship Bank, founded on Saltmarket in 1750, the first bank in the city, built a new headquarters here in 1842. Its Doric portico *(David Hamilton)* was replaced by Burnet's spectacular Renaissance façade. The Doric columns were relocated (see 410). Existing statuary *(John Mossman sculptor)* was remounted.

Place names on the façade refer to branches of the Union Bank of Scotland which absorbed the Ship Bank in 1843. The domed banking hall *(James Salmon senior 1853)* on Virginia Place has fine carvings outside *(John Thomas sculptor)*. Sumptuous interiors survived use as a courthouse in the 20th century. The glass-domed, barrel-vaulted and colonnaded salons have been restored as the Corinthian Club.

91
Trades Hall
85 Glassford Street
Robert Adam 1791–1794

This is the city's oldest secular building still used for its original purpose: home of the Trades House of Glasgow, a federation of 14 trades and a benevolent society established in 1605. Robert Adam was one of the few architects whose name became a style, associated especially with his interiors. Those here were replaced by Victorian interventions. The façade and dome are original, typical of Adam's work: prestigious, classical and scholarly without being pompous, and proportioned perfectly. The two small outer bays (not shown) are additions *(David Hamilton 1838, James Sellars 1888)*.

92
Virginia Court
Virginia Street and Miller Street
zm Architecture 2009

Old and new buildings in a courtyard accessed from an alley beside the **Tobacco Merchant's House** (see next entry) and through a pend in **Virginia Buildings** (43 Virginia Street, 1817).

Next door, on Virginia Street, is a ghost sign, 'Jacobean Corsetry', a shop here from 1946 until 2000. The mixed-use Virginia Court replaced Crown Arcade (1820), formerly the tobacco and sugar exchange, which should have been saved but was condemned as being unstable.

93
The Tobacco Merchant's House
42 Miller Street
John Craig 1775

The family home of merchant prince Robert Findlay, a founding member of the Chamber of Commerce (1783) and later Chairman of it. It is the only house left in the Merchant City from the era of the tobacco lords. It was subsequently occupied by cotton spinners, jewellers, glass and chinaware importers, and printers. It was derelict before being rescued and restored in 1995 by Glasgow Building Preservation Trust.

Next door (54 Miller Street) is a palazzo *(James Smith 1863)*, originally **Old Stirling's Library**. The library and warehouses replaced the other merchants' houses here. The warehouse at **81 Miller Street** *(James Salmon senior 1850)* is the finest.

94
Buck's Head Building
63 Argyle Street
Alexander Thomson 1863

'Greek' Thomson adapted classical forms to the contemporary city and to innovations in construction. This warehouse is essentially iron and glass, a McConnel patent load-bearing structure (see 47). Cast iron columns and a filigree balcony wrap around the corner, giving depth to the façade. Glazing extends to stone pilasters to maximise light inside. Decoration is delicate, Greek of course.

Built on the site of the Buck's Head Hotel (1790), with a stone deer *(John Mossman sculptor)* to say so. The extension on Dunlop Street (1864; rebuilt 1982) was reduced by demolition in 1975 to three original bays.

95
Guildhall
57 Queen Street
David Barclay 1903; Covel Matthews Architects 1987

The shop fronts, façade and majestic entrance of this mammoth warehouse for Hunter Barr & Co. were retained when the building was redeveloped with offices. A full height atrium, said to have been the first such intervention in a heritage building in Scotland, was hollowed out of the old light well. Architect Barclay's building replaced the National Bank which was disman-

tled stone by stone, re-erected and renamed **Langside Hall** (see 433).

96
Gallery of Modern Art (GOMA)
Royal Exchange Square
1778; David Hamilton 1827-1832;
Glasgow City Council 1996
Punctuating the end of Ingram Street is the former mansion of merchant William Cunninghame, who made a fortune from his hoard of tobacco after the price went up during the American War of Independence. The Royal Bank bought the house in 1817 and stayed until 1827 when a new building, the Greek Revival **Royal Bank of Scotland** *(Archibald Elliot),* was completed at the west end of Exchange Square.

The mansion—'the wonder of its time'—was reconstructed for the Royal Exchange by Hamilton. He wrapped it with Roman splendour: a portico, Corinthian columns, a pediment and clock tower, and extended the flanks

with more columns. There is a vast salon with a coffered ceiling and parallel colonnades where members of the Exchange, previously at the Tontine Building on Trongate, traded in coal, iron, shipping and colonial commodities. In 1880 a mansard was added to house the first telephone exchange in the city.

The building was bought by Glasgow Corporation in 1949 and reopened in 1954 as Stirling's Library. Heritage features, including the oval-domed hall of the original mansion, were retained in the 1990s when it was rehabilitated for GOMA. The new identity was announced on the portico's tympanum—a mosaic deconstruction of the city coat of arms *(Niki de Saint Phalle artist)*—and the gallery name engraved in Roman letters on the entablature.

The clock tower has been restored *(Austin-Smith: Lord 2016)*. The resulting stone patchwork followed conservation best practice—that the difference between new work and the original be clear. Passersby unaware of this wonder why the restorers didn't just clean the whole thing up.

Across the road is **110 Queen Street** *(Cooper Cromar 2015)*, a glass curtain-walled office block. Curvy corner and concave elevation on Ingram Street, like it's breathed in to seem less bulky.

97
Duke of Wellington Monument
Royal Exchange Square
Carlo Marochetti sculptor 1844
A noble equestrian statue of 'the Iron Duke' rarely without a traffic cone on

his head. The mischief was condemned in 2013 by no-fun officials who said the plinth should be raised to stop the habit. Council was ridiculed on social media and retreated.

The bronze statue was erected to commemorate the defeat of Napoleon

at Waterloo. Tableaux of Wellington's victory and other narratives are on the plinth. Marochetti also designed the equestrian figures of Victoria and Albert (1854, 1866) on George Square.

98
St. Vincent Place
Various architects 1871–1907
A passage on the north side Exchange Square leads to an alley and St. Vincent Place, an unexpectedly wide space in the dense downtown street grid. It features heritage buildings of exceptional variety and quality.

Clydesdale Bank *(John Burnet 1871–1874)* at 30 St. Vincent Place has a Venetian Renaissance façade and sculptures *(John Mossman)* of Father Clyde, St. Mungo, Industry and Commerce (classical figures, a blacksmith and a fabric seller). The façade is in-

complete because the *Evening Citizen* owned the adjacent lot. The paper's name appears above the entrance to its northern Renaissance façade *(Thomas Lennox Watson 1889)*. Next door is the **Anchor Line Building** *(James Miller 1907)*, built for the Glasgow steamship company. The façade gleams with Doulton Carraraware faience. A restaurant occupies the opulent interior.

At 2 St. Vincent Place is the **Bank of Scotland** *(John Thomas Rochead architect, William Mossman sculptor 1870)*. At the door two Atlantes support the bank's coat of arms—a shield with the Saltire, four coins, and the figures of Justice and Plenty. The domed banking hall is now a bar. The south side of St. Vincent Place is dominated by the **Scottish Provident Building** *(Peddie & Washington Browne 1906)*, nine storeys of faux Parisian grandeur.

99
George Square

c. 1772

The site was bought by the city and named for George III. It was edged with Georgian townhouses and laid out formally in 1825 as a garden for residents. It became a public space in 1862, and a grand one when the **City Chambers** (see 104) opened in 1888.

The first of many statues was of John Moore *(John Flaxman sculptor 1819)*, Glasgow-born hero of the Peninsular War. The square's centrepiece is the **Scott Monument** *(column David Rhind; figure by John Greenshields sculptor, completed by John Ritchie 1838)*. The fluted Doric column with the figure of Scott was paid for by public subscription. It was the first memorial erected to the writer, preceding the more famous Scott Monument in Edinburgh.

Across the square from City Chambers is the Italianate **Merchants House** *(John Burnet 1874)*. Atop the campanile is the merchants' symbolic sailing ship on a globe. J. J. Burnet added a baroque superstructure (1909). Directly north is **Queen Street Station** *(James Carswell 1880)* with an iron arched train shed.

There are no sculptures to record the square's most tumultuous event: Black Friday in January 1919. Shipyard and engineering workers campaigning for a shorter working week were read the Riot Act by the Lord Provost and confronted by police, backed up by English troops and six tanks. Glasgow's own regiment, the Highland Light Infantry (HLI), was confined to Maryhill Barracks lest its Jocks join the proletariat. The government in London was fearful 'Red Clydeside' might spark a Soviet-style revolution.

The only substantial 20th-century addition to the square is the **Cenotaph** *(J. J. Burnet 1924)*, unveiled by Earl Haig to commemorate Glasgow's dead of the First World War. The polished granite monument is flanked by two recumbent imperial lions. Burnet insisted the site in front of the City Chambers was the best place for it.

In 2012 an international design competition to reconfigure the square challenged the tired traditionalism of its public realm. The entries variously excluded traffic and sidelined the sculptures and Walter Scott. The winning design *(John McAslan + Partners)* kept Scott as the centrepiece of a land-

scaped, uncluttered civic space. But the jury was overruled by the leader of city council and the project abandoned. A *cause célèbre* and an opportunity lost.

100
George House
50 George Square
  Cockburn Associates 1979; Reiach
  & Hall Architects 2012
This office block replaced a rotting but reusable Georgian terrace, one of two (c. 1810) on the north side of the square; the other, formerly the North

British Hotel, still stands. George House escaped the wrecker's ball after a taller development was rejected by city council in 2009. A rethink and refurbishment made it a model of sustainability (BREEAM Excellent), gaining carbon credits rather than the debit of demolition and new construction.

More conventional is adaptive reuse of heritage buildings. **Z Hotel** *(Purcell architects 2014)*, 36 North Frederick Street, is a minimalist rehab behind the façade of a former printworks, originally a warehouse (1883). At 280 George Street is the Parisian roofline of the former Inland Revenue Office *(Walter W. Robertson 1885)* which, with the adjacent Parish Halls Building *(Thomson & Sandilands 1900)*, 266 George Street, is part of the **George Street Complex**. Renderings *(Hoskins Architects)* were released and planning permission sought in 2016.

cornice. The façade facing the square was originally to have been twice as long. The exterior was kept as a heritage mask for a recent rebuild.

The style was first seen in Glasgow when the **Phoenix Assurance Building** *(Alexander David Hislop 1912)* was constructed at 78 St. Vincent Street.

101
McLaren Warehouse
9 George Square
> *James Miller, Richard Gunn 1924;*
> *Glass Murray Architects 1998*

Gunn worked in the United States before joining the office of James Miller and was influenced by American skyscraper classicism. He achieved with several buildings in Glasgow the thrilling vertical emphasis of the early 20th-century Chicago Style, if without skyscraping height. The style adopted the three divisions of a classical column (base, shaft and capital) expressed, as here, with a strongly modelled main floor, pilasters and

102
General Post Office Building
47 St. Vincent Street, George Square
> *Robert Matheson, Office of Public*
> *Works 1875–1878; Cooper Cromar,*
> *Woolgar Hunter engineers 2010*

Now called G1 George Square, this was,

until 1995, the city's main post office. It was extended in two phases on Ingram Street and filled at the sides *(William Thomas Oldrieve 1894–1916)*, creating a mail sorting and delivery complex covering a city block. The extensions were converted to flats (2002). A proposal to make the original on George Square a national gallery of art and design failed to raise funds. Eventually the property was gutted and rebuilt with offices. Basement parking was excavated. The Renaissance façades were retained and restored. The upper levels of offices are covered with a French-style steel and glass canopy.

103
Cochrane Square
Cochrane Street
CZWG Architects 1998

A postmodern façade responding to the scale of the City Chambers and to local history. Pilasters punch out like the prows of ships; soffits and panels in the window bays look riveted, respectively references to maritime trade and shipbuilding. Frivolous but fun.

104
Glasgow City Chambers
George Square
William Young architect; various sculptors 1883–1888

Queen Victoria opened this Venetian Renaissance extravaganza, one of the most opulent city halls anywhere. Two design competitions attracted over 200 entries. For the prizewinner it was a homecoming. He was born in Paisley, trained in Glasgow but based in London, thus a controversial choice.

The enterprise was a tremendous expression of civic pride. The laying of the foundation stone in 1883 was declared a public holiday and a vast crowd watched the event. After the official opening a 10-day public viewing enthralled 400,000 visitors, among them the project's workers showing their families and friends what they had done.

Young supervised the sculptural programme, the most extensive and elaborate seen in the city. The exterior is a narrative of civic and imperial success. Classical friezes symbolise local arts, crafts, sciences and commerce. **The Jubilee Pediment** has Victoria paid homage by peoples of the empire; at its apex is Truth Shining the Light of Liberty, with the figures of Riches and Honour by her side. The elevation culminates with figures of the Four Seasons around the campanile's cupola.

The interior is stunning, decorated with the finest materials. On the floor of the **Loggia** (as the lobby is called) is a mosaic of the city's coat of arms;

more mosaics sparkle in the vaulted, domed ceiling. The cruciform plan makes the space feel like a shrine. Beyond are the **Marble Staircases,** each in separate but connected voids like a *capriccio* by Piranesi. Windows overlook an inner courtyard. The **Councillors' Corridor** is clad floor to ceiling with glazed ceramic tiles. The **Banqueting Hall** has a barrel-vaulted ceiling and murals illustrating the city's history and progress. On the *piano nobile* is the mahogany panelled **Council Chamber** with a view commanding George Square.

105
City Chambers Extension
John Street
Watson, Salmond & Gray 1914
The annex opened in 1923 having been delayed by the First World War. It is

linked to the original building by two splendid Beaux-Arts triumphal arches. The architects also sketched a proposal by the client to enlarge the Council Chamber in William Young's original building. This would have repositioned the Jubilee Pediment on a giant Corinthian portico above a three-bay arcade on George Square. Fortunately the sketch was as far as the idea went.

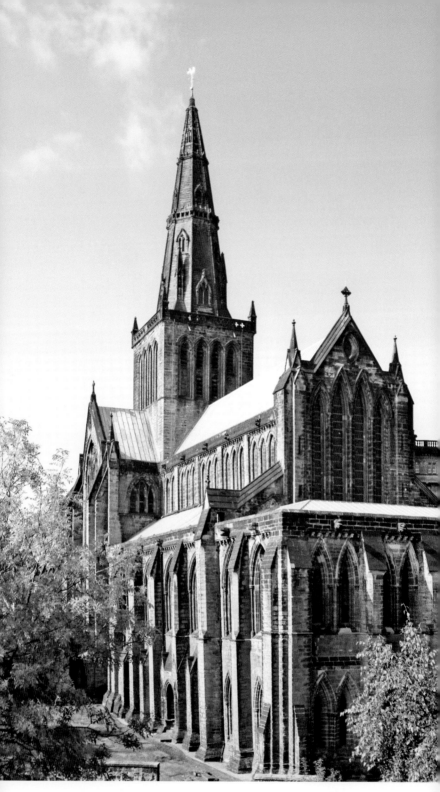

Glasgow Cathedral

3

Cathedral Street to Springburn

PERCHED ON THE EDGE of Townhead Interchange on the Glasgow Inner Ring Road (the urban section of the M8 motorway) is Martyrs School, designed by Charles Rennie Mackintosh. He was raised in a tenement in Townhead, a densely populated district north of Cathedral Street. Its character was caught memorably in the paintings of tenement children by Joan Eardley before it was wiped off the map in the 1960s, replaced with high-rise housing. The school narrowly escaped demolition when the interchange was constructed between 1968 and 1972.

The genesis of the Ring Road and 'comprehensive redevelopment' was the 1945 Bruce Report for Glasgow Corporation, a vision of a 'healthy and beautiful city' with separate zones for business, industry, housing and recreation, and corridors for transport. It was a Frankenstein monster of town planning: part Le Corbusier proposing to flatten central Paris for tower blocks; part Robert Moses, the freeway-obsessed planner in New York. The report, or Bruce Plan, was penned by city engineer Robert Bruce who should have been given counselling for megalomania. Had it been implemented fully the city centre would have been razed and rebuilt as a modernist Utopia. Of the historic buildings only Glasgow Cathedral would have been spared, with traffic on the Ring Road thundering in a cut below its front door.

The report was supported because it would have maintained the city's population and status. The rival Clyde Valley Regional Plan (Scottish

Office, Edinburgh 1946) proposed rehousing people in new towns out-side the city, and thousands were. Redevelopment went ahead in districts like Townhead. The Ring Road was not finished—Glasgow is never fin-ished, always in flux in different directions, part of its character and vitality. The north and west sections were built; the southern flank, now the M74 connector, opened in 2011; the so-called East End Regeneration Route is the substitute for the east flank, which was opposed. Had it been built, the cathedral would have been cut off, High Street destroyed and part of Glasgow Green despoiled. And yet . . . Were those who built the Ring Road exercising fearless foresight inherited from the merchants and engineers who made the Clyde navigable in the 19th century? For better or worse it is now as much part of Glasgow as the river.

Springburn was a 1960s Comprehensive Redevelopment Area (CDA), one of 29 in Glasgow. Like the others it has walk-ups and high flats. At the time, more than 200 tower blocks replaced tenements and changed the city skyline. Tenants liked the new flats but poor construction and maintenance, and social problems caused by industrial decline and unemployment made many housing schemes as bad as the slums they replaced. Writer William McIlvanney's detective Jack Laidlaw called them, memorably, 'architectural dumps where they unloaded the people like slurry. Penal architecture.' Since the 2003 transfer of council's stock of social housing to Glasgow Housing Association (GHA) and its neigh-bourhood off-shoots, the cityscape has changed, yet again. More than 30 percent of the residential towers have been demolished including the steel-framed Red Road flats, once the tallest in Europe. Others, however, are being refurbished sustainably.

Before industrialisation in the 19th century Springburn was home to agricultural labourers, quarry workers and weavers. The first signifi-cant industry was St. Rollox Chemical Works. In 1842 the Edinburgh & Glasgow Railway opened. Its arrival attracted the industry for which

Springburn became world renowned—locomotive manufacturing. Little is left. The largest relic is on Flemington Street, a heritage building with a steam engine in stone above the door, the headquarters of the North British Locomotive Company. It was formed in 1903 by a merger of three firms and became Europe's preeminent builder of steam locomotives. For 60 years folk on Springburn Road saw the company's gleaming engines hauled by flatbed trucks down to the docks for export. Most were built for railways in the colonies and dominions of the British Empire. When the empire collapsed and countries switched from steam to diesel and electric traction North British went bust, in 1962. Its workers had built more than 11,000 locomotives, a huge contribution to Glasgow's economy and reputation for engineering excellence.

Springburn's misfortune to lose its biggest employer was nothing to what followed. Springburn Road, lined with tenements and shops, the spine of the community, was bulldozed for an expressway, a legacy of the Bruce Report. The Burgh Halls (1902), a gift to the people from Hugh Reid of locomotive builders Neilson, Reid & Company, was neglected by council, declared dangerous and demolished in 2012. Springburn Park's iron and glass Winter Garden is derelict. It was donated by Reid in 1900. A statue of his father, pioneering locomotive builder James Reid, still stands in the park, which was established by the city in 1892.

Springburn has been sidelined by the new Glasgow. Restoration of the Winter Garden would help get it back on track. Glasgow Kelvin College, opened in 2009 across the street from the North British Locomotive building, is a rare sign of revival. Education is a catalyst for change, not just in Springburn. Colleges and universities are building facilities to attract research investment and students. Strathclyde University, established in 1964, its origin Anderson's Institution of 1796, continues to expand along George and Cathedral streets, the latter also the site of a new campus for City of Glasgow College (2016).

106

Glasgow College of Building and Printing

60 North Hanover Street

Wylie Shanks & Underwood

1958–1964

A modernist icon, the first International Style high-rise in Glasgow and still the best. No other building in the city looked like it or had such an array of Le Corbusier-style sculptural forms (and now a telecom mast) on the roof, or a lozenge-shaped plan similar to contemporary towers in Milan, New York and Vancouver.

The curtain walls gleamed with

Vitrolite and glass; the east and west elevations were clad with Italian travertine panels. A concrete podium resolved the steeply sloping site. The south-facing entrance features a cantilevered concrete canopy, and *pilotis* expressing the reinforced concrete structure. The low-rise pavilion to the north was added in 1969.

In 2015 the tower was advertised for disposal by City of Glasgow College, along with the seven-storey former **Central College of Commerce** on Cathedral Street (same style, same architects 1959–1963).

107

Royal College Building, Strathclyde University

204 George Street

David Barclay 1903–1909

Grandiose Italianate block said to have been the biggest single educational building in Britain at the time. The front elevation has a triple-arched Florentine entrance and Corinthian columns rising to a pediment. Side elevations stride up the hill. Edward VII laid the cornerstone, inscribed to record the event. The Royal College of Science and Technology became Strathclyde University in 1964.

108

McCance Building

George Street and Richmond Street

Covell Matthews & Partners
1964–1968

A megastructure composed in a striking hierarchy of forms typical of Brutalism, the style favoured by universities at the time. It was conceived as an arts, social sciences and commercial complex. Educational floors are above a parking and retail podium. At its east end is **Livingstone Tower**, designed for offices (there was no take-up, so it was leased to the university). An art gallery, the **Collins Building**, was added on Richmond Street in 1973.

109

Rottenrow Gardens

Gross Max landscape design 2003

Much-needed green space for the university, on the site of Glasgow Maternity Hospital which was demolished in 2001. Architectural features from it were kept as gateways to the gardens. The terraced layout was a response to the plunging terrain of the cleared site. Plantings and paving create areas of activity, contemplation and natural beauty. A seven-metre-high steel nappy pin, *Monument to Maternity (George Wyllie artist)*, was installed in 2004.

110

Sculpture Garden
Strathclyde University

Sixteen steel pillars like megalithic monuments *(Gerald Laing artist 1974)* stand in a park on the highest point of the campus. Commissioned by the university they were dubbed 'steelhenge' but inspired by and named *Callanish* after the prehistoric standing stones on the Isle of Lewis. On the south edge of the park is the brutalist former **School of Architecture Building** *(Frank Fielden & Associates 1967)*.

111

John Arbuthnott Building, Institute for Biomedical Sciences
27 Taylor Street
Reiach & Hall Architects 1998
On the north side of Strathclyde's sculpture garden, a high-tech, eco-friendly experiment in passive design. It was a pioneering investment in green technology with energy savings over the life of the structure. The break-even point was estimated to be around 10 years. The elevation has a double skin with catwalk access for window cleaning. Solar transfer is regulated with outer louvres. The void

between the two skins encourages the stack effect for natural ventilation and climate control. Hot air rises to be extracted; solar heat gain in cooler weather can be maximised. The strategy is widely accepted now.

112

Wolfson Centre for Bioengineering
106 Rottenrow East
Morris & Steedman 1971
A modernist box articulated powerfully with precast concrete vertical fins in zigzag profile. The effect is curiously classical, like a monolithic fragment of a fluted Doric column. It faces a plaza, below which is a galvanised steel

artwork *Prometheus, the Gift of Science to Liberty (Jack Sloan artist 1994).*

113

Institute of Pharmacy & Biomedical Sciences
161 Cathedral Street
Sheppard Robson Architects 2011

Designed for several faculties under one roof, to promote interaction. The interior programme reflects that idea with a see-through, triple-height entrance and reception with a coffee shop and common areas. A suspended stair serves three upper levels which have labs and other work spaces. Strong street presence and a public plaza.

114

City of Glasgow College, Cathedral Street Campus
Reiach & Hall Architects, Michael Laird Architects, Arup engineers, rankinfraser landscape architecture 2016

The college is the largest in Scotland following its creation by a merger of three older institutions in 2010. It embarked on an ambitious building

programme—two flagships, one at **Riverside Campus** (see 58) and the other here. Its gleaming modernist elevations are clad with precast *brise soleil.* The mass is dynamically distributed across a sloping site. Angled forms are echoed in a luminous, multilevel atrium. The public realm is generous: a sociable south-facing park, landscaped with trees and monumental steps arranged informally.

115

Barony Hall, Strathclyde University
Castle Street
J. J. Burnet 1889; David Leslie Partnership 1995

Barony Parish congregation worshipped in the crypt of the cathedral until 1798 when a church designed by James Adam opened on Cathedral Square. It was strange, castle-like, described by one minister as 'the ugliest kirk in all Europe'. It was replaced by this Gothic Revival design. No steeple: simply a flèche on a barn-like timber roof above a lofty, austere interior.

In 1986 Barony Church was bought by Strathclyde University and rehabilitated as a ceremonial and graduation

hall. Fine stained glass includes Bicentenary windows *(John K. Clark artist)*.

Across the street is an equestrian statue *(Peter Scheemakers sculptor 1734)* of William III dressed like a Roman emperor. Originally outside the Tontine Hotel on Trongate, it was relocated here in 1926.

116
Ladywell Housing Scheme
Cathedral Square and Drygate
Honeyman, Jack & Robertson 1964

Tenements on *pilotis*. Step through the gap and you're in a time warp of slab blocks and walk-ups like Soviet workers' housing. The scheme, built on the site of Duke Street Jail, was named after the Lady Well on Ladywell Street, closed for hygienic reasons after the Necropolis opened. Didn't bother brewers long established here (see 164).

117
Barony North Church
Cathedral Square
John Honeyman 1880
Built as Barony Free Church, Italian baroque with a single campanile at the north end (a second tower for symmetry was not built). Statues of the Evangelists stand like silhouettes, and niches contain St. Peter and St. Paul *(attributed to John Mossman or McCulloch & Co., London)*. Inside is a U-shaped gallery on cast iron columns, a Victorian pipe organ and Greek Revival-style stained glass, *The Transfiguration (W. & J. Keir)*. In 1978 the building was bought by Glasgow Evangelical Church and restored.

On the boundary wall is a memorial to the Townhead Martyrs, three Covenanters executed in 1684. Martyrs School (see 128) was named for them.

118
Cathedral Hotel
Cathedral Square
Campbell Douglas & Morrison 1896
A Scottish Baronial curio, originally the Discharged Prisoners Aid Society, a rehab centre for prisoners released from Duke Street Jail. Lord Provost

William Bilsland, the society's chairman, hoped the former jailbirds would learn trades and 'regain the paths of virtue and sobriety'.

119
Cathedral Visitors Centre
2 Castle Street
Ian Begg architect 1990
A rusticated stone pastiche of the Bishop's Castle, a tower house pillaged during the Reformation. The replica houses the St. Mungo Museum of Religious Life and Art. The museum features items representing the world's religions, from Christian stained glass to a Zen garden. The centre was a pivot for renewed urban design, creating a sense of enclosure which has made Cathedral Square (see 122) more visitor-friendly.

120
Provand's Lordship
3 Castle Street
1471
The oldest dwelling in Glasgow, originally a clergy house. Ceilings are low, wood-beamed above small windows in rubble stone walls. There are fireplaces and wood floors, and a stone spiral stair well worn.

The house was part of a cluster of ecclesiastical buildings around the cathedral. Most were abandoned after the Reformation. In 1906 a historical society was formed to preserve the building, which has been owned and renovated periodically by the city since 1978. The 17th-century furniture is from the Burrell Collection (see 467).

121
Tontine Heads, St. Nicholas Garden
3 Castle Street
David Cation 1736, Mungo Naismith 1760 masons; Gary Johnson architect 1995
At the back of Provand's Lordship is a re-creation of a medieval cloister and herbal garden. In the cloister are the Tontine Heads, grotesque keystones from the arches of the Tontine Hotel

(see 69) on Trongate. Some are thought to be caricatures of local worthies, others the Green Man. Also in the cloister is an eroded coat of arms, carved by master mason John Boyd, salvaged from the Tolbooth (see 61). The fence and gates *(Jack Sloan artist)* incorporate local symbols.

122

Cathedral Square

Page\Park Architects, Ian White Associates landscape design 1988

The space in front of the cathedral, a parking lot for the Royal Infirmary, was reclaimed after a public realm competition. The makeover reoriented the precinct to counter the distracting bulk of the Victorian hospital. An *allée* oriented to the west front of the cathedral was created along with an angled alignment from the southwest. Statues were rearranged, notably **David**

Livingstone *(John Mossman sculptor 1879)*, its plinth with bas-relief panels illustrating his adventures in Africa. Vintage lampposts are decorated with the city's bird, tree, bell and fish symbols. The Bishop's Palace Memorial Pillar *(James Miller architect, Robert Gray sculptor 1915)* marks the site of the 13th-century palace.

123

Glasgow Cathedral

Cathedral Square

The first stone kirk was dedicated to St. Kentigern, commonly known as St. Mungo, by King David I of Scotland in 1136. The sixth-century saint was the first bishop of the kingdom of Strathclyde and his tomb is in the crypt, which became a place of pilgrimage. Bishop Jocelyn gained the monastic settlement and town below it burgh status, granted by King David's grandson William the Lion in 1178.

The Gothic Cathedral is of the 13th to 15th centuries. The structure steps down to a glen where the Molendinar burn flowed. The roof ridge was extended but remained high. The interior is consequently long, lofty and luminous, with a descent to an undercroft (the Lower Church) and St. Mungo's shrine. In the novel *Rob Roy,* Walter Scott described the lower levels: 'an extensive range of low-browed, dark, and twilight vaults . . . regions of oblivion, dusky banners and tattered escutcheons . . .' These levels, including the chapel-like **Blacader Aisle** (15th century), have since been restored. Archbishop Blacader also

commissioned the stone choir screen. It is decorated with figures, possibly representing the Seven Ages of Man or Seven Deadly Sins.

Most of the stained glass is 20th century (a controversial 19th-century scheme of Munich glass was replaced). In the nave the **Great West Window**, *The Creation (Francis Spear 1958)*, and **The Millennium Window** *(John K. Clark 1999)* are outstanding. Memorial windows, plaques and cenotaphs line the walls. They commemorate distinguished citizens, and army officers from imperial conflicts. The city's 14 craft trades are here, as they should be—the guilds reputedly defended the cathedral during the Reformation because their members built it. The west front had two towers believed to have been medieval. The Victorians thought not and tore them down in the 1840s.

The timber roof, much rebuilt, is a medieval design. Continuing conservation and restoration of the building by Historic Environment Scotland includes stone carved to fit the existing work, and new gargoyles, pinnacles and window tracery. In 2009 it became the 100th landmark to be illuminated as part of city's Lighting Strategy to enhance the public realm.

124
Glasgow Necropolis Gates
Cathedral Square
1833

Glasgow Cathedral has two burial grounds. The older, at the entrance, predates the church; the newer to the north opened in 1801. Neither they nor Ramshorn churchyard (see 80) could be enlarged, so the Necropolis was laid out in Merchants Park on Fir Hill. To reach it, the triple-arched **Bridge of Sighs** *(David Hamilton 1834)* was built across the Molendinar burn. The name of the bridge came not from the one in Venice but, it is said, because the walk across the glen and up the hill exhausted coffin bearers. The bridge complements the cathedral and the setting. Artist J. M. W. Turner thought so and sketched the scene in 1834.

The path from the cathedral to the bridge is entered through ceremonial iron gates. They bear the ship on a globe emblem of Merchants House, the city coat of arms and signs of the zodiac (being symbols of navigation by the stars). Merchants House owned the hill and developed the new cemetery.

125
Glasgow Necropolis
Cathedral Square
Begun 1832

Valhalla for the great and good of Glasgow society—preachers and lord provosts, merchants, shipbuilders, iron founders, locomotive builders, professors and poets. Above them all, on a fluted Doric column, is the joyless leader of the Reformation, John Knox *(Thomas Hamilton architect; figure by William Warren, Robert Forrest sculptor)*; foundation stone laid in 1825.

A design competition for the cemetery was held in 1831. The winner was architect David Bryce; his brother John Bryce was runner-up. The judges preferred that a landscape gardener implement the scheme and appointed, as superintendent and head gardener, George Mylne. Whatever the attribution, the landscape design was inspired by Père Lachaise in Paris (1804). Catacombs were planned but the tunnel, at the entrance to the cemetery, collapsed leaving a cave with a baroque façade.

The Necropolis was declared multifaith (the first burial was a Jewish merchant and cholera victim) but the solemn monument to Knox reveals its Presbyterian personality and where power and influence lay. Knox is sur-

rounded by pathways stratified around contours crammed with mausoleums, obelisks and angels carved in stone, all in the architectural styles of the Victorian city they overlook.

Eulogies inscribed on the markers are self-serving but truth often undermines sanctimony: for 'West India planter' read slave owner. Below Knox is a flamboyant memorial to actor-manager John Henry Alexander *(James Hamilton architect, Alexander Handyside Ritchie sculptor 1851).* It has a bas-relief stage and proscenium originally with figures of Tragedy and Comedy, the cemetery's most honest comment on life.

126
Royal Infirmary
84 Castle Street
James Miller 1905–1915
The Victorians created some wonderful townscapes. The juxtaposition of this hulk next to the cathedral was not one

of them. The bulky block was erected to commemorate the 63-year reign of Queen Victoria whose figure *(Albert Hemstock Hodge sculptor)* is on the façade. The previous infirmary *(Robert & James Adam 1794)* was smaller and more respectful of the setting.

127
Royal Blind Asylum
90 Castle Street
William Landless c. 1880
An eccentric baronial pile with crow-step gables, turrets, battlements and a Gothic clock tower with gargoyles. There is a seated statue, *Christ Healing*

natural light. Timber roof trusses, iron brackets on the balconies and exterior stonework show Mackintosh's unique style emerging.

A plaque by the park outside has a street plan marking the tenement (demolished) where he was born. The street lamps are his design, revived in the 1990s. Public art (2008) in the nearby Townhead housing estate was inspired by his work. The school is now council offices.

the Blind *(Charles Grassby sculptor).* The asylum was founded in 1828 to provide accommodation, education and training for the blind. It was absorbed by the Royal Infirmary in 1935.

129
St. Mungo's Church
52 Parson Street
Goldie & Child 1869

128
Martyrs Public School
Parson Street
Honeyman & Keppie, Charles Rennie
Mackintosh 1898
The school was beached like a shipwreck when the M8 motorway was channelled through Townhead. Inside, you would not know this happened, the Victorian interior being well preserved. The atrium, a typical feature of school-board architecture, is flooded with

Franco-Italian Gothic with a half-built tower. Rose window with attached sculpted figures, *Christ and Madonna (Andrian Melka sculptor 2002).* High altar *(Gillespie, Kidd & Coia 1952)* and stained glass by Mayer of Munich (1898), which had supplied windows for Glasgow Cathedral. Energetic contemporary stained glass, *Adam and Eve (Lorraine Lamond artist 2002),* enlivens the quatrefoil and rose windows. Next door is the collegiate Gothic style **St. Mungo's Retreat** *(Father Osmund Cooke 1892).*

130

Townhead Blochairn Parish Church

176 Royston Road

Campbell Douglas & J. J. Stevenson 1866; John Gilbert Architects, Loci Design landscape design 2001

Buttressed tower with a spire like a rocket on Roystonhill. The Normandy Gothic landmark was saved by community action after the city declared it unsafe in 1997 and threatened to tear it down. The church, which had an interior by Daniel Cottier and stained glass by Morris and Co., had already gone (the Morris glass was salvaged by Glasgow Museums).

Part of the north front remains as a screen to **Spire Park**, a contemporary landscape intervention. The tower was stabilised and restored and the spire and finial reconstructed. Adjacent is **Rosemount School** (1866). Spire View Housing Association plans a community centre *(MAST Architects, MB Landscape Architects)* behind its Gothic façade.

131

St. Rollox House

130 Springburn Road

c. 1880

This former Caledonian Railway office belies the extent of St. Rollox locomotive works founded in 1854, and how

industrialised the area was in the 19th century. The skyline—when it could be seen above the smog—was dominated by the twin smokestacks of Pinkston Power Station and the 132-metre chimney (the world's tallest) at the sprawling, toxic St. Rollox Chemical Works, the largest in Europe, established in 1799 (all demolished). Pinkston (1900) powered the city's electric trams.

What's left of the locomotive works is a maintenance facility for ScotRail. The office was refurbished for a regeneration agency. The name St. Rollox is derived from an early 16th-century chapel to St. Roche, built at Townhead because an appeal to the saint was believed to cure the plague. Nothing remains of the chapel which was abandoned after the Reformation.

132

Sighthill Regeneration

Fountainwell Road

Collective Architecture, Linda Curr landscape design 2015

Ten multistorey slab blocks were demolished to make way for this Glasgow Housing Association development, a mix of flats and terraces for tenants displaced by the demolitions. In spirit and form the new buildings are Scottish vernacular, human-scale, with varied materials replacing the bleak uniformity of the slab blocks. Traditional streets and community amenities, absent from the Comprehensive Redevelopment Areas of the 1960s, are included in the masterplan for hundreds of new homes here.

133
Sighthill Cemetery
225 Springburn Road
1840

Sighthill Cemetery Company advertised this 'beautiful Garden Cemetery laid out in fine Walks and Parades at immense cost in its embellishment, the Père Lachaise of Glasgow'. Inspiration from the Paris cemetery had already been claimed by the Necropolis (see 125). Nevertheless, Sighthill's 'elevated situation and commanding views' match its rival. The embellishments include a pillared gateway and Greco-Egyptian chapel *(John Stephen 1839)*.

Sighthill's most famous monument is the **Martyrs Memorial** to leaders of the Radical uprising of 1820 hanged at Stirling, their 'slain and mutilated forms' reinterred here in 1847. Other dissidents were transported to a penal colony in Australia. Also buried here are architect William Leiper and the Mossman family of sculptors, whose work adorns many of the city's buildings and cemeteries.

134
North British Locomotive Company
120–136 Flemington Street
James Miller 1909
Edwardian baroque headquarters with a steam engine above the door flanked by two classical figures representing Speed and Science *(Albert Hemstock Hodge sculptor)*. North British was an amalgamation in 1903 of three local locomotive manufacturers: Sharp, Stewart & Co., Neilson, Reid & Co., and Dübs & Co. The deal made it the biggest locomotive builder in Europe.

The building's roof was ribbed and glazed for north light to drawing offices in the attic. A light-well brought daylight to lower floors. During the First World War armaments were produced in the locomotive works. The Red Cross had a hospital for wounded servicemen in the office building, where a stained glass war memorial window *(William Meikle & Sons)* was unveiled in 1921. North British went out of business in 1962. Springburn College occupied the building, now Flemington House business centre.

Nearby is the Carnegie-funded former **Springburn Public Library** *(William Brown Whitie 1906),* 179 Ayr Street, built on railway land donated by Neilson, Reid & Company.

135
Glasgow Kelvin College
123 Flemington Street
RMJM 2009

A great white ship of regeneration sailing in a sea of industrial decline. The campus evolved from Springburn College of Engineering, part of the district's industrial heritage. The serrated roof in the atrium is a homage to drawing offices once on the top floor of the North British Locomotive Company headquarters. The college building bisects the former site of the Sharp & Stewart's Atlas and Neilson's

Hyde Park locomotive works. The wedge-shaped part of the plan allowed for a landscaped public realm.

136
Balgray Tenements
Lenzie Street and Barclay Street
Beattie & Morton 1903

Lenzie Street was part of Balgrayhill Road until planners redrew the map with new roads, for which these tenements were lucky to escape demolition. They have characteristic features: bay windows, a domed corner and wally closes with floral tiles ('wally' means white china, hence closes with ceramic tiles on the walls). Adjacent new housing *(Page\Park Architects 2017)* in urban village style for Loretto Housing Association.

At the crest of Balgrayhill Road is **Viewpoint Place** *(Archibald George Jury city architect 1964–1968)*, four point towers once part of a huge housing scheme of linear deck-access blocks. Demolition has eliminated most of them. Those remaining, and the towers, have been refurbished by North Glasgow Housing Association. Nearby at 140–142 Balgrayhill Road is **Redclyffe**, a modest early work (1890) by Charles Rennie Mackintosh.

137
Balgray Tower
52 Broomfield Road
David Hamilton c. 1820

A belvedere like an 18th-century garden folly. The octagonal tower was built for Moses McCulloch to admire the panorama to the west. There are battlements and an internal spiral stair. McCulloch owned a foundry on Gallowgate. His name lives on at Mosesfield House (*David Hamilton 1838*) in Springburn Park.

138
James Reid Monument
Springburn Park, Broomfield Road
William Goscombe John sculptor 1903
A bronze statue on a plinth inscribed

'James Reid of Auchterarder and the Hyde Park Locomotive Works'. He is posed as if surveying the empire to which his steam locomotives were exported. Plaques with Pre-Raphaelite females holding tablets record he was a president of the Institute of Fine Arts and of the Institution of Engineers and Shipbuilders, and Dean of Guild in Glasgow.

In his sight line is a Doulton terra-cotta column (1912), originally the centrepiece of a fountain sited where Springburn Leisure Centre is now.

139
Winter Gardens
Springburn Park
Simpson & Farmer 1900
James Reid's son Hugh funded this spectacular glasshouse, once the largest in Scotland. Its builders, Simpson & Farmer, were based at Partick Bridge. The roof, ridged with cast iron thistles, was made by William Baird of Temple Ironworks, Anniesland.

The A-listed glasshouse was once

filled with exotic plants. None now because city council wanted to tear the place down, having left it to rot after closing it in 1984. In 2014 Glasgow Institute of Architects and Springburn Winter Gardens Trust held a competition to stimulate adaptive reuse. The city recently approved repairs to prevent the roof collapsing.

140
Stobhill Hospital Water Tower
Belmont Road
Robert Sandilands 1903
Water and clock tower in baronial style, with bartizans, fake gargoyles and a bulbous crown. Typical of the age when functional buildings were decorated to pretend the Industrial

Revolution had not happened, that somehow an idyllic past had not been lost. The former Superintendent's House also reflects the delusion, in half-timbered Tudor style. The hospital complex *(Thomson & Sandilands 1901–1903)* was built in the countryside to replace poorhouse wards in the city.

141
Ambulatory Care and Diagnostic Centre, Stobhill Hospital
133 Balornock Road
Reiach & Hall Architects 2009

A one-stop, same-day patient consultation and medical testing facility for NHS Greater Glasgow and Clyde on the existing campus. Trendy iconic design was resisted. The building is restrained and rational with clear and soothing spatial organisation designed for users, not for show.

Two blocks—north for treatment, south with clinics—are fused by a linear concourse which is projected in a long canopy onto the entrance plaza. The concourse is the circulation hub with access to all levels. The clinics are grouped around larch-clad courtyards. Artworks and poetic inscriptions were part of the programme.

Templeton's Carpet Factory

4

The East End

'LEARN FROM THE PAST, USE WELL THE FUTURE' was the motto on a plaque inside Bridgeton Working Men's Club. The building was opened in 1899 on Landressy Street near Bridgeton Cross. It had recreation rooms, a library and canteen. Booze and gambling were banned on the premises. Workers' well-being was the motivation of the employers who had established the club in 1865. By 1899 there were thousands of members. When it closed in 1978 and was demolished there were 20, a symbol of the rise and fall of the industrial East End.

The East End was an economic heavyweight in the 19th century. Among its enterprises were William Arrol & Company, builders of hammerhead cranes for shipyards, the Forth railway bridge and the 1960s road bridge; William Beardmore & Company whose Parkhead Forge was the largest iron and steel mill in Scotland; Tennent's Wellpark Brewery; and James Templeton & Company, known for its Venetian Gothic carpet factory on Glasgow Green. Only Tennent's brewery is still in business.

The 'future' in the motto at the Working Men's Club turned out to be grim. Deindustrialisation from the 1960s through the 1980s led to lives on the dole and slum clearances. Folk were moved to housing schemes miles away or to new towns built for Glasgow's 'overspill', the euphemism planners and councillors used meaning people, none of whom was consulted. The authorities wanted a quick fix for the city's slum housing. The East End lost two-thirds of its population.

The motto's 'past' was a potent brew of industrial progress and radical protest . . . the theme of *The Glasgow History Mural* by Ken Currie inside the dome at the People's Palace. The mural was created for the bicentenary in 1987 of the killing of the Calton Weavers during a strike. Weaving was the work of most folk in Calton village east of Glasgow Cross in the 18th and into the 19th centuries, and textiles became one of the main industries in the East End. Currie's tribute to industrial labour, from the weavers to Govan shipbuilders, was the most ambitious artwork commissioned for a Glasgow public building since the Banqueting Hall in the City Chambers was decorated a century before. Entry to the People's Palace, which opened in 1898 with a museum, art gallery and concert hall (the Winter Garden), was free and remains so today.

The post-industrial notoriety of the East End obscured stable communities like Dennistoun. It began as an upmarket suburb of terraces and villas proposed by landowner Alexander Dennistoun. He hired architect James Salmon (senior) to plan it. Some villas and terraces were built according to the plan. Tenements followed as the city grew. Architecturally the neighbourhood, complete with Victorian churches, schools and a Carnegie library, is comparable to the solidly built tenement areas of the Southside and West End. There are parks, notably Alexandra and Tollcross, both a legacy of the Victorian desire for urban green space and healthy recreation, and of course Glasgow Green.

The Gaelic for Glasgow, *Glaschu*, means Dear Green Place. It is still. Satellite images taken in 2016 of the ten cities in the UK with the largest populations showed Glasgow the second greenest (32 percent green); Edinburgh was first, almost 50 percent of land within its boundary being relatively undeveloped. Glasgow has more than 90 parks and gardens. The oldest, Glasgow Green, dates from 1450. It has been used for pleasure, public hangings and political demonstrations. In December 1745 troops led by Bonnie Prince Charlie camped on the Green, some billeted in a church, St. Andrew's in the Square, being built at the time. The Prince stayed at Shawfield Mansion by Trongate. He was not popular with the city's elite which was Hanoverian, a stance evident still in street names, but his demand that his soldiers be fed and clothed was met. The mood of the burghers of Glasgow was that the sooner the Jacobites left the better and the city could get back to business.

Glasgow Green was neglected during the years of comprehensive redevelopment. In 1976 the multi-agency Glasgow East Area Renewal (GEAR) shifted policy from new towns back to the city. The remaining crumbling tenements and derelict factories were demolished and new homes built, some with gardens which created a surreal suburbia amidst what was left of the past. Bridgeton Cross and Parkhead Cross retain impressive *fin-de-siècle* buildings which, like those in Dennistoun, are now protected in conservation areas. Glasgow Green was restored in the 1990s. On its north side is Homes for the Future, an innovative project which reinvented traditional urbanism, a legacy of Glasgow's year as City of Architecture and Design 1999.

What did not return despite GEAR's hopeful prospectus was industry, and it never will in its previous form. The latest regeneration effort, Clyde Gateway, formed in 2007, is a 20-year programme of investment in housing and business parks, environmental clean-ups, skills training and employment. Early efforts upgraded transport infrastructure and landscaped the routes to the arena and velodrome built for the 2014 Commonwealth Games, which were a boost to the East End's revival. The eco-friendly Athletes' Village was rehabilitated as housing. Across the river a woodland park opened in 2016 on previously derelict land. Clyde Gateway also sponsored the Olympia, an outstanding adaptive re-use of a derelict, century-old music hall and cinema at Bridgeton Cross. The old motto 'Learn from the past, use well the future' still applies.

St. Andrew's in the Square

1 St Andrew's Square

Allan Dreghorn architect, Mungo Naismith mason 1739–1755; Nicholas Groves-Raines 1999

The town council sought donations and levied a £1 head tax on citizens to pay for this church, for which a competition was held. The winning design was based on St. Martin-in-the-Fields, London *(James Gibbs 1726)*. The style is baroque, the exterior lacking Gibbs's polish but tougher. There is a noble portico, with the motto *Let Glasgow Flourish* and the bird, tree, bell and fish symbols carved on its pediment. The clock tower remains a landmark.

In 1993 the Church of Scotland announced it was leaving for the usual reasons: a declining congregation and the cost of maintenance. Glasgow Building Preservation Trust restored the building, now a Scottish cultural centre managed by St. Andrew's in the Square Trust. Victorian interventions were removed, except for stained glass *(Stephen Adam)* in the Palladian window. The vaulted ceiling springs from fluted Corinthian columns. There is gilded rococo plasterwork *(Thomas Clayton c. 1755)*. The 18th-century colour scheme was replicated after on-site analysis by conservationists from Historic Scotland. Extra space to generate income was created below by excavation.

When built, the church stood among fields and orchards. The square in which it is set was not laid out until 1774. Its terraces, once fashionable, became run-down and were demolished in the 1980s. Redevelopment *(Robert Johnston Associates 2000)* replicated their Georgian façades.

Nearby is the former **Central Police Headquarters** *(Alexander Beith McDonald, City Engineer 1903)*, red brick and sandstone, with finely-carved civic heraldry and figures of Law and Justice *(McGilvray & Ferris sculptors).*

143
St. Andrew's by the Green
33 Turnbull Street
Andrew Hunter mason 1751
An Episcopalian church, the oldest surviving in Scotland. It was called the 'whistling kirk' because music from the church organ could be heard across Glasgow Green. The Presbyterians, who banned instrumental music at the time, called it a 'temple of error', and accused mason Hunter of 'sin and scandal' for building it.

The last service was in 1975. Rehabilitated as offices (1988). Old gravestones in the burial ground. Next door (33–39 Greendyke Street) is the façade of Glasgow Corporation's **Skin and Hide Market** *(Honeyman & Keppie 1891).* Flats built behind (2000).

144
Homes for the Future
Greendyke Street
Page\Park Architects, Arup engineers, Elder & Cannon Architects, McKeown Alexander, Rick Mather Architects, Ian Ritchie Architects, RMJM, Ushida Findlay, Wren Rutherford, 1999

'How do you get across what architecture can be more clearly than through the idea of home?' asked Deyan Sudjic, Director of Glasgow City of Architecture and Design 1999. 'Rather than rely on exhibitions and talks, it makes more sense to give people the chance to build something.' Which is what he did.

Homes for the Future was the year's most exciting and progressive project. Its optimism recalled the Deutscher Werkbund 1927 housing exhibition in Stuttgart, an experiment in stylish, cost-effective modernist housing.

The masterplan *(Page\Park Architects)* reinterpreted the city's tenement block urbanism and posed alternatives to it, a mix of apartments and town houses. Some reinforce the traditional street wall; others are set back in a courtyard where landscape design was part of the plan.

Elder & Cannon's building on Greendyke Street has an angled penthouse pod and a high walkway along the elevation. The sleek, curve-fronted neighbour was the first in Britain by Tokyo-based Japanese-Scottish partners Ushida Findlay. In the courtyard Wren Rutherford sought a contemporary but traditionally rooted idiom that nods to Mackintosh. The project showed that place-making could be more than heritage pastiche; that fitting the urban scale and grain is what matters.

At Charlotte Street is the brutalist extension to **Our Lady and St. Francis Secondary School** *(Gillespie, Kidd & Coia 1964)*. The Georgian house (c.1790) of David Dale, co-founder of New Lanark, was on the street. It was demolished with three others in the 1950s. A fourth survives at 52 Charlotte Street.

145
Barrowlands Park
London Road and Gallowgate
Loci Design landscape design 2014
The site was derelict—one of city council's 'stalled spaces'—and a potential embarrassment on the route to the East End venues of the 2014 Commonwealth Games. The temporary

park deserves to be permanent. It has an artwork, *The Album Pathway (Jim Lambie artist)*, made with coloured concrete strips like the spines of vinyl record covers. These feature almost every band that has appeared at the nearby **Barrowland Ballroom** (1934; rebuilt 1960). Brilliant. So is Barrowland's neon sign.

146
White's Clay Pipe Factory
42 Bain Street
Matthew Forsyth 1877

Industrial vernacular in the emerging creative zone at the Barras flea market. Twins on Bain Street, and a sibling on Moncur, originally William White & Son's Clay Pipe Factory. The company produced tobacco pipes, pottery clay and, significantly in Glasgow, soap-like blocks of pipe clay. The clay, dissolved in water, was used to clean the stairs in tenement closes. Traditionally every week each resident took her turn—and it was the women who did the work— to sweep and mop the common stairs.

At 17 Bain Street is **Saint Luke's**, a Georgian church *(James Wylson 1836)* refreshed in 2015 as a performance and events venue, bar and kitchen. Grant aided by the Calton Barras Action Plan and Glasgow City Heritage Trust. One of numerous projects supported by the trust since its inception in 2007.

147
Gallowgate Tenement
Gallowgate at Claythorn Street
1771

A stone tenement, one of two here. Both feature a central chimney gable, and a cylindrical stair tower at the rear. This one is part of a 1983 Scottish Special Housing Association (SSHA) development; the other, Hielan Jessie, a traditional bar. They were built when the East End was a gateway to Glasgow. Travellers were fed and horses watered at stagecoach inns. The most fashionable was the Saracen's Head (1754; demolished 1904), recalled by the eponymous bar at 209 Gallowgate.

148
Doulton Fountain
Glasgow Green
Arthur Ernest Pearce designer;
various sculptors 1888
Four tableaux vivants of the British Empire decorate this fabulous fountain. It was gifted to the city by the Doulton Company after being a showpiece at the International Exhibition held in Kelvingrove Park in 1888. It was re-erected on the main promenade of Glasgow Green in 1890. Queen Victoria stands at the top of the structure guarded by her armed forces, including a Highland warrior. Australia, Canada and South Africa, and the British Raj are represented on the tableaux below.

Like all things Victorian it was

neglected during Glasgow's obsession in the 1960s with modernity and motorways and became a target for vandals. Eventually it was restored piece by piece (2004–2005) and relocated on a plaza outside the **People's Palace** museum (see next entry). It is the world's largest terracotta fountain.

149
The People's Palace
Glasgow Green
Alexander Beith McDonald, City Engineer 1893–1898

French Renaissance style with figures of Industry, Science and Arts *(William Kellock Brown sculptor)* on the façade. Attached at the rear is the cast iron and glass **Winter Garden**. At the inauguration Lord Rosebery called the unconventional ensemble 'a palace of pleasure and imagination around which the people may place their affections and which may give them a home on which their memory may rest.'

The memory palace tells the story of the people's city from 1750 to the present. In 1899 David Richmond, Lord Provost, called it the unique institution 'an experiment full of potentialities.' Its potential to be one of the most

popular museums in Scotland was realised fully in the 1980s, due largely to the work of former curator Elspeth King. Commissioned at that time, for the octagon inside the dome, was *The Glasgow History Mural (Ken Currie artist)*, eight panels of agitprop (see page 92).

Outside is one of several Commonwealth Games legacy sculptures *(Robert Coia 2014)* made for Glasgow parks. This one was inspired by First Nations' mythology on Canada's west coast.

150
St. Andrew's Suspension Bridge
Neil Robson engineer 1855
Built to replace a ferry for industrial workers. Cast iron pylons with fluted Corinthian columns look like classical porticos. The wooden deck was replaced, the ironwork repaired and painted saltire blue, and new lamps fitted (1998). The old lamps are in the garden of the Humane Society house.

151
Glasgow Humane Society
Glasgow Green
The oldest life-saving society in the

world, founded with a merchant's bequest in 1790 to rescue people from the river or recover bodies. A lifeboat shed and officer's house have been here since 1795. The present house was built in 1937. An inscription on the path at the suspension bridge records officer Ben Parsonage who 'single handedly rescued more people from drowning than any man in Britain.'

Nearby on the river bank is the historic, timber-framed **West Boathouse** *(Alexander Beith McDonald, City Engineer 1905)*, still used by the two original rowing clubs.

152
Nelson Monument
Glasgow Green
David Hamilton 1806
On the main promenade of the Green an Egyptian Revival obelisk on a classical plinth, the first civic monument to Nelson, erected by public subscription.

No embellishment was required other than the name of the hero and his naval victories—Aboukir, Copenhagen and Trafalgar, where he was killed.

Near the obelisk is a granite stone (1969) inscribed in memory of James Watt. Legend has it that while walking here he had the eureka moment which revolutionised steam power.

153
Templeton's Carpet Factory
Glasgow Green
William Leiper 1888–1892

James Templeton & Co. as 'patrons of the arts resolved to erect, instead of the ordinary and common factory, something of permanent architectural interest and beauty.' What they got was inspired by the Doge's Palace in Venice, after asking Leiper what his favourite building was. So the story goes.

The polychrome façade was as decorative as the carpets made inside (the drapery-clothed figure spinning thread on top represents the textile industry). Behind the façade was a functional factory. This was revealed tragically in 1899 when part of the front collapsed during a gale, killing 29 women weavers working in an adjoining shed.

Three thousand people once worked
here. Later buildings include an Art
Deco extension with zigzag brickwork
(George A. Boswell c. 1930). The complex
was rehabbed in 1982 as a business
centre, now an urban village *(ZM
Architecture 2005–2010)*, mixed-use,
trendy with a brewpub, West Brewery.

154
James Martin Memorial Fountain
Templeton Street
 Walter Macfarlane & Co., Saracen
 Foundry 1893
Moorish-style filigree design decorated
with lions, dragons, owls, swans and
herons, and an eagle on the dome.
James Martin was a councillor and
magistrate. Macfarlane's Saracen
Foundry, Possilpark, was one of the
biggest makers of architectural ironwork in the world, with a mail-order
catalogue and products which reached
the furthest corners of the empire.

155
Greenhead House
Greenhead Street
 Charles Wilson 1846; Carrick
 & McCormack Architects 2000
A palazzo for Duncan McPhail whose
cotton spinning mill (1824) was here.
The house was sold in 1859 and became

the Buchanan Institution for destitute boys. The adjoining Palladian façade with a student with chalk and slate *(William Brodie sculptor)* was added in 1873. The building became Greenview School in 1904. Converted to flats and renamed Buchanan Square with contemporary infill behind.

156
Logan and Johnston School
Greenhead Street at James Street
James Thomson 1890

Founded as a school of domestic economy to train poverty-stricken girls for household service. The name is on the stumpy tower; the date and a beehive symbol of productivity are on one of the gables. The style is Scottish Renaissance, slightly Flemish. Now part of Buchanan Square (see above).

157
Glasgow National Hockey Centre
Glasgow Green
Glasgow City Council 2013
Low-tech stadium stand with a high-tech look, appearing lightweight like a hang-glider. The dynamic roof form is steel-framed on column and strut supports. A legacy structure from the 2014 Commonwealth Games (see 182).

158
Glasgow Women's Library
23 Landressy Street
James R. Rhind 1906; Collective Architecture 2015
Formerly Bridgeton Public Library, one of seven Carnegie libraries in Glasgow designed by Rhind with sculptor William Kellock Brown. After a new library opened at **The Olympia** (see next entry) the old building was reha-bilitated for Glasgow Women's Library. The façades have figurative carvings revealed agreeably along the curve of the street. Heritage features remain inside following a structural upgrade and reconfiguration of the spaces for exhibitions, readings and reference. An extension for an elevator was built, decorated with a wall of words.

Also by Collective Architecture is **Red Tree Business Centre** (2013), 33 Dalmarnock Road, a smart retrofit on a tight site overlooking the railway at Bridgeton Station.

159
The Olympia
4 Orr Street

John Arthur & Frank Matcham 1911;
McNair & Elder 1938; Page\Park
Architects 2012

A Beaux-Arts beauty with an Ionic-columned corner and French dome, originally the Olympia Theatre of Varieties, a music hall. It was revamped as a cinema in 1924 and given a moderne makeover in 1938. By the 1970s cinema-going had declined. Many picture palaces like the Olympia were converted as bingo halls. The building was later a furniture store, then abandoned and, in 2004, damaged by fire.

Clyde Gateway, the regeneration agency, stepped in with a rescue plan. The façade was retained and a steel-framed structure built behind. Its minimalist glazed curtain wall makes the adaptive reuse clear. Bridgeton Library (see previous entry) was relocated here, and there is a BFI Mediatheque, a café, gym and offices. The dome was taken down and reconstructed. The canopy and sign recall the original ones. A curvy new stair captures the picture palace spirit perfectly. The intervention achieved a BREEAM Excellent rating.

160
Bridgeton Umbrella
Bridgeton Cross

George Smith & Co., Sun Foundry
1875

Bridgeton Cross Shelter and Clock, called for generations the 'Umbrella', was more than a public clock, tram-stop rendezvous and shelter from the rain: workers assembled to pick up day jobs. The cast iron classic was fabricated at Smith's ironworks at Townhead. It was restored (2010) and repainted in historically correct colours as the focus of a pedestrian-friendly public realm *(Austin-Smith: Lord, Gillespies landscape design),* for Clyde Gateway.

161

Calton Burial Ground

309 Abercromby Street

1787

The burial ground was founded by the Incorporation of Weavers of Calton and Blackfaulds. Eroded plaques on the wall inside the cemetery commemorate three weavers shot and killed in 1787 by troops deployed as strike-breakers. The strike was provoked by 'starvation wages' after the East India Company imported cheap material. The words are clearer outside new gates where inscriptions were made on the pavement: the weavers were 'martyred by the military, under orders of the Civic Authorities of Glasgow.' More than 6,000 people attended their funeral.

162

St. Mary's Calton Church

89 Abercromby Street

1842

Two angels fly across the pediment of this, the second-oldest Catholic church in the city after St. Andrew's Cathedral (see 51). The interior, illuminated from double-height windows, has an arcaded gallery with cast iron columns *(George Goldie architect 1877)* added after the ceiling collapsed. A Renaissance-style triptych dominates the altar. The parish has a historic connection with Celtic Football Club (see 181).

163

Graham Square

Gallowgate

McKeown Alexander, Page\Park Architects, Richard Murphy Architects, Arup engineers 2000

A redevelopment by Molendinar Park Housing Association of the city's Abattoir and Meat Market *(John*

Carrick, City Architect 1875), a sprawl of utilitarian iron and glass sheds. A heritage-listed Roman façade with paired Doric columns, filigree iron inserts and bull and ram's head keystones was reused as a screen for infill flats, with a void for privacy. A second old façade is at the top of the street. Forms and materials—butterfly roofs, glazed stairways and functional cladding and render—did not mean breaking with the past: across the street a second block responds to the urbanism of a 19th-century tenement (the Drover Bar on Gallowgate), and the old Market Hotel was rehabilitated.

The brief was focussed on place-making, with affordable, energy-efficient homes of mixed configurations. The scheme was design-led, with the three architectural practices selected to work together after a competition. Public art, *The Calf (Kenny Hunter sculptor)*, recalls the former purpose of the site.

A companion to Graham Square, also on the former meat and cattle market site with a heritage archway retained, is **Moore Street Housing** *(Elder & Cannon Architects, JM Architects, Page\Park Architects, Richard Murphy Architects, 2007).*

164
Drygate Brewery
85 Drygate
Graven Images 2014
In the shadow of Ladywell Housing Scheme (see 116) a craft beer outlet in a repurposed brewery packaging plant. Craft beers and groovy graphics. Architecture? Industrial

chic. The startup is part of Tennent's **Wellpark Brewery** (161 Duke Street), a site associated with brewing since the 1550s. Down the hill, at 100 Duke Street, is the former **Great Eastern Hotel** *(Charles Wilson 1848)*, originally a cotton mill, later a skid-road hostel. Closed in 2001. Rebuilt with flats behind the façade.

165
Wellpark/Kirkhaven Enterprise Centre
Duke Street and Sydney Street
Peddie & Kinnear 1858; Elder & Cannon Architects 1996, 2003
A Greek Revival church with carved relief decoration in the pediment above a Corinthian-columned porch. It was built as Sydney Place Presbyterian Church, latterly Kirkhaven Day Centre for homeless men until closed in 1986.

Retrofitted inside with workspace rental units. Original plaster ceiling in situ. Adaptive reuse by Glasgow Building Preservation Trust included the adjacent Italianate former Wellpark Institute (1867), a Free Church school.

To the east is the former **Duke Street Women's Hospital** (253 Duke Street). Nothing remains except a French Renaissance-style administration block (*Alfred Hessell Tiltman 1904*).

166

Westercraigs Court
Westercraigs at Duke Street
Campbell Douglas & Sellars 1877; 1988

Formerly Blackfriars Church, first established at the Old College on High Street. This Victorian incarnation closed in 1983. Its towers and entrance were retained when flanking flats were built, fitting the heritage context and streetscape. The taller tower originally had a German Romanesque steeple.

167

Reidvale Tenements
314–332 Duke Street
Elder & Cannon Architects 1992
A revival of the tenement form and its urbanism, where you could pop out for a pint of milk without driving an SUV

to a mall. Reidvale Housing Association, founded in 1975 to refurbish run-down but otherwise sound tenements, commissioned this new build. It was one of the first to show the typology was still viable, and adaptable. Five storeys were fitted to the usual four-storey height. Configuration is open plan, split-level in large flats with south-facing rooms overlooking a landscaped back court.

168

Dennistoun Public Library
2 Craigpark
James R. Rhind 1905

Delightful Italianate Carnegie library with a Venetian window centred on the *piano nobile*, figurative reliefs in the spandrels, and an angel reading a book on the dome. The sculptural work was by William Kellock Brown, the architect's collaborator at several other city libraries.

169
Reidvale Allotments
Reidvale Street
ASSIST Architects 2008

The first new allotments in the city since the Second World War, when self-sufficiency augmented government rations. Galvanised steel fencing secures the perimeter. Recycled railway sleepers were laid for planter beds which vary in height for different users (space was allocated for school children to participate). Cedar sheds were roofed with zinc and collect rain water for irrigation. Cedar resists rain, weathers to a pleasing patina and is maintenance-free. No paint required. All eco-friendly. A trend: community gardens have taken root across the city.

170
St. Anne's Catholic Church
21 Whitevale Street
Gillespie, Kidd & Coia 1933
The earliest church by the firm which replaced weary sermons of Gothic with idiosyncratic modernism (see next entry). The idiosyncrasy here is the mix of sources. The Greek cross plan rises to a vaulted interior. The west front is Italian baroque with the figure of Christ in the pediment *(Archibald Dawson sculptor).*

The expressive fan-shaped brickwork suggests the Amsterdam School. At the entrance is a trio of Romanesque arches with Celtic-patterned pilaster capitals and, in the centre, a Madonna and Child keystone. The style of the carvings and wrought iron gates is late Arts and Crafts, as is the clergy house in the garden.

171
Our Lady of Good Counsel
73 Craigpark
Gillespie, Kidd & Coia 1968

A different tune from St. Anne's, thanks to young talent playing in Jack Coia's band. The new members were Andy MacMillan and Isi Metzstein, to whom much work by the practice is credited. Coia cultivated the patronage of the Catholic Church and gained work on its rebuilding programme for which he embraced MacMillan and Metzstein's free modernist aesthetic.

Our Lady of Good Counsel is pure form with an interior volume expressed by a canted, copper-clad roof, timber-faced inside. The ridge peaks on the west side and drops in a vertical wall which is carried on a linear beam on columns inside. Soft light filters in from random small windows, a quote from Le Corbusier.

The columns and beam separate an aisle, sacristy, baptistery and confessionals from the body of the church. This was possible because the Catholic church altered its liturgy to better engage with the faithful. The architects' unconventional but rational response created a timeless space. It is the only A-listed, postwar church in Glasgow.

172
City Park
368 Alexandra Parade
1953; Cooper Cromar Architects 2001

Built by Imperial Tobacco, this office and factory complex with an Art Deco central tower was rehabilitated as a business centre with additional space added on the roof and corner stair towers elevated. The new levels look top-heavy but are clearly contemporary. Another former tobacco factory is **Wasps Studios** *(Elder & Cannon Architects 1997)* two blocks west.

173
Saracen Fountain
Alexandra Park
Walter Macfarlane & Co., Saracen Foundry; David Watson Stevenson sculptor 1901

Magnificent fountain with classical figures (Art, Literature, Science and Commerce), cherubs, sea monsters and a *tempietto*, all cast iron. It was made for the 1901 International Exhibition at Kelvingrove Park and to promote the company. When Kelvin Way was laid out the fountain was relocated here. A drinking fountain *(Cruikshanks & Co. 1880)* is at the main gate. The park (1870) was designed by Joseph Paxton.

174
St. Andrew's East Church
681 Alexandra Parade
James Miller 1904
Arts and Crafts medievalism like a fortress with a cavernous entrance

bay and traceried window flanked by Gothic towers. The pagoda-style bell tower was influenced by Japanese art and design, being discovered by Western artists and architects at the time. Above the door of the church hall *(James Salmon junior & John Gaff Gillespie 1899)* are angels and the tree of life in organic Art Nouveau style.

175
Vogue Bingo
772 Cumbernauld Road
  William James Anderson (11), John McKissack & Son 1938

Streamline moderne super-cinema, originally Riddrie Picture House, on the edge of suburbs being developed at the time east of Alexandra Park. Faience-clad frontage shaped like a ziggurat, a portal to the world of the silver screen. Renamed the Vogue in 1950. No movies since 1968; a bingo hall instead.

176
Barlinnie Jail
81 Lee Avenue
  Major General T. B. Collinson, Scottish Prison Department 1882–1897
The 'Bar-L' looms over suburbia like a dark satanic mill, a breaker or maker

of hard men. The site, chosen in 1879, was Barlinnie farm estate, way out of town. It is the largest prison in Scotland.

The layout of each cell block is typically Victorian, with cells in a long, galleried atrium. 'A' block opened in 1882 followed by four more. Prisoners quarried and broke stones used to build them. Workshops were built for various trades from which the prison service turned a profit. In the 1970s a 'special unit' gained fame, pioneering rehabilitation instead of punishment.

Barlinnie's buildings are notorious for overcrowding and to be replaced, unlikely to be missed. But a governor said recently, 'There's history here. You could imagine tours, the Alcatraz of Glasgow.'

177
Shettleston Housing Association
65 Pettigrew Street
  Elder & Cannon Architects 2010
Two structures a century apart linked

visually by thoughtful design. The old building is the former Co-operative Hall (1912). The scale and vertical thrust of its Edwardian classical façade inspired the extension's elevation, the old and new in harmony. The project won the Andrew Doolan Award 2010.

178
Tollcross House
Tollcross Park
David Bryce 1848

Country house built for James Dunlop, scion of one of Glasgow's founding mercantile families. The Dunlop assets included at various times a founding share in the Ship Bank, a Virginia tobacco trading house, Clyde Iron Works, and Tollcross estate which was acquired in 1810.

Architect Bryce was the doyen of Scottish Baronial style. The house is romantic with crow steps, scalloped quoins and the requisite French turrets. The estate's South and East lodges (Tollcross and Wellshot roads, respectively) are similarly picturesque. James Dunlop replanted the grounds, which were a refuge from the flaring furnaces and pollution of his nearby iron works.

Glasgow Corporation bought the property and opened it in 1897 as a public park. There are carriage drives, meadows, a wooded glen, a Victorian winter garden, children's farm, rose garden and the **Aquatic and Leisure Centre** (swimming venue for the 2014 Commonwealth Games). The house was for seven decades a children's museum. It was rehabilitated as sheltered housing following restoration in 1992 by the National Trust for Scotland.

179
Beardmore Park Steam Hammer
Westmuir Street at Shettleston Road
R. G. Ross & Son engineers 1915

A relic of heavy industry transformed as public art in a community park created on derelict land (*City Design Co-op landscape design 2005*).

No traditional sculpture could better express the power of William Beardmore & Co., or the passage of time. During the First World War the engineering and shipbuilding giant employed more than 20,000 people at Parkhead Forge making armour plate and guns for warships. It was the largest iron and steel works in Scotland. The site was cleared and is now **The Forge Shopping Centre** (*SBT Keppie Architects 1988*).

180

Savings Bank of Glasgow

1456 Gallowgate, Parkhead Cross

John Keppie 1908

Parkhead Cross, originally a weavers' village, was built up in the late 19th century with an array of tenements, most in Scottish Renaissance style. The highlight is the Savings Bank whose entrance led to a single-storey domed banking hall. There is no bank here now but its imprint remains on façades decorated lavishly with relief carvings and heraldry. High up by the baroque dome is a figure wrestling a wolf—*Prudence Strangling Want (Archibald Macfarlane Shannan sculptor).*

To the east on Tollcross Road are the **Public Library** *(James R. Rhind 1906)* and the **Corporation Baths and Wash-house** *(Alexander Beith McDonald, City Engineer 1905).* Another survivor of civic enterprise is **Parkhead School**, *(Hugh H. MacLure c. 1880),* 135 Westmuir Street, rehabilitated *(Purcell*

architects 2017) by Glasgow Building Preservation Trust with Parkhead Cross Townscape Heritage Initiative and Parkhead Housing Association.

181

Celtic Park

London Road

Celtic Football Club was founded in 1888. It was rooted in charity work by Brother Walfrid and St. Mary's Calton Church (see 162), to alleviate poverty and encourage healthy recreation.

The club moved to this site in 1892. The south stand (1898) was destroyed by fire in 1927. Archibald Leitch, the star of stadium planning at the time— fresh from a design at Ibrox Park (see 455) for rival club Rangers—designed a new stand (1929), since replaced by Celtic's centenary redevelopment.

In the 1990s two all-seat stands were built, named for manager Jock Stein and his team which won the 1967 European Cup. On the plaza outside is a statue of Stein *(John McKenna sculptor 2011)* and one of Brother Walfrid *(Kate Robinson sculptor 2005).* Celtic Park hosted the opening ceremony of the Commonwealth Games.

182

Commonwealth Arena and Sir Chris Hoy Velodrome

1000 London Road

3D Reid Architects, Sports Concepts,
Halcrow Group engineers 2009–2012

The arena and velodrome were the only major venues purpose-built for the 2014 Commonwealth Games. They are separate structures which morph into a glazed circulation zone. A frame attempts to visually bind their bulk together. Both are vast column-free halls. Each is spanned by two 300-tonne, 93-metre roof trusses which were assembled on site, each in two sections, then hoisted by crane and manoeuvred into place.

The arena reverted to a rebranding after the Games, the city having licensed naming rights to Emirates in 2012. Sustainability was a key feature of the event, 'the greenest Games ever'. A legacy is the Athletes' Village energy-efficient district heating system which the arena and velodrome share.

183

Athletes' Village

Springfield Road

Stallan-Brand Architecture + Design,
Brindley Associates landscape design
2014

Around 7,000 Commonwealth Games athletes stayed in this award-winning eco-friendly village. The flats and houses were rehabilitated after the Games and, in 2015, the first residents moved in. The 700-unit estate has 400 rental dwellings for housing associations; the other 300 were sold.

At a glance the scheme is 'new urbanist', a North American place-making mantra fashionable since the 1980s, recalling the English garden city movement of the early 20th century.

The Athletes' Village, however, looks built for the future, not the past. It has contemporary row houses with brick and timber cladding, pitched roofs, and gardens. There are higher density brick-clad four-storey blocks of flats. The row houses look vernacular but of no particular era; the flats utilitarian and no worse for that. There is no distinction between the social and private housing.

A structural timber system allowed off-site assembly of some components. Building envelopes were insulated for thermal performance, roofs have photovoltaic (solar) panels and there is a combined heat and power (CHP) district heating system: all for energy savings and reduced carbon emissions.

The character of the village is quite urban, with outdoor space shared and preference give to people, not cars. The street plan is a grid. Parking areas do not dominate the setting. But there are no shops. The site benefits from facing, on its east side, Cuningar Loop Woodland Park. There is a pedestrian and cycle bridge (*Robertson Civil Engineering 2016*) to the park, across a bend in the River Clyde.

The village won multiple Scottish Design Awards, was shortlisted for the international BREEAM Awards, won a Saltire Society Housing Design Award (all 2014) and the society's Landscape in Housing Award (2016).

184
Dalmarnock Station
Dalmarnock Road
1895; Atkins Group 2013

The previous entrance and ticket hall was a 1980s hole in a wall which treated commuters as if they were moles about to burrow underground. This upgrade, prompted by the Commonwealth Games, and part of Clyde Gateway's regeneration, is more than a shed with a funny shape. The structure bridges the tracks where they enter the tunnel to the city centre. Access to the platforms is efficient and the industrial aesthetic—steel frame and sandblasted glass—fits Dalmarnock's heritage. A car-free route (*Ares landscape design*) leads to Clyde Smartbridge (see 186).

185
Barrowfield Mill
121 Carstairs Street
Joseph Stott & Sons 1885

Italianate relic of the textile industry, built for the Glasgow Cotton Spinning Co. Modelled on cast iron and brick mills in Lancashire, where architect Joseph Stott worked. The site had a tall chimney; Dalmarnock was a forest of them, all gone as is the community.

Across the street is the repurposed **Strathclyde Public School** (*John McKissack 1903*). At 273–289 Dunn Street is a survivor, Andrew Muirhead & Son's historic **Dalmarnock Leather Works**, here since 1870. At 103–113 French Street is the former **Barrowfield Weaving Factory** (1899). The street was first named Papillon Street after Pierre Jacques Papillon, a master dyer from Rouen who knew the secret of Turkey Red dyeing, a profitable process for which the East End became known. He worked for George Macintosh and David Dale who, in 1785 at Barrowfield, opened the first Turkey Red works in Britain.

186
Clyde Smartbridge
Carstairs Street
Halcrow Group engineers 2014

A pedestrian and cycle link between the Shawfield and Dalmarnock regeneration zones. The bridge, part of Clyde Gateway's infrastructure, is 'smart' because the deck has built-in conduits

for broadband and power lines. Even smarter is the butterfly arched steel structure with a cable-braced deck, a model of simplicity, easily the most elegant of all recent Clyde crossings.

187
Police Scotland
2 French Street
Cooper Cromar 2014

The new national law enforcement agency was established in 2013. It absorbed Strathclyde Police which was based in an outmoded 1970s HQ and operations centre on Pitt Street in the city centre. The original City of Glasgow Police Force, from which Strathclyde took over in 1975, was the oldest in Britain, formed in 1800.

This modernist office block with a glass and aluminium façade and stone-clad colonnades accommodates more than 1,000 police officers and support staff on a riverside campus. The building, designed to BREEAM Excellent standard, was built on recycled industrial land and was Clyde Gateway's biggest single development at the time.

St. Vincent Street Church

5

Buchanan Street to Anderston

AT THE CORNER of Buchanan and Argyle streets is a Renaissance-style warehouse built for Stewart & McDonald, clothing makers and retailers who began trading at number 5 Buchanan Street in 1826. Like rival merchants J. & W. Campbell, founded on Saltmarket in 1817, Stewart & McDonald's start-up was a warehouse in a rented tenement. The two companies, which merged in 1922, were market leaders. Glasgow was known not only for its shipbuilding and engineering but also for commerce and, by the end of the 19th century, a culture of consumerism. The first shopping mall in Scotland, the Parisian-style Argyll Arcade, opened here in 1828. Glasgow Chamber of Commerce, established in 1783, is one of the oldest in the world.

The American War of Independence bankrupted some tobacco lords but not those who had begun to diversify. Glasgow's merchants and manufacturers found new markets. Exports to the British Empire boomed in the 19th century. By the 1890s, Stewart & McDonald had wholesale and retail outlets in Scotland, England, Australia, Canada and South Africa. Their factories in Glasgow, Leeds and Northern Ireland produced ready-made clothes for a mass market. The company employed hundreds of factory workers, and warehouse and sales staff.

The name 'Buchanan Street' recalls tobacco lord Andrew Buchanan who invested in real estate in the 1760s. He anticipated the expansion of the city to the west and built a house for himself at what became Stewart

& McDonald's corner. He would have developed the street but the war in America intervened. Buchanan's lands in Virginia were confiscated by the rebels and his businesses back home went bust. Banks took over his Glasgow assets and leased the land. The street was formed and built up from 1780 to 1808, mainly residential (the developer of Argyll Arcade had a villa here). The first public building was St. George's Church (1808), now St. George's Tron Church.

Buchanan Street became a fashionable business, media and retail address. Its historic architecture, with the Stock Exchange and The Herald façades among the most distinguished, is of the highest quality and variety. Frasers Department Store, for example, is an assortment of five heritage buildings: south to north are Stewart & McDonald's corner block (1903) and their earlier property (1879); the former Kemp's Shawl Emporium (1854) with the city's oldest surviving cast iron façade; the former Wylie & Lochhead store (1886) and Maclure & Macdonald lithographers & engravers (c. 1840). The street is now almost exclusively shopping, marketed as the Style Mile along with Sauchiehall and Argyle streets. It was pedestrianised in the 1970s and refurbished *(MBM Arquitectes, Gillespies landscape design c. 2000)* to match the best in Europe. Princes Square (1987) and Buchanan Galleries (1999) raised its profile. Buchanan Galleries, a multilevel shopping centre with a parking for 2,000 cars, is close to Buchanan bus station, the subway and Queen Street train station. It attracts shoppers from a wide catchment area and gave the city centre a boost at a time when it faced serious competition from out-of-town malls.

The city expanded westward in the 1790s when the street grid was extended to Blythswood Hill. The grid—the most efficient way to feu (lease) land for urban development and profit—gives parts of central Glasgow a North American look and so do some buildings. Victorian and Edwardian office blocks by J. J. Burnet and 1920s classical revival banks by James Miller and Richard Gunn could be in New York, Chicago or Montreal. The hilly streetscapes are comparable to the urban drama of San Francisco, with thrilling four-way intersections and perspectives on tumbling terrain.

Terraces, villas and churches were built on Blythswood Hill, which was developed as a residential quarter after the Napoleonic Wars. Some of the domestic architecture survives, converted to offices; other houses were replaced by *fin-de-siècle* office blocks. Thereafter, the streets stayed as they were until the 1960s when modernist offices were built, none of much merit apart from Heron House *(Derek Stephenson & Partners 1971)*, a megastructure with British Telecom offices and the first Habitat store outside London, next to 'Greek' Thomson's St. Vincent Street Church. Its Brutalism, not unsympathetic to Thomson's plan and massing, was bowdlerised by recladding during a makeover for flats in the 1990s. The flats were a good idea. Residential adaptive reuse of buildings in central Glasgow has been encouraged by planners since the 1980s.

New buildings have to conform to height and density restrictions. A marriage of heritage preservation and progress has resulted in façadism. Old buildings look the same but have been retrofitted with the open-plan floor plates contemporary offices require. Interiors are lost but façade retention is better than demolishing everything and starting over, which was the way things were done in the 1960s. Planners and developers have thus maintained the city centre as the region's commuting core without completely destroying its Victorian fabric. The façades are alive with sculpture: if you look up you will see ancient gods, mythical creatures, saints and sea monsters carved on old buildings everywhere.

The lower slopes on Blythswood Hill are part of the Central Business District (CBD). It extends to Anderston, an old neighbourhood completely obliterated by the Ring Road and redevelopment. Its concrete jungle of the 1960s has new growth, Glasgow again remaking itself.

188

St. George's Tron Church
Nelson Mandela Place

*William Stark 1808; CRGP Architects
2007*

The church is centred on what used to
be St. George's Place, an open-ended
square originally on the edge of the
city and residential. In 1986 the square
(then the address of the South African
Consulate) was renamed for Nelson
Mandela. Glasgow had honoured him
with the Freedom of the City in 1981,
the first council in the world to do so.
He returned the compliment with a
visit in 1993.

The urban design here is similar to
Royal Exchange, St. Andrew's and St.
Enoch squares—an architectural focal
point closing street-end views. The
front of St. George's Tron is baroque
with giant Roman Doric columns,
obelisks, a cupola, and a Georgian fanlight above the entrance (the obelisks

were to have been statues until money
got tight). The west elevation is a plain
classical gable. Interior decoration is
confined to coloured glass on the west
windows (1852) and a ceiling rosette.
The windows were exposed when the
organ was removed during a makeover
which created a luminous, multi-
purpose space. The original U-shaped
gallery remains in place.

189

Royal Faculty of Procurators
12 Nelson Mandela Place

Charles Wilson 1856

The faculty was incorporated in the

17th century. Faces of law lords appear as carved keystones. The members' library is an exquisite Palladian room on the upper floor. Of the secular buildings on Nelson Mandela Place only this Venetian-style gem remains in original use. The former **Glasgow Stock Exchange** (see 194) is on the south side of the square. The north side, into Buchanan Street, was occupied from the 1930s to 1987 by the **Royal Scottish Academy of Music & Drama** (RSAMD; see 254) which evolved from the Athenaeum.

190
The Athenaeum Building
8 Nelson Mandela Place
John Burnet 1886

The Glasgow Athenaeum was founded in 1847 to 'provide a source of mental cultivation, moral improvement and delightful recreation to all classes.' The society was based at the Assembly Rooms (see 60) on Ingram Street until moving to this purpose-built neo-Roman clubhouse, fitted out with a library, classrooms, restaurant and concert hall.

Sculptures on the façade (*John Mossman*) expressed the society's aspirations: figurative groups Science and Literature; above them statues of John Flaxman, Christopher Wren, Henry Purcell and Joshua Reynolds. The venue was enlarged with a new theatre at 179 Buchanan Street (see next entry). The original building was gutted and redeveloped behind the façade c.1991.

191
Athenaeum Theatre
179 Buchanan Street
J. J. Burnet 1893

The first of several 'elevator' buildings in Glasgow, tall and thin on a narrow lot. The stairwell still has the lift cage, no longer for the Athenaeum Theatre. Instead there are electric guitars in the shaft, displayed for the Hard Rock Cafe. The makeover (2013) converted the auditorium as a diner. Original columns, arches and the galleried volume were retained. The vertically inventive and eclectic façade and sculptures (*William Kellock Brown*) are unaltered.

192
Liberal Club Building
4 Nelson Mandela Place
Alexander Nisbet Paterson 1909

Edwardian baroque with opulent façades, originally a gentlemen's club, the only one in the city centre to retain its interior décor. The pedimented doorway is corbelled with lion masks. The lobby is vaulted; the vast dining room boasts an extensively plastered ceiling. Rehabilitated (2012) over four floors as Chaophraya Thai restaurant.

193
Buchanan Galleries
220 Buchanan Street
Jenkins & Marr 1996–1999
Multilevel shopping mall with façades trying to fit with the Victorian city centre. It revived a run-down zone at the top of Buchanan Street. Adjacent is **Glasgow Royal Concert Hall** (*Leslie Martin & RMJM 1990*), built for Glasgow's reign as European City of Culture, and to make up for the loss of St. Andrew's Halls (see 294). It required 450 rubber dampers to prevent the rumble from subway trains which pass below being heard and felt. Postmodern exterior coldly classical, retro 1930s.

194
Glasgow Stock Exchange
Buchanan Street and Nelson Mandela Place
John Burnet 1877; J. J. Burnet 1898
Victorian capitalism clothed in Venetian Gothic with tighter-fitting fabric stitched on by Burnet junior. Embroidered with figures of Commerce, Industry and Agriculture, and roundels with busts of Science, Art, Building, Engineering and Mining (*John Mossman sculptor*). Façades and the French roofline owe much to an unbuilt design (*William Burges 1867*) for the Law Courts on the Strand, London.

Trading floor and offices rebuilt (1968–1971). Heritage interior lost. The institution, founded in 1844, joined the London Stock Exchange in 1973. The former **Western Club**, 147 Buchanan Street (*David and James Hamilton 1842*), was gutted as part of the Stock

Exchange scheme, one of the first examples in Glasgow of façadism, where historic preservation is a two-dimensional illusion masking change.

195
Rogano Oyster Bar
11 Exchange Place
Weddell & Inglis 1935
Moderne-style Vitrolite fascia with period lettering and a painted lobster announce this legendary marine-themed eatery. The ritzy interior is said to have been inspired by Art Deco salons on the ocean liner *Queen Mary*, launched at Clydebank in 1934.

196
Royal Bank of Scotland
10 Gordon Street
David Rhind 1853–1857
An elegant palazzo built for the Commercial Bank of Scotland, designed by the architect of the bank's Roman temple-style headquarters in Edinburgh (1847) and many of its branches. Decorative carvings

(John Thomas, Alexander Handyside Ritchie) include *putti* minting coins. The domed addition *(Sydney Mitchell 1887)* at Buchanan Street continued the Italianate style, bigger but not better.

197
Clydesdale Bank Building
91 Buchanan Street
George Washington Browne 1896

Glasgow's coat of arms is on the Dutch gable of this northern Renaissance façade, commissioned by Kate Cranston for one of her famed Lunch and Tea Rooms. Their brand identity was bohemian décor which thrilled and shocked the clientele. The interiors here were by George Walton and Charles Rennie Mackintosh, who created Art Nouveau stencilled murals. Nothing remains inside, later a branch of the Clydesdale Bank.

Another Cranston tea room was at 205 Ingram Street. The building is still there but not the interiors, which were by Mackintosh. After a long saga

to save them, furnishings and fittings were transferred to Glasgow Museums in 1977. They have been reinstated in part at the **Mackintosh and Glasgow Style Gallery** at Kelvingrove (see 312) See also **Willow Tea Rooms** (entry 262) for a flavour of what once was here.

198
BOAC Building
85 Buchanan Street
Gillespie, Kidd & Coia 1970

One of the few outstanding postwar buildings in the city centre, this steel-framed, copper-clad office was built for the British Overseas Airways Corporation. The airline's walk-in flight centre was on the ground floor, a sleek, jet-set space like a James Bond movie set.

The exterior was contextual long before much thought was given to crafting contemporary buildings to fit Glasgow's Victorian streetscapes. The metal-clad and glazed elevations reference 19th-century commercial façades, specifically cast iron fronts (see 47).

199
North British Rubber Company
60 Buchanan Street
Robert Thomson 1896

The company was founded in 1856 by two Americans who arrived with a Goodyear patent. They moved to Edinburgh and built a factory which made tyres and supplied 1.2 million pairs of wellington boots to soldiers during the First World War. The office in Glasgow is from the J. J. Burnet mould, like the Athenaeum Theatre (see 191). The façade is baroque and Scottish Renaissance. Spandrels have louche angels, and niches figures of Justice and Truth.

200
Princes Square
34–58 Buchanan Street
John Baird (1) 1842; Hugh Martin
& Partners 1987
Spectacular galleried shopping mall under a steel and glass canopy, created in a 19th-century courtyard with a her-

itage façade highlighted like a stage set. The development was the first to re-brand post-industrial Glasgow as 'style city'. The design was Belle-Époque with an Art Nouveau decorative theme. The Italianate façade on Buchanan Street is animated with fan-shaped peacock plumage *(Alan Dawson, metalwork)* completed in 1990, City of Culture year. The peacock now flies out from a

nest of metal foliage *(Timorous Beasties designers, Kenny Mackay sculptor)* which completed a makeover of the mall in 2011.

Princes Square won a public vote for Scotland's favourite building of the last 100 years, part of the Royal Incorporation of Architects in Scotland (RIAS) 2016 Festival of Architecture.

201
Argyll Arcade
Buchanan Street and Argyle Street
John Baird (1) 1828
The L-shaped arcade is the oldest shopping mall in Scotland, similar to those of the period in Paris where covered *passages* through city blocks were popular. Its promoter, John Robertson Reid, is said to have seen them. It was the first significant retail venture on

the western edge of the Merchant City.

The upper floor was built for offices and workshops (the arcade has a long association with skilled trades, notably watchmakers and jewellers). The novelty was that shoppers were protected from the weather by a hammer-beam iron and glass roof, an early example of this technology.

Also here is **Sloans Arcade Café**, the oldest in the city (1797; décor c.1900). It began as a coffee house in Morrisons Court (through a pend off Argyle Street) where a stagecoach service to Edinburgh was based. The only horse ever seen in the arcade was when an army lieutenant galloped through it for a wager in 1838. He and his pals were prosecuted by Reid and posted in punishment by their regiment, the 15th Hussars, to India.

The arcade was restored (2008–2010). Glasgow City Heritage Trust grant-aided individual properties. Historic colours found under layers of paint were reinstated and globe lights replicated. The Buchanan Street entrance,

below the baroque façade of **Argyll Chambers** *(Colin Menzies 1904),* has two semi-domes with mosaics.

202
Burton Building
Buchanan at Argyle Street
Pierce & Martin 1938

In the 1930s this men's clothing chain was rebranded in Art Deco style. The buildings were like billboards, clad in faience tiles. The former Glasgow store has all the trimmings—zigzags, chevrons, scalloped setbacks, stylised pilasters—as if the client saw a catalogue of Art Deco and ordered the lot.

203
St. Enoch Subway Station
St. Enoch Square
James Miller 1896
Jacobean style with gables and turrets, and toy-town scale like the Glasgow

District Subway it served. The office was above a ticket hall where passengers descended to the trains. The station was excavated and enlarged (1977–1980). The old building became a travel centre. New entrance structures were built, replaced in 2015. No loss: they looked like coal bunkers. The latest ones are transparent pods *(AHR Architects)*, part of an upgrade to the subway. The toy station is now a café.

St. Enoch Square dates from the mid 18th century. A Georgian church stood in the centre until 1925. The square was dominated by St. Enoch Hotel, a Gothic pile which fronted St. Enoch Railway Station (1876). The station had a train shed similar to St. Pancras, London. In the late 1970s it was reduced to scrap iron and the hotel to rubble dumped to fill Queen's Dock. The site is now **St. Enoch Centre** *(Reiach & Hall Architects, GMW Architects 1981–1989).* Its glass roof was the largest in Europe when built. Storefront extensions *(Cooper Cromar 2014)* conceal it.

office. William Teacher & Sons moved out in 1991 and the building was rehabilitated for IET Glasgow (Institution of Engineering and Technology).

205
Stewart & McDonald Warehouse
134–156 Argyle Street
Horatio Kelson Bromhead 1899–1903
Clothing makers and retailers Stewart & McDonald started in a rented room in a tenement here in 1826 and prospered. They built a Renaissance-style wholesale drapery warehouse at 21–31

204
Teacher's Building
14 St. Enoch Square
James Boucher 1875
William Teacher began trading in a grocery store in Anderston in 1830, following the 1823 Excise Act which regulated the whisky trade. In the 1850s he opened a chain of respectable bars called 'dram shops' when others were notorious for hooch. In 1863 he launched a best-selling own-brand whisky. That success was expressed in this Venetian Renaissance-style head

Buchanan Street *(William Spence 1879)* and enlarged it with this domed corner block. The Argyle Street entrance has two Atlantes *(William Vickers sculptor)* nicknamed 'Stewart' and 'McDonald'. The pediment has carved figures representing imperial trade. The store was absorbed by House of Fraser in 1951.

206
Wylie & Lochhead Building
45 Buchanan Street
Campbell Douglas & Sellars 1886

Wylie & Lochhead started on Trongate when two brothers-in-law, Robert Wylie and William Lochhead, set up as coffin makers in 1829 and made money from the 1832 cholera epidemic by disposing of corpses competitors refused to touch. They diversified into cabinet making, upholstery and interior design, and furnished Clyde-built passenger ships. As house furnishers the firm brought bohemia to the bourgeoisie. Its Art Nouveau, Glasgow Style products were exhibited at the city's

1901 International Exhibition and the Turin expo in 1902.

William Lochhead designed an early cast iron store on this site in 1855. It was gutted by fire in 1883 and replaced by the present 'fireproof' iron-framed, concrete-floored, Doulton terracotta-clad emporium. Above the entrance are figures of Art and Industry. The interior has an awesome barrel-vaulted atrium. In 1957 the retail business was bought by Frasers. Wylie & Lochhead still trades, as 'Glasgow's oldest funeral director.'

207
Glasgow Herald Office
69 Buchanan Street
James Sellars 1882
Caxton and Gutenberg *(John Mossman sculptor)* and Mercury the messenger headline this former home of *The Herald*, one of the oldest newspapers in the English-speaking world. It was first published as *The Advertiser* in 1783 and re-titled *The Herald and Adver-tiser* in 1801. Its office on Saltmarket

was relocated several times—Bell Street (1813), Trongate (1837), St. Vincent Place (1859) and Buchanan Street (1868)—keeping up as civic and commercial power shifted west. A new building opened in 1895 (see next entry). The Buchanan Street office was rebuilt behind the Renaissance façade after the paper relocated to Albion Street (see 79).

208
The Herald Building
Mitchell Street and Lane
  Honeyman & Keppie, Charles Rennie
  Mackintosh 1895
The Herald and *The Evening Times* were printed on thundering machinery in the basement press room of this

industrial-strength structure. The newsroom, editorial departments, library, and composing (typesetting) room were on the upper floors. Papers were distributed from five loading bays on Mitchell Street.

The exterior is like a 17th-century tower house stacked up to urban scale, a castle for the crusaders of the free press. Mackintosh punctuated it with a typical Glasgow corner, like a watch-tower or beacon, hence the name of the 1990s edition (see next entry). The Art Nouveau tower disguised a water tank, its decorative shields styled as elephant trunks ready to spray water.

209
The Lighthouse
11 Mitchell Lane
  Honeyman & Keppie, Charles Rennie
  Mackintosh 1895; Page\Park Archi-
  tects, Thorburn Colquhoun engineers
  1999
Scotland's Centre for Design and Architecture is an adaptive reuse of **The Herald Building** and a legacy of

Glasgow's year as UK City of Architecture & Design 1999.

The entrance, identified with trendy graphics *(Javier Mariscal designer),* is in Mitchell Lane because the A-listed Mackintosh building could not be altered. To gain space, a full height addition was slotted into a gap in the alley. It worked magic with light in the canyon-like void—an instant atrium for vertical circulation. The architects called it 'the battery pack' because it clips to the side of Mackintosh's building which it re-energised without shocks. A glass pod to view the cityscape was plugged onto the battery pack's roof.

Behind the Herald Building's masonry walls are high-ceilinged, open plan floors on steel beams supported by cast iron columns. Rising like a campanile through the new atrium is the 1895 brick chimney, its style influenced by sketches Mackintosh made in Italy on an Alexander Thomson Travelling Scholarship in 1891. The Art Nouveau corner tower became a belvedere with a suspended spiral stair in its shaft. The centre includes a café, shop and the **Mackintosh Interpretative Display** *(Gareth Hoskins Architects).*

210

Gordon Chambers
Mitchell Street and Lane
Frank Burnet & Boston 1906
Edwardian baroque office block with a balustraded balcony and Roman Doric columns. The building is relatively unchanged—that is, it isn't a piece of façadism gutted for some corporate

makeover. The owner was publican David Ross, whose bar at the corner was familiar to the *Herald*'s journalists from across the lane. There are three vintage elevators with sliding birdcage doors and operators to open them. Unexpected and atmospheric.

211

The Horse Shoe Bar
Drury Street
1887
The name was chosen by John Scouller who took over the business, established in 1846. He had two pubs with horsey names, the Spur and the Snaffle Bit, and went all the way here with horseshoe motifs everywhere. The 32-metre island bar, horseshoe in plan,

is claimed to be the longest in Europe. There are huge mirrors and other period features. In 1923 owner and manager J. W. Whyte added his initials to the décor, now A-listed heritage.

212

Northern Assurance Building
84–94 St. Vincent Street
John Archibald Campbell 1909

The company, founded in Aberdeen in 1836, had branches from Melbourne to Montreal. It made the largest single payout in the wake of the San Francisco earthquake of 1906. Not so much that it couldn't afford to build this landmark in Glasgow, the first completely steel-framed building in the city and the first clad with Portland stone.

It looks Italian, soaring like some

Stile Liberty (Art Nouveau) block in Milan but undecorated except for a baroque pediment and saltire heraldry. The rear elevation is strikingly modern: simply glazed white brick and glass to pull in north light.

213

Royal Bank of Scotland
92 West George Street
James Miller, Richard Gunn 1930

A sky-scraping wannabe with a veneer of 1920s North American classicism in marble and Portland stone. The exterior of the banking hall, originally the Commercial Bank, is defined by fluted Art Deco pilasters; those above divide recessed cast metal and glass window bays. There are Art Deco friezes and a snappy cornice. Altogether elegant, Chicago Style. The full volume of the hall has been restored and retrofitted *(Jestico + Whiles Architects 2016)* as a brewpub, the Shilling Brewing Co.

214
One West Regent Street
Ryder Architecture, Woolgar Hunter engineers 2015

Miesian bronzed metallic, glazed curtain walls recall the skyscraping International Style of 1960s America. Height here was limited by planning controls but the vertical emphasis is uncompromising and acknowledges the Chicago Style proportions of the nearby Royal Bank (see previous entry).

The project took forward preliminary work *(Gordon Murray Architects with Atelier Ten)*. It includes retention of the streamline moderne frontage on Renfield Street of the **Paramount Theatre** *(Frank Verity & Samuel Beverley 1934)*. The auditorium extended to West Nile Street until demolished in 2013.

Across from the cinema is the Jacobean style **Prudential Building** *(Alfred Waterhouse & Son 1893)*, 71 Renfield Street, with an astonishing glazed ceramic-tiled former business hall in Moorish style.

215
Sun Life Assurance Building
117–121 West George Street
William Leiper 1894

French Renaissance style with an array of allegorical sculptures: Aurora on a chariot with prancing horses, Apollo, Michelangelo's Dawn and Dusk and much more *(William Birnie Rhind sculptor)*. Art dealer Alexander Reid, who introduced French Impressionism to Glasgow's *haute bourgeoisie*, had a gallery here (117 West George Street), revived (2014) as Leiper Fine Art. Sun Life's marble banking hall at the ground floor corner is accessible, occupied by a Fratelli Sarti restaurant.

216
The New Club
144 West George Street
James Sellars 1879

Novel take on French Renaissance style, every detail drawn with delight; 'modern French' the architect called it. There are balconies in cast iron, a trio of oculi and a rococo frieze on the façade and a chateauesque roofline. The offset entrance is a grand elevated archway with fluted pilasters, a pediment and vestibule. Sculptural work *(William Mossman)* includes Hermes on the keystone and, in the spandrels, reclining figures of Summer (with scythe and a sheaf of wheat) and Autumn (grapes and a jug) suggestive of bacchanalian pleasure. Originally a gentlemen's club. Interiors lost in a 1980s rehab for offices, Sellars House.

217
Bank of Scotland
110–120 St. Vincent Street
James Miller, Richard Gunn 1927;
Holmes Partnership, Lee Boyd
architects 2007
A magnificent pile of North American classicism, originally the Union Bank of Scotland, whose general manager had visited the United States and liked what he saw. Giant Ionic columns march along the sidewalk outside a double-height banking hall with more columns and much marble. The hall was preserved as a foyer for an ingenious steel-framed rebuild with new office floors behind the old façades.

Outside is a bronze plaque from the building's previous life: 'Bank of Scotland estd. 1695, Glasgow Chief Office.'

218
Daily Record Building
Renfield Lane
Charles Rennie Mackintosh; Honey-
man, Keppie & Mackintosh 1904
Mackintosh's watercolour perspective for the client was shown at the 1901 Glasgow International Exhibition. The image—a modern tower house—was saturated with national romanticism masking an industrial structure, like the rival **Herald Building** (see 208) by the same design team. The site in the lane is claustrophobic. Mackintosh

responded to it with a gleaming façade of bay windows and glazed white bricks which bounced daylight off the building opposite, into the newspaper's editorial and production departments.

219
Egyptian Halls
84–100 Union Street
Alexander Thomson 1873

A Victorian photo *(Thomas Annan 1874)* because this warehouse—Thomson's last and finest—has been clad in a safety wrap since 2010. Decades of water ingress and decay have reduced it to a perilous condition.

It was built for iron founder, James Robertson. The façade conceals a historically significant wrought and cast iron frame, the sensible side of Thompson's architecture. The façade shows his eccentricity. The proportions are of the Renaissance but the eaves gallery is a phalanx of Egyptian columns, and exotic repeat patterns are incised in the stonework.

The building is a key to the revival of down-at-heel Union Street, but plans for adaptive reuse have so far failed. The neglect is scandalous and may limit preservation options.

Also by Thomson is the **Grosvenor Building** (1861; redeveloped 1967 and 1992) at 72 Gordon Street. Only the façade remains. The incongruous baroque superstructure is an addition *(Clarke & Bell 1907).*

220
Ca' d'Oro
Union and Gordon streets
John Honeyman 1872; 1990

Built for F. & J. Smith as a furniture warehouse of similar construction to **The Iron Building** (see 47). The popular name comes from the Ca' d'Oro Restaurant and Venetian Tea Room, opened in 1921 by City Bakeries. The eatery featured quick lunches, and dining accompanied by an orchestra.

The iron elevations above stone arches were cast at Saracen Foundry and shown in its catalogue. They survived a fire in 1987 and were restored to pristine appearance. The Union Street façade was extended with two bays matching the originals. The original Ca' d'Oro is a palazzo on the Grand Canal in Venice.

The building diagonally across Renfield Street was 'ladies and gents outfitters' **R. W. Forsyth** (see 441) for whom the original building *(Boucher & Cousland 1858)* was rehabilitated and enlarged *(J. J. Burnet c. 1900)* in fashionable Parisian style.

renamed Grand Central Hotel (2010).

Outside is a bronze statue, *Citizen Firefighter (Kenny Hunter artist 2001)*, commissioned by the Scottish Fire & Rescue Service, part of the Firefighters' Heritage Trail.

222
Central Station
Gordon Street

Blyth & Cunningham engineers 1876–1879; Donald A. Matheson engineer 1901–1906; Glass Murray Architects 1998; Gordon Murray + Alan Dunlop Architects 2002; Atkins Group 2014

The station is the biggest and busiest in Scotland, with platforms and tracks supported on a cavernous undercroft of brick arches. An old neighbourhood was cleared for the construction. Urban myth says its ghostly streets are still there. Intriguing, but investigation had proved this is not so.

The concourse and platforms are spanned by a prodigious roof. The older east section has multiple trusses and ridge and furrow glazing; the western extension elliptical arched trusses. They spring from masonry walls and meet at a colonnade of riveted steel columns. The steelwork was fabricated by Motherwell Bridge and Engineering.

On the concourse, newsstands and shops occupy wooden kiosks and pavilions *(James Miller c. 1905)*. The largest had manual panels with train times in the windows on the upper level. The antiquated but efficient method was replaced with an electronic board suspended from the roof in the 1980s.

Upgrades, including replacing the

221
Central Hotel
99 Gordon Street

Robert Rowand Anderson 1879–1883; James Miller 1901–1906

A rammy of gables, four on the corner pinnacle. The hotel is stone-clad; the station is all steel girders and glass, pure engineering. The two juxtaposed illustrate a very Victorian tension: engineering was the future, the hotel's northern Renaissance style the past.

The building was to have been offices for the Caledonian Railway but was reconfigured to compete with the newly opened St. Enoch Station Hotel. The block intended as the railway's hotel *(Peddie & Kinnear 1877)* was renamed Central Chambers and is directly across Hope Street. Central Hotel was extended later down the street by James Miller. It was refurbished and

glass in the roof, have kept the station fit for purpose while maintaining its character, recognised in 2002 by a *Europa Nostra* heritage award. Two long-established fixtures are a First World War howitzer shell used as a charity box and rendezvous and a Caledonian Railway war memorial, both at the Gordon Street exit where there is a cast iron and glass *porte cochère*.

223
Waterloo Chambers
19 Waterloo Street
J. J. Burnet 1899

Burnet visited America in 1896 and returned with fresh ideas to clad steel-framed office blocks with a classicism that would be creative but not scare off conservative clients. This example, with Beaux-Arts columns in a deep recess and an Italianate eaves gallery, was to have been two storeys taller. In the same idiom is **Atlantic Chambers**, 45 Hope Street *(J. J. Burnet 1899)*.

224
Clydesdale Bank Exchange
20 Waterloo Street
Keppie Design 2004

The bank celebrated the completion of this office by printing its image on £20 notes. The built form fits the Glasgow grid and townscape. The elevations are flush to the street, there is a corner

tower and eaves gallery; the flat roof imitates a classical cornice. Mannered but effective.

225
Mercantile Chambers
53 Bothwell Street
James Salmon (junior) 1898

An idiosyncratic façade with classical, Renaissance and Art Nouveau features composed with complete originality. Mercury shelters in a baldachin on a bracket of cherubs. A ribbon frieze spells out 'Trees grow, birds fly, fish swim, bells ring', alluding to Glasgow's coat of arms whose symbols appear between the words. Above are caryatids representing Prosperity, Prudence,

Industry and Fortune *(Francis Derwent Wood, McGilvray & Ferris sculptors).* The eaves gallery and dormer with a cupola are flanked by Gothic gables and baroque balconies more Barcelona *modernisme* than Bothwell Street. In the back lane, Salmon introduced a modern elevation of bay windows to gain natural light.

226
Scottish Legal Life Assurance Society
81–107 Bothwell Street
Wylie Wright & Wylie 1927–1931

Monumental steel-framed classicism, the architecture of 1920s North American capitalism. It weathered the Wall Street Crash. The Scottish financial stereotype of Prudence and Thrift is expressed in words on the heraldic crest above the entrance and symbolised on Art Deco figurative relief panels *(Archibald Dawson sculptor),* along with Courage and Industry. Window bays feature lions rampant on cast metal frames with chevron patterns. The arcaded vestibule, iron gates and the lobby are original.

227

Central Thread Agency

36–62 Bothwell Street

Hugh & David Barclay 1891–1901

Built in three stages for J. & P. Coats, the cotton thread manufacturer established in Paisley in 1830. Construction started after the family firm went public in 1890. The first stage was built at Bothwell and Wellington streets, followed by the central and western

structures. The individual façades coalesce in a tapestry of carved reliefs *(McGilvray & Ferris sculptors)* and energetic Renaissance style.

J. & P. Coats amalgamated with local rival Clark & Co. in 1896. The enterprise was one of the five largest companies listed on the London Stock Exchange and one of the first multinationals. Its managers oversaw a global empire of thread mills and their products. Masks representing parts of that empire—a native American wearing headdress, a bearded turbaned man, a pharaoh (Egypt being a producer of cotton)—are on the attic gables at Bothwell and Wellington streets.

The complex was redeveloped as

Britannia Court *(SBT Keppie Architects c. 1992)*, one the most extensive heritage façade retentions in Europe.

228

Commercial Bank of Scotland

30 Bothwell Street

James Miller, Richard Gunn 1935

Powerful composition of Portland stone façades in truncated Chicago Style, with fluted Corinthian columns and a recessed metal and glass screen at the entrance and pilasters on the side elevation. Art Deco figurative panels symbolise Commerce, Contentment, Industry, Justice, Prudence and Wisdom *(Gilbert Bayes sculptor)*. Banking hall gussied up as a bar.

229

St. Vincent Lane

The street grid drawn by the city's surveyor James Barrie in 1780 was extended west across Buchanan Street when the Campbell clan on Blythswood Hill feued their estate, starting in 1792. The urban design, focussed on Blythswood Square, was almost certainly by James Craig, famed for the layout for Edinburgh's New Town. Streets were lined with Georgian terraces and townhouses imitating those in the capital. Unlike the enclosed plan in Edinburgh, Glasgow's version was open-ended, a vision of unlimited growth.

Back lanes, originally for servant's quarters and coach houses, bisect the grid. Around 1900 it was partly overlaid with multistorey office buildings which make it feel North American. The topography is dramatic. The lanes are cobbled canyons where shadows fall. Steep streets catch long shafts of sunlight. There are sudden views and surprises at every corner.

and (on top) Temperance on a cheerful Flemish gabled façade decorated with *putti*, medallions and masks *(McGilvray & Ferris sculptors)*. In the alley the rhythm of bay windows was picked up by Mackintosh at the Daily Record Building (see 218). The paper got a street-front presence in 1919 when it bought the Temperance property.

231
Liverpool & London & Globe Insurance
Hope Street at St. Vincent Street
James Thomson 1901

230
Scottish Temperance League
106–108 Hope Street
John Gaff Gillespie 1894
Admonitory figures of Faith, Fortitude

Great name, great building, sailing up Hope Street like an over-decorated galleon. Victorian architecture like this was vilified in the 1960s as not worth preserving. The architect was pleased with it—he had his portrait

as a keystone of the arched window at
the corner, where a dome anchors two
northern Renaissance façades crowded
with granite columns and sculptures
(*James Young*). The exteriors were retained during an infill redevelopment,
123 St. Vincent Street (c. 2000), which
also kept two neighbouring heritage
façades. **Norwich Union Chambers**
(*John Hutchison 1898*) at 125 St. Vincent
Street is northern Renaissance style,
like Liverpool & London & Globe but
tougher.

232
The Hatrack
144 St. Vincent Street

James Salmon (junior) 1899–1902
Salmon was the only local architect to
come close to rivalling Mackintosh and
this is his most famous achievement.

The Art Nouveau building shoots up
on a narrow lot—eight storeys and an
attic expressed vertically and individually in bay windows and recessed massing. Stone cladding on the steel frame
is minimal to maximise glazing and
natural light from the street (and the
back lane where the elevation has twin
glazed bays).

Above the doorways are leaded
lanterns, one with stained glass ships
(*Oscar Paterson artist*), and fierce gargoyles (*Francis Derwent Wood sculptor*). The lobby has an Art Nouveau
elevator cage. The façade is Glasgow
Style 'spook school', with wrought iron
balcony railings on the upper levels. It
reaches a scary summit—a Gaudíesque
turret and finial which gave the building its nickname. The turret is a replica

(1990) of the long-removed original.

Next door (142 St. Vincent Street at
Hope Street) is the boisterous baroque
former **Royal Bank Chambers** (*Frank
Burnet & Boston 1900*).

233
Scottish Amicable Life Assurance
150 St. Vincent Street
King, Main & Ellison 1976

Fits the urban grain and grid without resorting to heritage pastiche. Vertical glazed bays are a modernist homage to the Hatrack. The elevations on a semi-podium respond to the slope of the street; also a lesson in how to greet it with civility, the entrance steps being integrated with the sidewalk.

234
157–167 Hope Street
Hope Street and West George streets
John Archibald Campbell 1903

Spectacular Iberian style commercial block with a double-height Roman eaves gallery and a cornice pierced by a squared-up corner tower with obelisk finials. Clues to its life as legal and financial chambers are the keystone above the entrance on West George Street (a blindfolded face of Justice) and *putti* (one with a money bag, the other consulting a ledger) on Hope Street. The bow-windowed bay and turret (conventionally these would have defined the corner) animate the West George Street façade.

235
196 West George Street
John Brash c. 1830

A Georgian style, miniature stately home from a time when Blythswood Hill was residential, populated by the merchant and professional classes. Most had moved to the suburbs by the late 19th century as office blocks like the adjacent **Ocean Chambers** (see next entry) were built. Most of the townhouses and terraces were sold for demolition or converted to offices.

236
Ocean Chambers
190 West George Street
Robert Alexander Bryden 1900

Built for the Ocean Accident & Guarantee Corporation. Above the entrance is its emblem: a lighthouse in bas-relief along with sailing ships and walruses evocative of Arctic exploration. The nautical theme continues high up on the façade with figures of Neptune and Amphitrite. Now apartments, one of many rehabs since the 1980s which have helped revitalise the city centre.

237
North British & Mercantile Insurance
200 St. Vincent Street
J. J. Burnet 1926–1929

Roman-inspired office block, Burnet's last commission in Glasgow, now a conference and events venue; interiors not original. The composition on a sloping site is simple—arcades, plain elevations, emphatic cornice. Marine themed sculptural work: St. Andrew on the prow of a ship *(Archibald Dawson sculptor 1927)*; a seafarer and his wife *(Jack Mortimer c. 1952)*. Capitals by the door are carved as a Viking longship and a galleon. The company's monogram appears on an escutcheon with a sea monster high on the outer corner.

238
Sentinel Building
103 Waterloo Street
Gordon Murray + Alan Dunlop Architects, Halcrow Group engineers 2005

'Not just a modern office building, it is a piece of public art'. So said its citation in the British Council for Offices Awards 2006. State-of-the-art LED lighting was embedded in the glazing to colour-shift at night in programmed sequences. Curtain walls are divided by contrasting verticals in slate. It meets the ground with transparency (the see-through lobby is recessed under a cantilever), and engages with the public realm in the Anderston regeneration zone.

239
St. Vincent Street Church
265 St. Vincent Street
Alexander Thomson 1859

An Ionic-columned acropolis, 'Greek' Thomson's most striking and three-dimensional work. The building, commissioned by the United Presbyterian Church of which Thomson was an elder, expressed the power of his faith and his desire for ordered geometry leavened with the romance of classical antiquity. Assyrian, Egyptian and Greek architecture, and the Temple of Solomon, have been cited as influences; even a devotion (not proven) to Freemasonry.

The structure stands on a massive podium wedged into the steep south slope of Blythswood Hill. As at **Caledonia Road Church** (see 400) the tower is offset, punctuating the composition and its raised Greek Revival porches. The interior is bathed with light from clerestories above a U-shaped gallery. The church organ, added later, is behind an elaborate wooden pulpit where the preacher could appear like a magician from a hidden door. The gallery is supported on cast iron columns which have capitals described by Thomson devotee Gavin Stamp as 'extraordinary, exotic . . . possibly Thomson's attempt to create a new Semitic order.'

Thomson was an unlikely Orientalist. He never went abroad, but there was plenty of published material and art which would have been influential—the apocalyptic imagery of artist John Martin springs to mind. Whatever else, there is a fierce intensity here too strong for contemporary taste, which is why Thomson, for all his talent, will never match Charles Rennie Mackintosh in popular affection.

This sublime, now city-owned building has yet to receive the complete conservation and restoration it deserves. Caledonia Church is a ruin; Egyptian Halls (see 219) is at risk. His third great church, Queen's Park United Presbyterian, was destroyed by a stray German bomb in 1943.

Across the street is the legendary live music venue **King Tut's Wah Wah Hut**, its Egyptian name from a New York club, not Thomson's Greco-Egyptian fantasy.

240

**St. Columba Gaelic Church
of Scotland**

300 St. Vincent Street

Tennant & Burke 1904

The parish was established in 1770 for
Gaelic-speakers who migrated from
the Highlands and Islands to find
work in Glasgow, a consequence of the
Clearances and because the booming
city offered more opportunity than a
meagre living crofting.

The Gaels worshipped at a church
on Hope Street near the **Hielanman's
Umbrella** (see 46) until the early 1900s.
The congregation moved when Central
Station was enlarged. Compensation
received from the Caledonian Railway
Company funded this Gothic Revival
church, built to accommodate 1,000
people. Services in Gaelic are still held.
Rusticated and smooth stonework
animates the exterior, where a statue
of St. Columba stands in a niche on the
tall, buttressed tower.

241

Eagle Building

215 Bothwell Street

sbt *Keppie Architects 1992*

An elegant steel-framed office tower

with cylindrical, glazed elevator shafts.
It was named to recall the Venetian
Renaissance style **Eagle Buildings**
(Alexander Kirkland 1854) previously
on the site. During demolition the
best bits, including a stone eagle, were
stone-cleaned and reassembled in the
tower's lobby where they stand like a
Palladian stage set.

Directly north is the former **Britoil
Building**, 301 St. Vincent Street *(Hugh
Martin & Partners 1983–1988)*. The
temptation to make it look high-tech
like an oil rig was resisted.

242

Malmaison Hotel

278 West George Street

John Stephen 1839

Greco-Egyptian church, too early to

be by 'Greek' Thomson but no less bizarre. The entrance pavilion was crowned with a *tempietto*, removed in the 1960s. Built as St. Jude's Episcopal Church, converted to offices (1975). Now a boutique hotel *(Jestico + Whiles Architects 1994),* designer chic behind the intriguing façade.

243
Lusitania Window, Scottish Opera Building
39 Elmbank Crescent

A Venetian baroque palazzo, formerly headquarters of the Institution of Engineers and Shipbuilders *(John Bennie Wilson 1908)*, now Scottish Opera rehearsal space and offices with original features retained. In the foyer is a memorial to the engineers (including two Glaswegians) of the *Titanic* 'who all died at their duty when the ship was lost in mid-Atlantic' *(William Kellock Brown sculptor c. 1912).*

A marble staircase leads to Rankine

Hall, named for William MacQuorn Rankine, professor of civil engineering and mechanics at Glasgow University and co-founder (with railway locomotive manufacturer William Neilson) of the institution, and its first president. Stained glass *(Stephen Adam)* includes a portrait of Rankine and an image of Henry Bell's *Comet*, the first commercial steamship in Europe. The highlight is the Lusitania Window illustrating the eponymous transatlantic liner, the world's largest passenger ship when launched at Clydebank in 1906.

Across the street is the Renaissance-style former **Glasgow High School** *(Charles Wilson 1848)*, built originally for Glasgow Academy. On plinths are statues *(John Mossman sculptor)* of Cicero, Galileo, James Watt and Homer.

244
Scottish Power Headquarters
330–336 St. Vincent Street
 Page\Park Architects, Ortiz León Arquitectos, Arup engineers
 2014–2017
The first major purpose-built corporate HQ in Glasgow since Britoil. The site was occupied by the former Strathclyde Regional Council offices, a 1960s slab block. A mixed-use development, Elphinstone Place, with an elliptical 39-storey skyscraper to have been the tallest building in Scotland, was cancelled by the crash of 2008.

The Scottish Power building is welcome on a site that needed architectural presence, and for the city's prestige. The massing responds to the scale of

the M8 motorway and neighbouring
buildings and reinforces the street grid
(the pedestrian arcade is thoughtful).
It reboots 1960s modernism, a time
when technology was the future. In the
energy and renewables sector it is still.
The HQ accommodates staff, most previously at the Cathcart site (see 441),
and basement parking. The building
is straight-up, rational without trendy
frills, and rated BREEAM Excellent.

Across the street is **St. Vincent Plaza**
(Keppie Design 2015), also BREEAM
Excellent. Landscaped steps *(LDA Design)* lead to William Street, a pleasing
intervention in an area not pedestrian-
friendly.

245
The Buttery
652 Argyle Street
1869

The M8 motorway cut Anderston in
two and redevelopment destroyed the
community. This strip of Argyle Street

became a dead end, with the Buttery
isolated in an urban wasteland. A
footbridge across the M8 was built in
the 1970s but left stranded in mid air.
Eventually 'the bridge to nowhere' was
completed in 2013, with a ramp at the
west end of Waterloo Street giving
pedestrians and cyclists a link between
the city centre and what's left of the
neighbourhood.

This tenement survived because,
the joke went, the planners needed
somewhere for lunch. The eatery was
established in 1856 and noted then
for its merchant clientele. Intriguing

sculpted details on the façade. Good period interior.

246

Argyle Street Housing

Collective Architecture 2014

Three brick-clad blocks of flats interleaved with units clad in zinc. These recessed parts have Parisian attics and French balconies; the brick-faced blocks are taller, like a tenement streetscape. Flemish bond brickwork is a subtle textural shift at ground level.

The development, for Sanctuary Scotland Housing Association, won a Saltire Housing Design Award 2014. It is part of the Anderston regeneration, to replace 1960s slab blocks with a reinstated street pattern and more new housing by the same architects for the same client.

247

Savings Bank of Glasgow

752 Argyle Street

*James Salmon (junior) & John Gaff
Gillespie 1900*

A tenement with a complete repertoire of Glasgow Style. Art Nouveau carvings *(Albert Hemstock Hodge sculptor)* mix of medievalism, Celtic mysticism

and the city's motifs. Eroded angelic figures probably represent Prudence and Prosperity. The carved portrait of the founder of the bank, Henry Duncan, certainly does: he appears in a roundel with a ring of coins, holding a money bag and tapping his forehead knowingly.

The entrance to the bank is offset from the corner, allowing a baronial facet as a bracket for bay windows which rise to a corner tower, the most original in Glasgow. Its ascent, to a dome with a weathervane in Mackintosh style, is punctuated with extended columns and foliated capitals. The dome animates the roofscape, along with a turret, deep-set eaves and chimneys. The arched entrance to the banking hall has wrought iron gates, the name 'Savings Bank of Glasgow' in period typography, stylised stone coats of arms of Glasgow and Scotland, and peacocks on a mosaic in the tympanum. Wonderful.

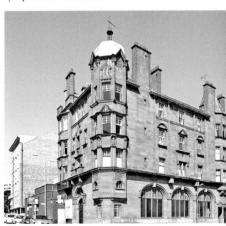

Reid Building foyer, Glasgow School of Art

6

Cowcaddens to Charing Cross

COWCADDENS until the end of the 18th century was cattle grazing land
north of the city centre. In 1790 the Forth & Clyde Canal opened. A link
to it, funded in 1777 by Glasgow's merchants who feared they would be
bypassed by the canal's peripheral route, created Port Dundas, a freight
transit and industrial zone. Cowcaddens, below the port (which bizarrely
was up a hill), was filled with tenements and factories, and became a
densely populated slum. Around 1970, comprehensive redevelopment
and the M8 motorway swept it away. Among its handful of notable buildings was the Caledonian Railway's Buchanan Street Station (1849), built
on the site of East Cowcaddens Quarry (much of the area was worked for
stone in the early 19th century). It was one of four Victorian rail termini
in Glasgow; the others being St. Enoch (demolished 1977), Central and
Queen Street. The station, on Port Dundas Road, was described as 'the
gateway to the Highlands'. The Caley called it Buchanan Street for prestige which it never gained. It closed in 1966 and was demolished. Its
freight yards are the site of Glasgow Caledonian University.

The district is a gritty patchwork of renewal and preservation. There
is Dundasvale, a modernist housing scheme built to replace the slums.
A row of 19th-century warehouses at Speirs Wharf, Port Dundas, has
been rehabilitated as flats. A derelict church is now the National Piping
Centre. A culture quarter, Speirs Locks, is emerging on the canal towpath and Garscube Road with facilities for the Royal Conservatoire,

Scottish Opera and the National Theatre of Scotland.

Cowcaddens is a short walk from the bright lights of Sauchiehall Street, famed for its cinemas, theatres and shopping. The Empire, at Sauchiehall and West Nile streets until demolished in the 1960s, was one of the largest variety theatres in Britain. The Pavilion, Theatre Royal and the Glasgow Film Theatre are among the few traditional venues left. The street was Glasgow's premier shopping promenade until the 1970s, when Copland & Lye and Pettigrew & Stephens department stores were torn down for the cheerless Sauchiehall Centre. Such high-profile vandalism was typical of city council's disregard for the city's architectural heritage at the time. The redevelopment could have been slotted inside Copland's and Pettigrew's Victorian façades, common practice now. Preservation groups like the Scottish Civic Trust and the New Glasgow Society stepped up their efforts to save what Andor Gomme, writing in *Architecture of Glasgow* (1968), called 'the Victorian city *par excellence*'.

Five blocks on Sauchiehall Street were pedestrianised and landscaped in the 1970s but the street never recovered its status. Rival Buchanan Street has gained investment and pizazz. Sauchiehall Street does have the Willow Tea Rooms building, designed by Charles Rennie Mackintosh, which is being restored. The honky-tonk strip from Rose Street to Charing Cross was declared a Business Improvement District in 2013. A Sauchiehall and Garnethill district masterplan, commissioned by the city, went to community consultation in 2015. The plan is part of a nine-zone City Centre Strategy, unrolled in 2014 to promote a 'liveable city centre'. Its main thrust is to civilise the public realm. Sauchiehall Street and the fractured zone of Cowcaddens would benefit; Charing Cross too, where the M8 could be decked to create a public plaza and park in front of the Mitchell Library.

In the early 19th century Sauchiehall Street was part of a residential suburb which included Bath Street, Blythswood Hill and Garnethill. It continues through Charing Cross into the West End. Much of Charing Cross was destroyed by the M8. A view of Charing Cross Mansions, the most spectacular tenement in Glasgow, was opened up by chance. The M8 boxed in Garnethill, a mini Montmartre, grittier and more diverse than the Paris *quartier* but with similar steep topography and bohemian personality. Glasgow's 19th-century street grid was overlaid precipitously on its drumlin, one of those Ice Age outcrops which give the cityscape as much character as its architecture. Garnethill has its own Sacré-Cœur, the Jesuit St. Aloysius Church which, with St. Aloysius College, has been in Garnethill since the 1860s. Ethnic diversity is embedded here thanks to a pattern of migration since the late 18th century: Highlanders, Irish, Jews, Italians, South Asians and Chinese.

Garnethill and Blythswood Hill have a long association with the arts. The Glasgow Institute of Fine Arts, founded in 1861, exhibited at the McLellan Galleries. Glasgow School of Art, established in 1845, moved into the galleries in 1869, and to the Mackintosh Building in 1899 (the school recently leased the galleries again). The Glasgow Art Club (1867) has been on Bath Street since 1893. Thomas Annan opened a photography studio on Sauchiehall Street in 1904. The Roger Billcliffe Gallery occupies a Victorian building formerly The Fine Art Society on Blythswood Street. The Centre for Contemporary Arts, founded in 1974 as the Third Eye Centre, is in the Grecian Buildings, designed in 1865 by Alexander 'Greek' Thomson.

From Thomson to Charles Rennie Mackintosh and today, architecture here is as diverse as the people. The most recent high-profile project is the controversial, award-winning Reid Building at the GSA, commissioned to make the multi-disciplinary campus fit for the 21st century.

248

Glasgow Caledonian University Saltire Centre

70 Cowcaddens Road

Building Design Partnership, Nomad RDC, Struer engineers 2006

A multilevel library and learning centre with one-stop student services. The concept was unconventional, widely praised as an exemplar: 'A university but not as we know it . . . it rewrote the design book for academic libraries', said *The Guardian*. In 2006 it won an RIBA (Royal Institute of British Architects) design award.

The façade is a steel and Douglas fir glue-laminated timber screen with fritted glass to reduce solar gain and glare. The spatial focus is an atrium, colourful and convivial like an Italian piazza complete with campanile—a cylindrical stair tower from which bridges access several levels. The atrium, a big buzzy forum with a hinterland of quieter spaces, contains an info desk, pop-up study pods, a café and chill-out zones.

249

St. Andrew's House

48 Milton Street

Skinner, Bailey & Lubetkin 1970

Headquarters of St. Andrew's First Aid, founded as a charity in 1882 to teach emergency care and run an ambulance service, the first in Scotland. Construction of the M8 motorway forced its move from North Street to this

purpose-built modernist design. The carving of St. Andrew on the west elevation was salvaged from the previous building. The stylised saltire on the north elevation, the structural clarity and powerful posture owe much to émigré architect Berthold Lubetkin and his memory of Russian Constructivism in post-revolutionary Moscow. The former **Scottish Ambulance Service Building** round the corner on Maitland Street was part of the project.

250
Orient Buildings
16 McPhater Street
William James Anderson 1895

Fantasy façades in concrete and stucco with machicolations like a *castello* in a Renaissance painting. The architect had visited Italy in 1888 having won the first Alexander Thomson Travelling Scholarship at Glasgow School of Art.

The structure was industrial, with iron columns and beams and concrete floors. It was intended for workshops and warehousing but soon became the Orient Model Lodging House, subsequently offices abandoned in the 1970s. Rehabilitated (2006) as lofts.

251
National Piping Centre
32 McPhater Street
Campbell Douglas & Sellars 1873

Built as Cowcaddens United Free Church, closed in 1968 when comprehensive redevelopment bulldozed the district. Nearby **Dundasvale Housing Scheme** (*Walter Underwood & Partners 1973*) and the M8 are the most visible reminders of that upheaval.

The Italianate church lay empty until repurposed (*McGurn, Logan, Duncan & Opfer 1996*) as the Piping Centre. There is an auditorium, a museum, library, and a hotel (the Piper's Tryst) next door. Three stained glass windows (*John K. Clark*) were installed above the centre's entrance. They represent Pibroch, the classical music of the Highland bagpipe.

252
Theatre Royal
282 Hope Street
George Bell 1867; Charles Phipps 1879 and 1895; Derek Sugden, Arup engineers 1975; Page\Park Architects 2014
Originally the Royal Coliseum and Opera House, converted in 1957 as studios for Scottish Television (STV) which broadcast from here until 1974.

It was bought by Scottish Opera and reopened in 1975 as Scotland's first national opera house. The auditorium is essentially as decorated by Charles Phipps, after fires in 1879 and 1895. It is lustrous with Renaissance plaster-work.

The Victorian Italianate exterior is rudimentary. It now has a dramatic drum-shaped new foyer and box office, cantilevered around the street corner. Every second vertical stack around the drum acts as a ventilator; the alternate stacks conceal columns which restrain the moment of the internal cantilever. The drum picks up the rhythm of the McConnell Building across the street and lights up like a chandelier. Circulation is focussed around a flamboyant spiral staircase.

253
McConnell Building
Hope Street at Cowcaddens Road
John Keppie 1907
A baroque tenement built by Glasgow Corporation which was proud of it—the city coat of arms appears four times high up on the façades. These ripple with bay windows which rise

to curved pediments alternating with iron railings on the flat roof which was a clothes-drying area because there was no back court. The name is from McConnells, one of the original shops.

254
Royal Conservatoire of Scotland
100 Renfrew Street
Leslie Martin, William Nimmo & Partners 1988

Built for the Royal Scottish Academy of Music & Drama, the Royal Conservatoire since 2011. Its previous properties still stand (see 190–192). The new facility was conceived in the 1960s and the exterior has the same retro style as Glasgow Royal Concert Hall. The highlight inside is the **New Athenaeum Theatre**, named to recall the previous venue and designed in traditional manner. The complex includes the **Alexander Gibson Opera Studio** *(BMJ Architects 1998)*, named after the founder and conductor of the Scottish National Orchestra (SNO) and Scottish Opera. Acoustic isolation was required for the opera studio, a big box on rubber dampers fitted to absorb vibrations from subway trains directly below.

The conservatoire's latest venture is **Wallace Studios** *(Malcolm Fraser Architects 2011)*, a rehabbed warehouse at Speirs Locks culture zone.

255
Cineworld
7 Renfrew Street
AWW Architects 2001

A Gotham city montage, at 62 metres high the tallest cinema on the planet. It might also be the ugliest—it received a 'carbuncle' award from *Urban Realm* magazine. The 18-screen cineplex can seat around the same number of people as its predecessor, Green's Playhouse (1927), the biggest cinema in Europe, which accommodated more than 4,000

fans. It became the Apollo live music venue, demolished in the 1980s.

256
Pavilion Theatre
121 Renfield Street
Bertie Crewe 1904

Opened as the Pavilion Theatre of Varieties, one of many music halls run by impresario Thomas Barrasford. The frothy interior—Marie Antoinette meets Punch and Judy—is classic music hall, a perfect setting for pantomimes traditionally performed here. The French Renaissance exterior is clad with terracotta. There is a French turret at the corner, lively signage on the marquee and period lettering on the Renfrew Street façade. The auditorium was refurbished and original features highlighted in 2013.

257
Lion Chambers
172 Hope Street
James Salmon (junior) & John Gaff Gillespie, Louis Gustave Mouchel engineer 1907
An aesthetic and structural *tour de force*—an imaginary tower house built with reinforced concrete pioneered by French engineer François Hennebique.

It rises to eight storeys on a deep, narrow lot. The novelty of the Hennebique system was that it maximized floor space and natural light, with a slim but robust fireproof frame and non-load bearing walls.

The client was lawyer, writer and Glasgow Art Club member William Black. There was a printing plant in the basement, shops on the ground floor, offices for lawyers midway up and artists' studios on top. Their vertical integration is massed in Scottish Arts and Crafts style. Decoration is confined to some Art Nouveau appliqué, an armorial bas-relief and busts of two judges. The lane elevation has a wall of windows for north light.

This was the second Hennebique structure in Glasgow and it has degraded like the first, **Sentinel Works** *(Brand & Lithgow, Archibald Leitch 1903)*, a factory at 61 Jessie Street on the Southside. Lion Chambers since 2004 has been wrapped in chicken wire to prevent fragmented concrete from

corroded rebar falling on passersby. It is one of Glasgow's architectural treasures, in desperate need of a saviour.

258
Watt Brothers
Hope Street
> *Alec S. Heathcote 1915; Keppie*
> *& Henderson 1932*

Family firm founded by farmer's son Allan Watt who opened a shop on Elmbank Street in the early 1900s. It evolved into this department store. The style is Italianate at Sauchiehall Street and Art Deco at the Hope and Bath street corner. Original ground floor display windows in situ. The two parts are connected by a bridge across the mid-block lane. There were several department stores on Sauchiehall Street. Watt Brothers alone still trades. The top floor has been refurbished for Willow Tea Rooms (see 262).

259
Savoy Centre
140 Sauchiehall Street
> *David Barclay 1895; Gavin Paterson*
> *& Sons c. 1975*

Only the Roman-style Victorian frontage and fine sculptural work *(William Birnie Rhind)* remain of this former

260

Reid & Todd Building
200 Sauchiehall Street

James Thomson c. 1900

Nineteenth-century consumer culture spread from the boulevards, arcades and department stores of Paris. French style appealed to high-end retailers like Reid & Todd, who commissioned this French Renaissance medley of double height dormers, turrets and a roof as if flown in from the Louvre.

The building had business tenants in offices above Reid & Todd's two retail floors. Their bourgeois clientele also shopped at Copland & Lye and Pettigrew & Stephens, two grand emporiums across the street. They were demolished in 1972 to make way for the Sauchiehall Centre, a regrettable exchange. Its only benefit is rooftop parking deck from where there is a fine view of the Reid & Todd relic.

furniture store converted in 1910 as a movie theatre, the Picture House (later the Gaumont). Another cinema, the Savoy *(James Miller 1911)*, was on Hope Street. Both were torn down in 1972 for the Savoy Centre, an office and shopping mall combo to which the popular cliché 'concrete monstrosity' applies.

261

Dunnes Stores

222 Sauchiehall Street

North, Robin & Wilsdon 1930;
RPP Architects 2001

The store was rehabilitated for Dunnes after C & A pulled out in 2000. C & A's 1960s chequerboard curtain wall was removed revealing the original modernist faience and glass façades. Originally the bay windows extended to the ground floor displays.

262

Willow Tea Rooms

217 Sauchiehall Street

Charles Rennie Mackintosh 1903
A radical makeover of a conventional Victorian building, commissioned by Kate Cranston (see 197). The contrast of plain stucco surface and intricate metalwork, mosaic tiles and leaded glass recalls the Vienna Secession, familiar to Mackintosh from a visit to that city in 1900.

The interior was transformed with a galleried atrium and tea rooms in a stimulating spatial sequence. The symbolist decorative scheme—stylised tree branches, leaves and flowers (birds too, flying on wrought iron signs)—perhaps recalls a lost Arcadia (Sauchiehall or *Saughiehaugh* means 'alley of willows'). The most celebrated space is the **Salon de Luxe**. The doors to the room are fitted with Art Nouveau leaded glass of exceptional artistry. Daylight from the wide window glows on a gesso panel designed by Margaret Macdonald.

Kate Cranston sold the tea rooms when she retired in 1919. They closed in 1928, the Mackintosh furniture was dispersed and the rooms absorbed by a neighbouring store. In 1980 they were refurbished *(Keppie Henderson & Partners)* and reopened to exploit commercially the renewed interest in CRM.

In 2014 the building was acquired by the Willow Tea Rooms Trust and closed in 2016 for a two-year restoration (the tea room business relocated to Watt Brothers store; see 258). Restoration *(Simpson & Brown Architects)* will create a Mackintosh visitor centre, exhibition and learning spaces and reinstate the tea rooms' original design.

263
Art House (Abode Glasgow) Hotel
129 Bath Street
Henry Edward Clifford 1912; 1999

Former headquarters of Glasgow School Board, later Glasgow Corporation Education Department. Original features—Edwardian baroque façade, main door with fanlight, barrel-vaulted foyer—contrast with boutique hotel chic. The stairwell has an antique birdcage elevator with a wood-panelled cab made locally by A. & P. Steven. The top floor features 'art in the atrium' hence the original name of the hotel.

264
Sovereign House
158 West Regent Street
Robert Duncan 1893
A bas-relief scene, *Christ Healing the Deaf and Dumb Man*, identified this

mini chateau as the Institute for Adult Deaf and Dumb. Next door was John Ross Memorial Church for the Deaf *(Norman Dick 1931)*, incorporated into existing townhouses. The two buildings were rehabilitated as offices for architects *(SBT Keppie 1989)*. Ornate entrance with the bas-relief, cast iron railings and lamp standards, and bay windows crowned with Loire-style turrets.

265
Lady Artists' Club
5 Blythswood Square
Charles Rennie Mackintosh 1908

Blythswood Square was laid out with four classical terraces *(John Brash architect c. 1825)* facing a residents' garden. Number 5, an office rehabilitation called Mackintosh House (2004), was the Lady Artists' Club whose members commissioned the front door, an Art Nouveau take by Mackintosh on the square's neoclassicism. Number 4 was from 1906 to 1910 the office of Honeyman, Keppie & Mackintosh.

Number 11, formerly the Royal Scottish Automobile Club, is now the 5-star **Blythswood Square Hotel** *(Novo Design Studios 2011)*.

Number 7 is known as the **Madeleine Smith House**, after a scandal in 1857. Madeleine Smith (daughter of architect James Smith), having acquired a rich fiancé, was accused of murdering her French former paramour and potential blackmailer with poison. The 'notorious temptress' went to trial. Verdict: not proven.

266

Glasgow Art Club

185 Bath Street

> *Honeyman & Keppie, Charles Rennie Mackintosh 1893; MAST Architects 2014*

Part of a neoclassical terrace called Athol Place (1830s), bought by the Art Club in 1892. A timber-roofed skylit gallery was added, with a stencilled Art Nouveau frieze of stylised thistles by Mackintosh. The frieze was later covered with plaster. It was recreated during recent restoration, the original

being too fragile to be uncovered. Mackintosh visualised a frieze in the same relative position for the similarly skylit Museum at the GSA (see 281) but it was shelved to cut costs.

267

McLellan Galleries

254–270 Sauchiehall Street, 145 Renfrew Street

> *James Smith 1855; Frank Burnet, Boston & Carruthers 1904; Alexander Beith McDonald, City Engineer 1914*

Art collector Archibald McLellan planned to leave his treasure trove of old masters and this building to the city but both were put on sale to cover his debts after he died in 1854. The city bought the unfinished gallery and the artworks which became the nucleus of the civic collection, at Kelvingrove House from 1872 to 1899 and subsequently at the Art Galleries (see 312).

Behind the Italianate frontage on Sauchiehall Street was a department store, Trerons et Cie, Magasin des Tuileries (1896), known simply as 'Trerons'. It closed in 1986 after a fire gutted the store and collapsed the dome, rebuilt when the galleries were refurbished (*SBT Keppie Architects*) for Glasgow European City of Culture

1990. Their Beaux-Arts interiors and Renfrew Street façade date from 1914, the dome from 1904.

Across the street is the **Bank of Scotland** *(Keppie & Henderson 1932)*, a chunky commercial palazzo in North American classical style with two allegorical figures *(Benno Schotz sculptor)*.

268
Glasgow Film Theatre
12 Rose Street
William James Anderson (II), John McKissack & Son 1939

Dutch modernism with an Art Deco tower, originally the Cosmo Cinema. It was famed for foreign programming, symbolised by a globe above the marquee and 'Mr. Cosmo', a cartoon logo welcoming patrons. Alterations since the 1960s subdivided the auditorium for a second screen, and a bar in the foyer. The Scottish Film Council rebranded the venue the GFT in 1974. Upgrades since 2011 *(NORD Architecture)*, including a third screen, are sympathetic to its intimacy and character.

269
St. Aloysius Church
25 Rose Street
Charles Jean Ménart 1910
Jesuit church designed by a Belgian architect who studied at Glasgow School of Art. Corinthian pilasters rise to a pediment. The baroque campanile towers above a ferroconcrete roof, vaulted and arched inside where lavish Renaissance style prevails as if in Rome.

270
Haldane Building
24 Hill Street
Horatio Kelson Bromhead 1892
A former army drill hall built with rusticated stone walls to look like a fort. The soldiers decamped in 1967. Glasgow School of Art took over the building which was reconfigured inside (1976). The name recalls James Haldane, a local engraver whose trust helped establish the GSA.

271
Garnethill Park
Hill Street at Rose Street

Garnethill Community Council was
formed in 1975 to revive the neighbourhood following the negative
impacts of the M8 motorway and city
planning policies. One of its initiatives
was much-needed play space and,
assisted by Third Eye Centre, the Garnethill Mural Project. The park's pop
art mosaic *(John Kraska artist 1978)*
was part of the project.

The site was landscaped *(Dieter
Magnus environmental arts)* by the
Goethe-Institut as its contribution
to Glasgow's year as European City
of Culture 1990. There is a sandstone
amphitheatre, performance space and
play areas. The design is intriguing—it
looks part park, part archeological dig.

On the neighbourhood's streets are
Chookie Burdies (Shona Kinloch artist),
metal birds perched on lamp posts
installed for the Garnethill Lighting
Project *(Page\Park Architects 1993)*.

272
The Normal School
40 New City Road
David Hamilton 1837

Founded by educational innovator
David Stow, the Glasgow Normal
Seminary was the first teacher training
college in Scotland (the name was
taken from the French *École Normale*).
Teacher training was transferred to the
new Jordanhill College of Education in
1922. Redevelopment of Cowcaddens
in the 1960s destroyed the school's
Victorian urban context (New City
Road ran from Woodside until severed
by the M8). The façades are Italianate
with a neoclassical porch and baroque
clock tower. Refurbished as offices and
renamed Dundas Court.

273
The Phoenix Flowers
Garscube Road
*7N Architects, rankinfraser landscape
architecture 2010*
Public art and landscape design defuse
the hostile environment below an ele-

vated section of the M8. The pedestrian route was widened, resurfaced and planted with 50 colourful aluminium flowers. The name refers to Phoenix Foundry and a park once here. The foot and cycle path connects the city to **Speirs Locks** culture zone—the Glue Factory arts space, the National Theatre of Scotland (see 348) the Whisky Bond (see 347) and Speirs Wharf.

274

Speirs Wharf, Forth & Clyde Canal
Craighall Road

1790; 1812–1865; James Cunning, Young & Partners, Nicholas Groves-Raines 1988–1993

The canal, approved by Act of Parliament in 1768, was the first constructed in Scotland. Work stopped when cash ran out in 1775. Some of the navvies joined the British army during the American War of Independence. The project was completed in 1790.

Historic buildings line the wharf at Port Dundas. The canal company's Georgian office stands at its south end. To the north is a row of masonry and cast iron 19th-century structures—City of Glasgow Grain Mills and

Stores, Port Dundas Sugar Refinery, and Wheatsheaf Mills—now flats.

To the east is **Pinkston Watersports** *(7N Architects 2014),* North Canal Bank Street, with a whitewater course in an abandoned canal basin. Its architecture is low-tech and low-cost, with shipping containers cheerfully recycled. Five are stacked up like a giant drive-in sign; others in a waterfront row are meeting and storage rooms.

275

Savings Bank of Glasgow
New City Road

Neil Campbell Duff 1910

The Savings Bank commissioned several landmark branches on prominent corner sites across the city. This one is a tenement dominating the gushet, like a great ship stranded after the M8 cut the street. The banking hall was on the ground floor. The prow is embellished with pairs of *putti,* cornucopia, allegorical figures of Shipbuilding and Commerce, lion and unicorn heraldry and a baroque dome.

276
St. Aloysius Junior School
45 Hill Street

Elder & Cannon Architects 1999
St. Aloysius College is in a traditional
tenement area, a challenge to architects
commissioned for new designs. This
one, with a façade of *brise soleil*, sits
mid-block facing the school's Italianate
original building *(Archibald MacPher-
son 1883)* to which it does not defer. No
need for heritage pastiche: contextual
scale was preferred to mere style. Two
companions –the **Clavius Building**
(2003; Andrew Doolan Award 2004)
and a priests' residence (2006)—both
by Elder & Cannon, are at Hill and
Scott streets.

277
Breadalbane Terrace, Peel Terrace
97–113 Hill Street and 102–112
Hill Street

Charles Wilson c. 1845
Wilson introduced to the city's domestic architecture the first four-storey bay
windows on a tenement here. They are
at the back, south-facing. By the 1890s
no tenement or terrace was complete
without fashionable bay windows
overlooking the street.

Breadalbane Terrace has an air of
Georgian urbanism and style, with

neoclassical porches, window pediments, cornice balustrades and cast
iron railings. Stair wells are circular.
Apartments on the *piano nobile* were
designed for well-to-do families and
decorated accordingly. Peel Terrace
was built a few years later. Its east side
steps steeply down Garnethill Street,
an effect typical of the neighbourhood's topography.

More prosaic is **The Tenement House**
(145 Buccleuch Street; 1892), a fascinating time capsule owned since 1982 by
the National Trust for Scotland.

278
Garnethill Synagogue
Hill Street

*John McLeod, Nathan Solomon
Joseph 1879*

 The oldest
synagogue
in Scotland,
decorated
in Roman-
esque style
favoured by
the Jewish
diaspora for
association
with the Holy Land. Interior barrel-
vaulted, Byzantine, with a stained-
glass dome. The sanctuary was built

at right angles to the entrance to avoid existing properties and to observe the tradition that temples should be angled toward Jerusalem.

279
Almandine Apartments
145–167 Hill Street
Austin-Smith: Lord 2010

A design competition by Charing Cross Housing Association and the Royal Incorporation of Architects in Scotland (RIAS) produced this group of apartment blocks (some social housing, others for sale) which feature glazed stair towers instead of tenement closes.

The project took on a gap site where Hill Street stops above an artificial cliff edge. The street's tenements stepped steeply down to St. George's Road before they were torn down and the street severed by the trench excavated for the M8.

280
Garnethill Viewpoint
Hill Street
This panorama of the West End skyline was revealed by tenement demolitions for the M8. **Glasgow University** (see 313) is in the distance; on the right the French Gothic steeple of **Woodlands Church** *(John Burnet 1875)*; **Park Towers** (301) are above **St. George's Mansions** (291). St. George's Mansions was part of the neighbourhood around Charing Cross, a contiguous townscape before the motorway ploughed through leaving a wide fissure below Garnethill, creating the view.

281

Mackintosh Building, Glasgow School of Art

167 Renfrew Street

Honeyman & Keppie, Charles Rennie Mackintosh 1897–1899; CRM, Honeyman, Keppie & Mackintosh 1907–1909

the Art Nouveau bas-relief with roses and female guardian figures, and the typeface with the school's name, above the main door.

The school, originally called Glasgow Government School of Design, opened in 1845 on Ingram Street. Classes were held in the McLellan Galleries (see 267) from 1869 until 1899, when Mackintosh's masterwork opened.

It was built in two stages, east and west respectively. The Renfrew Street façade, designed in 1897, ties them together. There are wide eaves and a grid of studio windows with steel lintels. The effect seems modern, industrial even, yet Mackintosh's aesthetic was out of the past: of the hand-drawn and hand-made; medieval, Arts and Crafts. He designed almost everything here, from light fittings and furniture to

The building programme evolved from national guidelines set by the Department of Science and Art, South Kensington. An architectural competition was held to which 11 local firms were invited. Utility was stressed, and cost. The size of the studios and their windows (to be north-facing) was fundamental. The winner was Honeyman & Keppie, for whom Mackintosh was then an assistant. By the time the second stage of the school was financed he was a full partner and the building's lead architect. He was fortunate from the start in having a visionary and supportive client, Francis Newbery, the school's director, under whom he had studied. He also benefited from partnership with the more experienced John Keppie.

The entrance, part of the east block, is set in an asymmetrical tower, with steps over the basement light well, like a drawbridge to a castle. There are balconies for the director's room and studio, the latter recessed. The tree and bird weathervane on the stair turret symbolises Glasgow's coat of arms. Street railings have finials like samurai banners. Japanese design was part of Mackintosh's artistic armoury. Scottish motifs too—the wrought iron brackets on the windows look like Celtic basket-hilt broadswords (their practical purpose was to support window cleaners' planks).

The 17th-century fortified tower house theme is here, its height and massing adapted already by Mackintosh to fit Glasgow's urban scale (see 208). The back of the 'Mac' is harled and rears up on the hill like some ancient fortified crag. The west block's stone gable with vertical glazing on Scott Street transcended the stylistic expectations of the time.

Sculptural figures of Art, Architecture, Sculpture and Music planned for the west elevation were dropped due to cost (cylindrical stones show where they would have been). A frieze for the skylit, timber-trussed **Museum** was never stencilled.

Mackintosh's gift and continuing inspiration to students was his ability to create magical spaces. The most famous, arguably his finest

achievement, was the **Library** (1909), a Zen-like glade in the forest of the city. Latterly, access to it was restricted to set times, to accommodate students and the increasing numbers of tourists for whom it had become a shrine. The vertically glazed, double height room overlooking Scott Street was gutted in 2014 by a fire that threatened to engulf the whole building, and would have but for rapid response by firefighters. The Library was well documented, an aid to reconstruction *(Page\Park Architects)* and an opportunity to reconsider its purpose.

282
Bourdon Building
Scott Street at Renfrew Street
Keppie Henderson & Partners 1979

A brutalist block striding across Renfrew Street on *pilotis*, passing the Mac with a contextual gesture of big studio windows. Named for Eugène Bourdon, the first Professor of the GSA School of Architecture founded in 1903. It completed an ensemble, with the Foulis Building and Newbery Tower, all by Keppie Henderson & Partners 1970 (a direct descendent of Honeyman, Keppie & Mackintosh).

283

Reid Building, Glasgow School of Art
164 Renfrew Street

Steve Holl Architects, JM Architects,
Arup engineers 2011–2014

A landmark, named for Seona Reid,
Director of the GSA during the project.
It replaced the Foulis Building and
Newbery Tower, judged no longer fit
for purpose. The former had three
storeys and had been altered; the tower,
a brutalist campanile which would
have merited a retrofit, stood on a plaza
set back from Renfrew Street to avoid
clashing with the **Mackintosh Build-**
ing. The GSA Students' Association
Assembly Hall *(Keppie & Henderson*
1930), was retained because students
wanted it kept. Also, its stone façades
were seen to mediate between the

shock of the new and the Mac.

How to respond to the Mac while
obeying the brief to house the school's
design faculties was the challenge set
by the design competition for the new
building. The winner's Renfrew Street
elevation is face to face with the Mac.
To prevent sunlight bouncing into the
latter's studios the Reid Building is
veiled with sand-blasted matt glass. In
some conditions it does a vanishing
act, a good thing critics would say.

Sustainable measures, which include
rainwater harvesting and connection
to a biomass heating plant shared with
the Mac and Bourdon Building, rate
the Reid Building BREEAM Excellent.
To gain north light artists prefer, workshops and studios have windows to the
back alley. This pragmatic response re-

flects century-old practice in Glasgow of maximising light to rear elevations in lanes. Office and refectory spaces face Renfrew Street where the entrance features a stained-glass artwork by GSA alumnus Martin Boyce. A Mackintosh visitor centre is off the foyer.

Top light penetrates the building from oculi on three structural light wells—cylindrical, poured in place concrete shafts described by lead architect Steve Holl as 'driven voids of light'. Their smooth surfaces were achieved by curved steel plate rather than wood formwork. The shafts, and associated circulation ramps, are a key feature (they also act as chimneys for stack-effect ventilation). Eddies of natural light over five levels of spatial intrigue recall the genius of Mackintosh. The Reid Building is said by its architect to be a homage to him. The question is, were CRM to revisit Renfrew Street today what would he say?

284

Centre for Contemporary Arts
350 Sauchiehall Street
Alexander Thomson 1865; Page\Park Architects, Arup engineers 1996–2001

A Greek Revival commercial block, originally called Grecian Buildings, with an eaves gallery of chubby Egyptian columns . . . Thomson in a dream of antique lands.

Its origin as an arts venue was The Third Eye Centre, founded in 1974, a popular hangout, very Glasgow, being both avant-garde and unpretentious. It was relaunched as the CCA in 1992. Interventions created a three-storey, glass-roofed atrium in the former front yard of a previously hidden 19th-century townhouse.

Dominating the CCA is the tower-on-podium **Dental Hospital and School** (*Wylie Shanks & Partners 1970*). It backs up to the hospital's previous building (*Wylie Wright & Wylie 1932*) which has an Art Deco façade on Renfrew Street. The ornate wall of sandstone at 396–450 Sauchiehall Street is the ebullient Edwardian baroque **Ashfield House**, built in two phases (*Thomas Lennox Watson 1903, 1908*).

285

Renfield St. Stephen's Church
260 Bath Street
John Thomas Emmet c. 1850; CRGP Architects 2001

Classical terraces and two churches, Renfield St. Stephen's and **Adelaide Place Church**, 209 Bath Street (*Thomas Lennox Watson 1877*), are clues that the street was once part of a residential neighbourhood, Blythswood Hill.

The Roman-style Adelaide Place was reconfigured in 1995 as a multi-functional facility. Renfield St. Stephen's was almost destroyed in 1998 when

the steeple was toppled by a storm and crashed through the roof. *Christ and the Apostles* on the east window *(Norman McLeod MacDougall, stained glass 1905)* escaped damage but the Gothic arcades, timber roof and the slender spire had to be reconstructed. The church has evolved: for worship, concerts and as a conference centre. The adjoining hall, chapel and pocket plaza *(Monro & Partners)* date from 1971.

286
The Griffin
266 Bath Street
William Reid 1903
Glasgow Style in wood and etched glass, the Art Nouveau woodwork influenced by detailing on The Hatrack

(see 232) completed the year before. The bar opened as the King's Arms, named for its location across from the Edwardian baroque **King's Theatre**, 355 Bath Street *(Frank Matcham 1904)*, which provided a clientele. Its ornate auditorium has been restored *(Simpson & Brown Architects 2011)*.

287
The Beresford
460 Sauchiehall Street
Weddell & Inglis 1938; 3D Reid Architects 2007
Full-frontal American Art Deco with bow windows framing tiled vertical fins which shoot up from a marquee like a movie theatre. It opened as the 200-room Beresford Hotel. The first guests were visitors to the 1938 Empire Exhibition at Bellahouston Park.

During the Second World War it was requisitioned by the government as a billet for American and Canadian forces. It was converted to offices by Imperial Chemical Industries (ICI) in 1952. In 1964 it became Baird Hall, student digs for Strathclyde University. There was a bar on the ground floor called Ocean's Eleven (from the 1960 Sinatra movie) with a backlit skyscraper skyline on the fascia, a Hollywood noir image which fitted the building perfectly.

The Beresford has since been rehabilitated as apartments. Galleried deck-access for flats was attached around the inner courtyard. The lobby and revolving doors were restored and the original colour scheme revived.

288
Royal Highland Fusiliers Regimental Museum
518 Sauchiehall Street
John Keppie 1904
Dutch-gabled northern Renaissance façade with classical figures in the style of Michelangelo, a popular source (*McGilvray & Ferris sculptors).* Built as a gallery and studio for T. & R. Annan & Sons, founded in 1855 by pioneering photographer Thomas Annan. His best known portfolio, *Old Closes and Streets of Glasgow 1868–1877,* was commissioned by the slum-clearing City Improvement Trust.

The building became a recruiting centre for the Royal Highland Fusiliers in 1959 and a museum. The initials RHF and Regimental Colours were added to the façade and gable when the building was refurbished and the storefront restored (1999). An elevator cage and other features were attributed to Mackintosh but there is no evidence he was involved here. Hidden by the Fusiliers' façade is a house, once part of a 19th-century terrace called Albany Place.

Next door was T. A. Ewing's **Piano and Harmonium Emporium**, hence the angelic statue of Harmony on top and, at the rear on Renfrew Street, a bust of Beethoven, both (c. 1897) by the owner's brother, sculptor James Alexander Ewing.

289
Charing Cross Mansions
540–546 Sauchiehall Street
J. J. Burnet 1891
Glasgow's most flamboyant Victorian apartment block. Its Parisian roofline and French Renaissance façade recall the Hôtel de Ville in Paris which Burnet had seen. The centrepiece is a *grand horloge* with Roman numerals and the signs of the Zodiac. Below it are Father

Time, St. Mungo and two *putti* pulling aside a curtain to reveal the city's coat of arms. Carved figures *(William Birnie Rhind sculptor)* reclining on the arch above the clock were modelled on *Night and Day* by Michelangelo in the Medici Chapels. Others represent the Four Seasons. The initials of Burnet's client, Robert Simpson & Sons, are carved on a cartouche. A lion rampant rises above the loggia and cornice. *C'est formidable.*

The full sweep of the façade, which is crowned with an octagonal cupola, lantern and cast iron filigree, was revealed by the demolition in 1969 of the Grand Hotel (French Renaissance style, 1880s). It was in the way of the M8 which was blasted through Charing Cross in a cut-and-cover tunnel. Victorian survivors here include **Albany Chambers** *(J. J. Burnet 1899)* at 534 Sauchiehall Street. Like Charing Cross and St. George's Mansions (see 291) it

was built as an upmarket, mixed-use tenement with shops, business chambers and flats, a typology which helped form, populate and enliven the city's dense urban grain.

290

Cameron Memorial Fountain
Sauchiehall Street
Robert Alexander Bryden 1896

Terracotta drinking fountain made by the Doulton Company, London. Its subject, Charles Cameron, was a newspaper editor, member of parliament and a leader of the temperance movement. Not his fault that the fountain leans like a drunk. Urban myth blames excavations for the M8 but the lean was noticed in the 1920s.

The motorway left gap sites. One was filled by **Fountain House** *(Walter Underwood & Partners 1981)*, its facetted form an echo of the roofline at Charing Cross Mansions.

291
St. George's Mansions
St. George's Road and Woodlands Road
Frank Burnet, Boston & Carruthers 1902

A grand tenement block perched on the edge of the M8 cut. Façades with curved pediments flank a showy corner capped with a Parisian roof, turrets and cast iron cresting. Built by Glasgow Corporation, hence cherubs holding cartouches with the city's symbols in the upper level's spandrels.

292
Tay House
300 Bath Street
Holford Associates 1991

One-armed office block with vertical outriggers trying to be high tech. Shiny cladding was intended until city planners insisted that the colour be contextual, that is to the Cameron Fountain and Charing Cross Mansions. The arm rests on a bridge-like deck across the M8. The deck (c.1970) was part of a tower-on-podium scheme, with an elevated walkway and offices and flats replacing the Victorian terraces on Sauchiehall Street west of Charing Cross, fortunately not constructed.

Before Tay House appeared there were calls for the deck to be removed and the M8 covered to create a public plaza between Charing Cross Mansions and the Mitchell Library (see 293). That was deemed inconvenient and rejected by the authorities because to take down the deck required temporary closure of the M8. A 2015 report for city council recommended the plaza idea be revived.

Art Galleries, Kelvingrove

7

The West End

IN 1870 a menagerie of stuffed animals which included a polar bear
was hauled on horse-drawn carts from the Old College on High Street
to Glasgow University's new campus on Gilmorehill in the West End.
The Old College had been sold to the City of Glasgow Union Railway to
fund the relocation to Gilmorehill, a country estate which the university
bought in 1865. The strange convoy was part of William Hunter's gift
of 1783 to his alma mater. The eclectic bequest was installed in the new
campus library and the Hunterian Museum; the artworks established
the Hunterian Art Gallery; the stuffed animals eventually found a home
in the Zoology Building.

The Hunterian Museum is a medieval-style hall by George Gilbert
Scott who was commissioned to design the Gilmorehill campus. His
Gothic Revival buildings and tower command a bluff above the River
Kelvin. Their only rival in the world of picturesque Victorian Gothic is
Parliament Hill in Ottawa, Canada, similar in style, scale and topog-
raphy. Kelvingrove Park is spread out below between Gilmorehill and
Woodlands Hill. Both had been private estates of Glasgow merchants.

In the 1845 Woodlands Hill was proposed as a site for the campus but
the idea was not pursued. The hill, along with Kelvingrove, was bought
by the city in 1852. Architect Charles Wilson was commissioned to design an upmarket residential development of terraced townhouses. They
flow around the contours, lending Park District a pleasing informality.

Terraces on the south slopes were by various architects who played classical themes. Wilson's orchestration is Italianate with contrasting notes. Park Circus, an ellipse of palazzo façades with gardens in its centre, was constructed on the hill's plateau; Park Terrace has a Parisian roofline like a tiara above Kelvingrove Park. The skyline is punctuated by Gothic and Florentine church pinnacles known as Park Towers.

The district attracted wealthy buyers, notably Walter Macfarlane, owner of Saracen Foundry, who commissioned one of the city's most ostentatious interiors for his townhouse at 22 Park Circus (1874). Changing fortunes and lifestyles in the 20th century saw most of the homes converted to offices and consulates. The Alliance Française and the Goethe-Institut are here. Macfarlane's palazzo became Casa d'Italia, a club for Scots-Italians and, until recently, was the city's marriage registry office. The trend now is to return the townhouses to residential use. Park Quadrant, the only unfinished part of Wilson's plan, is to be developed with new homes.

Kelvingrove Park (originally called The West End Park) was laid out to a design by Joseph Paxton, implemented between 1853 and 1867 by John Carrick, Superintendent of Public Works and City Architect. The land was previously Kelvingrove Estate, which was acquired along with its mansion, Kelvingrove House, by the city for the park, the cost covered by feuing building lots on Woodlands Hill. Glasgow's Victorian parks, created for the pleasure of all classes, are a joy thanks to the foresight and investment in public enterprises by the city fathers. Glasgow Corporation owned and operated not only parks but also public baths, libraries, art galleries, markets, tramways, the subway, gas, electricity, water and more. The Stewart Memorial Fountain in Kelvingrove celebrates one of the most ambitious schemes, the supply of fresh drinking water by pipeline, aqueducts and tunnels from Loch Katrine, 60 kilometres away. The biggest civic ornament in the park is Kelvingrove

Art Gallery & Museum (aka the Art Galleries), opened for the 1901 Glasgow International Exhibition and to house the municipal collection previously in Kelvingrove House, which was demolished. At the summit of the park is a sublime view from Park Terrace, with the baroque mi- radors of the Art Galleries and the Gothic spire of the university on the skyline.

George Gilbert Scott's buildings dominate the campus but other prominent architects are present here. The Hunterian includes a re- construction of a house on Gilmorehill once occupied and decorated by Charles Rennie Mackintosh and his wife Margaret Macdonald. Expansion of further education in the 1960s required new buildings. Brutalism was their style, not generally popular but now embedded in the historic texture of the campus—the Boyd Orr Building, Library and Hunterian Art Gallery for example. The university continues to expand. Acquisition of the Western Infirmary site increases the size of the cam- pus by up to 25 percent. A study *(Page\Park Architects 2014)* to guide its evolution has been published.

The university principals moved because they got a good deal from the railway company, and the Old College was no longer fit for pur- pose in an area increasingly slummy and industrialised. The West End, roughly the area between Charing Cross, Anniesland and the Clyde Tunnel, offered open space and clean air—the prevailing wind kept the air pollution of the East End's industries away. Land owners diversified into real estate, subdividing their holdings and feuing or selling build- ing lots. By 1900 villas, terraces and tenements for the bourgeoisie filled the area. The main drag is Byres Road. The dynamic of gentrification has seen previously run-down Finnieston and much of Partick absorbed.

To make the West End manageable, Great Western Road, its hinter- land and Botanic Gardens are featured in Tour 8, *Woodside, Maryhill & Great Western Road.*

293
Mitchell Library
North Street

William Brown Whitie 1907–1911
Over one million items are in the varied collections of the Mitchell, one of the largest public reference libraries in Europe. It was funded by the bequest in 1874 of tobacco merchant Stephen Mitchell, and located in the Merchant City. The bequest of bibliophile and traveller Robert Jeffrey in 1902 prompted the city to buy the site on North Street for a new building, for which a competition was held. The foundation stone was laid in 1907 by Andrew Carnegie, who helped fund the project.

A splendid marble staircase under the dome leads to the Jeffery Room, designed for the aforementioned bequest. The vast Edwardian reading room, now an events space, has a glazed barrel-vaulted ceiling. Sculpted figures of Wisdom *(Johan Keller)* and

Literature *(Thomas John Clapperton)* are, respectively, at the North Street entrance and on the dome. Neither the statues nor the dome were contemplated initially but the baroque building is better for them. Demolitions for the M8 motorway opened up a wide view of it.

On Granville Street is the façade of **St. Andrew's Halls**. Inside is the Mitchell Theatre, part of the Mitchell extension *(Frank Mears & Partners)*, announced in 1966 to make use of the site after the halls burned down but not completed until 1981. The enlarged library was refurbished in 2007. Its Glasgow Collection and the Glasgow City Archives are primary sources of historical reference.

294
St. Andrew's Halls
Granville Street
James Sellars 1873–1877
Great halls have great acoustics, and

St. Andrew's Halls, once the principal venue of the Scottish National Orchestra (SNO) was no exception. The auditorium was shoebox-shaped like the Concertgebouw, Amsterdam and the Musikverein, Vienna—Europe's best with which it ranked until destroyed by fire in 1962.

It was built in an era of cultural aspiration and civic pride. The exterior expresses the idea that the Victorians were heirs to classical traditions in music and other arts. The architecture is Greek Revival, severe like Schinkel's Berlin. There is an Ionic colonnade and a formidable collection of statuary—caryatids, Atlantes, and classical groups representing the Arts—created by the local Mossman firm. The accompanying lamp holders with patterns of laurel, acanthus and anthemion were cast at Macfarlane's Saracen Foundry.

The fire left a gutted shell which was propped up for two decades until filled by the Mitchell Library and the Mitchell Theatre. Decades of dithering to commission a replacement ended when **Glasgow Royal Concert Hall** (see 193) opened in 1990.

295
Central Gurdwara
138 Berkeley Street
Calford Seaden Architects 2015

This Sikh temple and community centre, the largest in Scotland, was built to replace a previous temple in a former Salvation Army hall still standing on Berkeley Street. It is not the first purpose-built—that distinction goes to Glasgow Gurdwara (see 422) opened in 2013. The golden onion dome was fabricated in GRP (glass reinforced plastic) on a steel frame. The façades have decorative panels carved in India.

Close by is the deconsecrated Gothic Revival **Trinity Church** *(John Honeyman 1864)*, a pioneering example of adaptive reuse *(Jack Notman c. 1980)* when rescued as rehearsal space and renamed Henry Wood Hall for the SNO. In 2015 the orchestra, now the Royal Scottish National Orchestra (RSNO) moved to the purpose-built RSNO Centre *(Glasgow City Council, Arup engineers)* at Glasgow Royal Concert Hall.

296
Minerva Street Tenements
8–32 Minerva Street
Alexander Kirkland c. 1850
Street corner curving with Corinthian pilasters, as if on a stately home. The classical pretension promoted the Stobcross Estate Company's suburb along **St. Vincent Crescent** *(Alexander Kirkland 1850–1855).* A twin tenement curved into Finnieston Street until demolished in 1972 to make way for traffic from the Clydeside Expressway. The planners then had no regard for homes, stately or not. By the 1880s railways, industry and construction of Queen's Dock discouraged further residential development here.

297
The Hothouse
1073 Argyle Street
Elder & Cannon Architects 2007

Finnieston was a down-at-heel post-industrial through-route to the West End until rediscovered by urbanites in search of affordable flats. The Hydro (see 34) gave a further boost to the local economy. Nineteenth-century tenements have been refurbished, their ground floors refreshed with trendy bars and bistros. The old Finnieston was more fish suppers than sushi—the least likely location for a whole-foods store, as there is now on Argyle Street, or the steel-framed Hothouse, advertised as 'boutique two-bed apartments'.

In plan the building is a sandwich, with the north and south slices offset to maximise daylight on all sides and minimise the bulk (the upper level to Argyle Street is set back). There are sun decks on the south side. It fits the scale and density of neighbouring tenements but is clearly 21st century.

298
The Hidden Lane
1103 Argyle Street

Back courts across the city were home to light industries and tradespeople in the 19th century. Buildings from that period survive here, through a cobbled pend, hidden behind a funeral parlour. There are workshops, studio spaces and a tearoom. Vibe alternative, with gussied-up brickwork, solar panels and start-ups. The Hidden Lane Gallery was a catalyst, opened in 2009 in the undertaker's former garage on Argyle Street.

299
The Queen's Rooms
1 La Belle Place
Charles Wilson 1857

Originally assembly rooms and a concert hall. The Italian Renaissance exterior is exceptional, with a decorative theme and classical frieze symbolising the evolution of Western civilisation.

Façades front and rear are pedimented, the latter with an inscription for posterity: 'Erected by David Bell of Blackhall, merchant in Glasgow'. Also recorded are the architect, sculptor (*John Mossman*), wright and builder. On the east elevation are portrait medallions thought to be (left to right) James Watt, Robert Burns, Joshua Reynolds, David Hamilton, John Flaxman, George Frederic Handel and Robert Peel.

The original interior was lost when the building was converted to a Christian Scientist church (c.1948). Since the mid 1990s it has been the **Hindu**

Mandir Glasgow, temple and cultural centre. At 2–5 La Belle Place are two very fine tenement façades, also by Wilson in the same style.

300
Claremont Terrace
John Baird (1) 1842–1847

From the 1830s onward, terraces of townhouses were built on Woodlands Hill (see next entry) west of Charing Cross. They snake around the contours, the city centre grid plan not being extended here. The effect is picturesque with gardens alternating with the streets. The lower terraces were styled individually by different architects. Claremont Terrace is Regency style, with Ionic porches and delicate wrought iron balconies. The centrepiece was originally a single villa, Claremont House, once the home of philanthropist Isabella Elder (see 2, 3 and 371).

301

Park District

Charles Wilson 1854–1863

The French Second Empire roofline of **Park Terrace**, the monumental **Park**

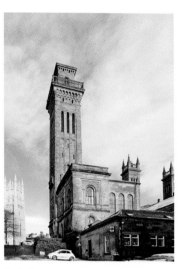

Steps and the classical plan of **Park Circus** were part of Charles Wilson's design for a residential district similar to Edinburgh's New Town. It commands the plateau at the top of Woodlands Hill, which had been proposed as a site for **Glasgow University** (see 313). The townscape he created is one of the finest and best preserved of its period in Europe, but it was not finished. Park Quadrant, on its north side, remained unbuilt following the crash of the City of Glasgow Bank in 1878. A controversial scheme to the fill the overgrown site with apartments, its architecture a parody of the district's Victorian terraces, was approved by council in 2016.

The Italianate *campanili* of Wilson's **Free Church (Trinity) College** (1856–1861) punctuate Park District's skyline. The neighbouring **Park Parish Church** (*John Thomas Rochead 1858*) is Gothic Revival. A unique ensemble. The tower of Park Church was saved after the nave was demolished in 1968 for an office building, now reclad as

Park House, an apartment block (*RMJM 2009*). Trinity College was converted to flats (c. 1985).

302

Lord Roberts Memorial

Park Terrace at Park Gate

Harry Bates sculptor 1916

Park Circus leads to a dramatic edge overlooking the valley of the River Kelvin and Kelvingrove Park. On the horizon are the spire of Glasgow University and the pinnacles the Art Galleries. The viewpoint was the obvious place for a monument and there is one—a statue portraying Lord Roberts vigorous and tense on his charger.

It was copied for convenience and cost from the original erected in Calcutta in 1898. It recalls a recruiting drive in Glasgow in 1913 when Roberts called for a citizen's army to serve the empire. The Victorian campaigns that made his name are inscribed on the pedestal. A frieze illustrates an epic march he led in 1880 from Kabul, to win the Battle of Kandahar during

the Second Afghan War. Victory is symbolised by a classical maiden; War by a medieval crusader.

Kelvingrove Park *(Joseph Paxton 1853–1867)* is a hilly carpet of wooded meadows dotted with *fin-de-siècle* public art. Sculptures include the Bengal Tigress *(Auguste Nicolas Cain 1867)*, a Highland Light Infantry soldier of the Boer War *(William Birnie Rhind 1906)* and Thomas Carlyle, as if hewn from a rock *(William Kellock Brown 1916)*. The most prominent building is the **Art Galleries** (see 312).

303
Stewart Memorial Fountain
Kelvingrove Park

James Sellars 1872

Named for Lord Provost Robert Stewart who promoted the supply of fresh drinking water to the city after several outbreaks of cholera. The enterprise,

completed in 1859, was a heroic feat of engineering. Aqueducts and tunnels were built and a pipeline laid from Loch Katrine in the Trossachs.

The infrastructure was upgraded recently by Scottish Water. Glasgow City Heritage Trust aided restoration of the fountain. Its decorative scheme was inspired by the flora and fauna at the water's source and Walter Scott's narrative poem *The Lady of the Lake* which was set there. The poem's heroine, Ellen Douglas, appears as the fountain's figurehead. Stewart appears on a commemorative plaque.

304
Kelvingrove Parish Church
49 Derby Street
Campbell Douglas & Sellars 1880

Greek Revival style, with an Ionic columned portico and octagonal domed lantern. Converted to flats (2009), a now common adaptive reuse of redundant churches, the Victorians having built so many. A blessing for architects in Scotland after the Disruption of 1843 when 450 ministers broke away from the established church. This building was originally Finnieston Free Church, one of many commissioned by the breakaway sect.

305
The Argyle Street Tree
1223 Argyle Street

Nature's gift to Argyle Street, an ash, long regarded as the only tree on the street between Glasgow Cross and Kelvingrove, and one of the city's tallest. It might be as old as **Franklin Terrace** (1850), the range of tenements where it seeded, reputedly having been mixed in plant roots brought from the country by a resident.

306
Yorkhill Barracks
172 Yorkhill Street
Leiper & McNab 1901; Riach Partnership 2000

A Tudor castle with dummy battlements, formerly a Highland Light Infantry (HLI) drill hall, 6th Battalion as noted above the entrance. Polish soldiers were based here during the Second World War. **The Polish Church** (St. Simon's) where they worshipped still stands at 33 Partick Bridge Road (south of Partick Cross). The distinctive drill hall is now flats, part of a residential adaptive reuse of the barracks.

307
The Galleries
Sauchiehall at Argyll Street
Cooper Cromar c. 1990

A postmodern pastiche of the Glasgow Style with the ghost of Mackintosh present, willing or not. Plays with the tenement form and responds to the setting. Effective elevations, and a square tower at the gushet.

308
Kelvin Hall
Argyle Street
Thomas Gilchrist Gilmour, Thomas Somers engineer, Glasgow Corporation 1927; Page\Park Architects 2016
Domes and ziggurats bristling with obelisks and metal globes, like a train station perhaps, in 1930s Shanghai. It followed the plan of its predecessor, the Machinery Hall at the International Exhibition of 1901 where Glasgow-built locomotives were displayed. Kelvin Hall's vast interior was used during the Second World War to assemble anti-aircraft barrage balloons. It was better known for its Christmas carnival and

circus before being repurposed for the Museum of Transport and a sports arena (1987). In 2011 the museum was relocated to **Riverside** (see 27).

The hall has been re-roofed and reconfigured as a cultural and storage facility for Glasgow Museums, the National Library and The Hunterian Collections Study Centre along with sports and fitness facilities for Glasgow Life. The change of use is announced by an elegant linear reception pavilion (2016) attached to the west side of the Beaux-Arts frontage.

309
Bishop's Mill
206 Old Dumbarton Road
c. 1850
The only remaining grain mill near Partick Bridge where there were several, well into the 20th century. The River Kelvin was channelled and accelerated to power their water wheels which were geared to milling machinery. The original mill on this site was destroyed by fire in the 1830s. This replacement

closed in the 1960s and was converted to flats (1985). The stone wheat sheaves on the gable crests indicate its former function. **Partick Bridge** *(Bell & Miller engineers 1878)* is on the boundary between Glasgow and the former Burgh of Partick. Below its north parapet is the previous bridge of 1800.

310

Cameronians War Memorial
Kelvingrove Park

Philip Lindsey Clark sculptor 1924
A dynamic tableau of the First World War. Three soldiers symbolise Courage, Duty and Sacrifice, the enduring narrative of Remembrance Day. The sculptor was a war veteran. The memorial was unveiled by Earl Haig.

311

Sunlight Cottages
Kelvingrove Park

James Miller 1901
Tudor Revival style cloned from the Arts and Crafts model village of Port Sunlight, then being built by Lord Leverhulme for his workers. His soap company, Lever Brothers, sponsored the cottages as part of the 1901 International Exhibition and he gave them to Glasgow after the event, when they became dwellings for park staff.

312

Kelvingrove Art Gallery & Museum
(The Art Galleries)
Kelvingrove Park

Simpson & Allen 1897–1901
Built as a permanent home for the municipal art collection and for the 1901 International Exhibition following a design competition in 1891 won by London-based architects. Their extravagant taste and self-confidence to exercise it expressed the spirit of the age. The building sprouts towers, turrets, cupolas and lanterns. The style? Spanish and French Renaissance, Baltic . . . take your pick. The ensemble is saved from the lunatic asylum by a rational Beaux-Arts plan.

The central hall is baroque, barrel-

vaulted with a coffered ceiling above arcades and an Italianate tiled floor which originally displayed classical sculptures (some now in the Kibble Palace; see 373). There is a Lewis & Co. pipe organ for concerts. Its sound penetrates two lesser but spacious galleried halls and salons in symmetrical wings, and echoes eerily in far colonnades and corners.

The sculptural programme (George Frampton supervising) was lavish inside and out. The finest piece (by Frampton) is St. Mungo as patron of Art and Music in the north porch. Access from the south is through a *porte cochère*. The two entrances and the taller north towers prompted the urban myth that the building is the wrong way round. In fact it was oriented to fit the expo plan.

Kelvingrove was closed in 2003 for a three-year refurbishment and re-display *(Building Design Partnership, Event Communications)*. At the

north porch the lower ground floor was opened up for a gallery shop and café, and to increase exhibition space. Upstairs, the **Mackintosh and Glasgow Style Gallery** evokes the *fin-de-siècle* bohemian city. The complete collection, a cornucopia, is one of the best and most diverse in Europe.

313

Glasgow University, Main Buildings Gilmorehill

George Gilbert Scott 1866–1870; spire by John Oldrid Scott 1887

Towering above Kelvingrove Park are the landmark buildings of the campus (see 318–332). They provided it with instant Gothic heritage. The selection committee, having declined to hold a competition, chose George Gilbert Scott for his 'eminent talent and taste'. Scott claimed that the design was 'his own invention . . . a 13th- or 14th-century secular style with the addition of certain Scottish features peculiar to

that country.' Local critics thought it too English. Alexander 'Greek' Thomson said so in a lecture to the Glasgow Architectural Society in 1886. He condemned the Gothic style and its architect as an 'invasion from the south' and dismissed Scott's self-justification as patronising nonsense. Thomson would have made it an acropolis.

Scott flattened the top of the hill for the foundations of his medieval fantasy. Its stonework clads machine-age construction. More than 1,000 workers were employed. They were laid off temporarily in 1870 when money ran out. The ceremonial **Bute Hall** (see 322) was not opened until 1884 and the tower lacked a spire until 1887.

The spire has an open framework in stone, chosen because the wind would blow through it and it would be durable but not too heavy (there was concern about the tower's stability). John Oldrid Scott cited the spires (1880) of Cologne Cathedral as a 'picturesque'

engineering precedent. From the archway at the base of the tower there is a panoramic view across the city.

314
Kelvin Way Bridge
Kelvingrove Park

Alexander Beith McDonald, City Engineer; Paul Raphael Montford sculptor 1914

Four sculptural groups in bronze

decorate the parapets: War and Peace (northeast), Navigation and Ship-building (southeast), Commerce and Industry (southwest), Philosophy and Inspiration (northwest). They were the result of a 1914 competition but not cast until 1926 because bronze had been reserved by the War Office for artillery shell casings during the First World War.

During an air raid in 1941 the bridge was near-missed by German bombs. Philosophy and Inspiration and War and Peace were blown into the river. They were hauled out and repaired (*Benno Schotz sculptor 1951*). The bridge is part of Kelvin Way, a tree-lined avenue through the park.

315
Kelvingrove Park Bandstand
Kelvin Way
James Miller 1924; Page\Park Architects 2014

Glasgow's only surviving heritage bandstand was derelict, vandalised and tagged with graffiti. Council planned to demolish it. The Friends of Kelvingrove Park campaigned to save it. Work was partly grant-aided by Glasgow City Heritage Trust and completed by Glasgow Building Preservation Trust. The building and amphitheatre were restored and upgraded without loss to their character.

316
Hillhead Primary School
110 Otago Street
JM Architects 2011

The school, commissioned by city council, sits in a hollow below Gilmorehill. The site is by the River Kelvin and Kelvingrove Park. Victorian tenements are to the north and east. A challenging context.

The design is contemporary, concrete, scaled to students' needs: a miniature campus with a sequence of pavilions connected by a bridge, sidestepping an existing property. Communal facilities are to the north; classrooms are in the sylvan south setting where intrusion into green space was mitigated by reuse of the former park works depot. The north pavilions step back from Gibson Street's traffic and expose the former Hillhead Congregational Church (see 318). Full marks for respecting heritage. The enduring lesson is that good design respects teachers and students, creating an inspirational learning environment.

317
Otago Lane

Early 19th-century lane with a mews
terrace, originally stables, a blacksmith's workshop and coach houses
with two cottages on a deck at the rear.
The historic ensemble is home to small
independent businesses: Voltaire &
Rousseau bookshop, horologist Kenneth Chapelle, Tchai-Ovna teahouse
and Mixed Up Records. A 'Save Otago
Lane' campaign defended this diversity
against a development of flats. They
were granted planning permission by
city council in 2012 despite thousands
of objections and the likely loss to the
lane's character and green space. The
permission was extended in 2016.

318
Glasgow University Union
32 University Avenue
Arthur & McNaughtan 1930
Drum-towered, crow-step gabled entrance fit for a 16th-century Highland
fancy dress ball. Bold composition
of the entrance bay influenced by

Art Deco as much as by the national
romanticism of the interwar years.

Next door is the new **Stevenson
Building** *(ECD Architects, Page\Park
Architects 2015),* a sports and social
hub connected to the Union, and to
the earlier Stevenson Building *(Keppie
Henderson & Partners 1961)* at Oakfield
Avenue. The contemporary interven-
tion, on the conspicuous corner at
Gibson Street, acts as a gateway to the
campus.

Across the street are **Hillhead Congregational Church** *(Hugh & David
Barclay 1895)* and **Gilmorehill Church**
(James Sellars 1878), both French Gothic, now occupied by the university.

On Oakfield Avenue is the **Rankine
Building** *(Keppie Henderson & Partners 1970),* brutalist but civilised, oriented like a terrace. Named after William MacQuorn Rankine (see 243). At
41–53 Oakfield Avenue is **Eton Terrace**
by Alexander 'Greek' Thomson *(1864);*
also **Lilybank House** (1830s), with distinctive touches following a makeover
by Thomson (c. 1864). Lilybank House
is at Bute Gardens, behind the Modern
Languages Building (see 328).

319
Pearce Lodge, Glasgow University
University Avenue
Alexander George Thomson 1887

A resurrection of the entrance to the
Old College (1656; demolished c. 1870)
on High Street. Stonework was numbered and re-erected here. It includes
an archway, the coat of arms of Charles
II, thistle, rose, harp and *fleur-de-lis*
ornament, corbelled balconies, crow
steps and axial chimney stacks. The
turret and the gateposts were new, to fit
in with Gilmorehill's Gothic. The **Lion
and Unicorn Stair**, at the southeast
corner of **Professors' Square** *(George
Gilbert Scott 1870),* was part of the
salvage, funded by William Pearce of
Fairfield shipyard.

The lodge inspired the handsome
fakery of the **James Watt Engineering Building** *(J. J. Burnet 1901)* inside
the gates. In all other respects it was
modern, based on engineering schools
Burnet had seen at McGill, Columbia,
and Yale universities on a research trip
in 1896. It was promoted by professor
Archibald Barr, to make Glasgow's
faculty world-beating in the tradition
of Watt.

320
Wellington Church
76 University Avenue
Thomas Lennox Watson 1884

A Roman temple built for a United
Presbyterian congregation previously
at Wellington Street in the city centre.
The porch, perched on a podium and
pedimented on Corinthian columns,
was inspired by the Maison Carrée in
Nîmes, France. Side elevations have
colonnades, and arched windows
illuminate the Renaissance interior.

321
McMillan Round Reading Room
University Avenue
Hughes & Waugh 1939

Brick-faced concrete rotunda with a
dome above a galleried interior which
radiates from an information desk at
the core. Decoration was confined to
a carving of St. Mungo above the Art

Deco entrance, aligned to reflect Scott's Gothic tower.

Across the avenue are the **Quincentenary Gates** *(Keppie Henderson & J. L. Gleave 1951)* erected to mark the 500th anniversary of the foundation of the university, the fourth oldest in Britain. The ironwork symbolises a tree in fruit, the fruits being the names of distinguished alumni, among them Adam Smith, James Watt and Lord Kelvin.

tracery. A flèche, shown on an early drawing by Scott, was not fitted. The adjoining **Randolph Hall**, smaller but striking with a timber vaulted ceiling, was named for benefactor Charles Randolph, shipbuilder. The halls separate two quadrangles, a feature of the Old College. In the west quad is the **War Memorial Chapel** *(J. J. Burnet 1923–1929)* to which was added a flèche like that drawn for Bute Hall.

322
Bute Hall, Glasgow University
George Gilbert Scott, John Oldrid Scott 1884

The design for this ceremonial hall was in preparation when Scott died in 1878. His son John Oldrid completed it. The primary patron was the Marquess of Bute, a devotee of Gothic Revival. The interior is magnificent, faux-medieval. Stained glass *(Burne-Jones, Douglas Strachan, Morris & Co. et al.)* showing writers, philosophers, scientists and theologians is outstanding.

The exterior is an imaginary Loire chateau, Gothic though, and Scottish Baronial. There are turrets on round towers at each corner, crow-step gables, buttressed walls and window

323
Bute Hall Undercroft
George Gilbert Scott, John Oldrid Scott 1882

At ground level under Bute Hall a mysterious vaulted Gothic space with rows of columns reminiscent, perhaps knowingly, of the crypt at **Glasgow Cathedral** (see 123) where the university was founded in 1451. The practical function was to provide a covered route between the south and north ranges of the original campus plan and its east and west quadrangles.

324
The Hunterian Museum, Glasgow University

George Gilbert Scott 1870

The museum was established at the Old College in 1807 in a domed neoclassical building designed to house the bequest of Dr. William Hunter, citizen of The Enlightenment and collector extraordinaire. A model of the original building *(William Stark architect)* is exhibited here, along with Roman artifacts from the Antonine Wall, ethnographic objects from 18th- and 19th-century global exploration and much more, including George Gilbert Scott's design drawings for the Gilmorehill campus. The Victorian interior of the Hunterian looks like a medieval guild hall, but with cast iron colonnades and riveted iron beams supporting its gallery and timber roof, the visible mix of modernity and medievalism a Scott trademark.

Hunter's bequest included taxidermy which formed the zoology collection in the **Graham Kerr Building** *(J. J. Burnet 1924)*; manuscripts and books went to the Library (in 1870 on the west quad). The Hunterian (in the east quad) was refurbished in 2007. It is the oldest public museum in Scotland.

325
The Mackintosh House & Hunterian Art Gallery
Hillhead Street

William Whitfield & Partners architects, Lowe & Rodin engineers 1973–1981

The gallery and house form a restless composition, brutalist in form and use of concrete. External walls were cast and bush hammered to expose the aggregate. Parts of the house are harled. The effect is tough and grainy, in context very Scottish as is the gallery's cylindrical stair tower. In the foyer, four cast aluminium doors with pop art relief patterns *(Eduardo Paolozzi sculptor 1977)* open to the main exhibition space. It is contemporary, lit softly by indirect light from rows of slanted skylights and feels domestic, perfect for the scale and styles of the paintings displayed.

The **Mackintosh House** is a reassemblage of the principal interiors from a Victorian end-of-terrace property on Southpark Avenue where Mackintosh and Margaret Macdonald lived from 1906 to 1914. The terrace was

demolished for campus development in 1963. The rebuild faces east and south to catch the same light as the original. The couple's white and dark rooms and Glasgow Art Nouveau decorative scheme were reinstated over three levels, with the original Mackintosh-designed furniture. The sandstone exterior of Southpark was reproduced in roughcast and concrete. Steps to the front door were not fitted. The door hangs in mid air which, intentionally or not, makes the reinterpretation clear.

Between the Hunterian Art Gallery and the University Library is the **Sculpture Courtyard** where a Mackintosh curio stands like a gazebo. This is the lantern and metal finial from the dome of Pettigrew & Stephens department store *(Honeyman, Keppie & Mackintosh 1901)* demolished in 1972.

A rival personality to Mackintosh at the Hunterian is James McNeil Whistler whose art had much in common with the evolving Glasgow Style. Part of the gallery is a shrine to him. The Hunterian holds the largest collection of his work outside his native America, and has the largest single holding of Mackintosh's work.

326
Glasgow University Library
Hillhead Street
William Whitfield & Partners architects, Lowe & Rodin engineers 1965–1968

Top international talent—Le Corbusier, Alvar Aalto and Arne Jacobsen—was suggested by the university's consulting architect Joseph Lea Gleave for this commission. Gleave added he could do it. In the event an English modernist, William Whitfield, was appointed. Gleave thought the building should be monumental, formidable on its hill, and it is. Whitfield cited as inspiration medieval castles in his ancestral Northumberland.

The library was a glazed, open-plan reinforced concrete 'warehouse for books'. Around its perimeter were placed structurally separate service towers. How they would appear from different points of view was studied before construction started on the frequently wet and windy hill. Water ingress became a persistent problem and thermal performance was poor. These defects have been fixed by reglazing, recladding and reroofing the structure (c. 2012). An extra floor was added for Special Collections. The retrofits diminish the force of the original but gain credits for sustainability and accommodate the library service conveniently in one place.

327
Fraser Building
Hillhead Street
Frank Fielden & Associates 1966;
Page\Park Architects 2009
Originally the Refectory, one of several brutalist buildings added to the campus in the 1960s. It stood on a podium to cope with sloping ground to the east, where it crossed the footprint

of the Mackintosh house on Southpark Avenue (see 325). The podium was removed and a landscaped plaza created during a recent makeover which saw the block reclad with coloured glass panels. It houses student services. Among them is John Smith & Son's university bookstore. Smiths, established in Glasgow in 1751, is the oldest bookselling company in the English-speaking world.

328
Salmon House
12 University Gardens
John Gaff Gillespie 1900

Infill terrace house with touches of Art Nouveau—a wrought iron insert on a balcony, stained glass above the door and an ogee-roofed turret, the latter inspired by Mackintosh. Glass was by Oscar Paterson, whose studio produced numerous pieces for villas and tenements in the West End and elsewhere. The cornice was aligned with the existing terrace (1882–1896) designed by J. J. Burnet. He also designed **14 University Gardens** (1904). Its porch is Italianate; the Arts and Crafts roofscape complements Salmon House. Cast ironwork is original and some windows retain Art Nouveau glass.

Academics, professionals and merchants lived here. The terrace, like others on Gilmorehill, has been absorbed into the university campus. On the south side of the gardens are remnants of a row lost to redevelopment.

At 16 University Gardens is the **Modern Languages Building** *(Walter Ramsay 1959)*, a 1952 competition design with overtones of modernism in Italy where the architect had been on an Alexander Thomson Travelling Scholarship in 1935. It sits on a raft of reinforced concrete because the site was thought to be above old mine workings, a common hazard in the West End. The artwork on the façade is titled *Knowledge and Inspiration (Walter Pritchard artist)*.

is visible, with timber louvres to monitor solar heat. The building gained a BREEAM Very Good rating and is connected to the campus combined heat and power (CHP) district heating system installed in 2015.

330
Kelvin Building
James Miller 1902–1906

Miller, known more for his work for the Caledonian Railway, could turn his hand to any style, here Scottish Renaissance as the Old College had been. The building shows how the campus might have looked had the style been chosen instead of Gothic. Indeed, a Scottish Renaissance design with Jacobean turrets was proposed *(John Baird 1)* in 1847 when Woodlands Hill was being

329
Computing Science Department
Lilybank Gardens
Reiach & Hall Architects 2007
Filled gap site between **Queen Margaret Union** *(Walter Underwood & Partners 1968)* and Victorian row houses on Lilybank Gardens (c. 1880). Public realm improvements provided a plaza and pedestrian link between Lilybank and University gardens. The building programme adopted environmentally low-impact materials and natural ventilation. The energy-efficient strategy

considered as the site for the successor to the Old College.

The Kelvin Building, also known as the Old Natural Philosophy Building, was named in honour of Lord Kelvin. A newer **Natural Philosophy Building** *(Basil Spence & Partners 1947–1952)* is directly north. It was designed for advanced physics, with a synchrotron particle accelerator in a concrete chamber below ground. It's doubtful that the boffins in the basement were bothered how the building looked but Spence was keen—it was his first big commission and he drew inspiration from Le Corbusier. It looks shabby now, but then its Portland stone gleamed with postwar faith in progress.

Across from the Kelvin Building is the **Graham Kerr (Zoology) Building & Museum** *(J. J. Burnet 1924)* bulging with muscularity. Named for the professor who lobbied for it, to escape from an overcrowded basement at the Hunterian. At the end of the lane by the Kerr building is one of two modernist glazed stair towers at the much altered **Chemistry Building** *(Hughes & Waugh 1937–1954).*

331
Boyd Orr Building
University Avenue

J. L. Gleave & Partners 1964–1972
This sciences tower was part of an invasion of reinforced concrete and aggregate-clad brutalist buildings built for the expansion of further education in Scotland in the 1960s. Lecture theatres are expressed as cantilevered pods, and stair and elevator shafts empha-

sised. The floor slabs are interlocked in an offset plan which made the building look less boxy and maximised natural light. It retains the power of pure form and uncompromising materials that distinguished the best of Brutalism. Renderings released in 2016, for a redevelopment to replace the adjacent, contemporaneous Mathematics Building, show the Boyd Orr tower reclad, not happily.

It was named after University Rector and Chancellor John Boyd Orr, who was the first director of the UN Food and Agriculture Organisation and a Nobel laureate.

332
Wolfson Medical School
University Avenue

Reiach & Hall Architects, Arup engineers 2003
A medical and biomedical research and teaching centre on a triangular site with a typical Glasgow gushet. The design team's response was imaginative

age interior. Home-made ice cream—all 'Tally' cafés produced their own. They used to be in every neighbourhood, a benefit of immigration in the late 19th and early 20th centuries. This one is still owned by the descendants of founder Alfredo Verrecchia.

and elegant. The wedge-shaped corner was transformed with a curved, double skinned glass curtain wall. Noise, glare and solar gain were minimised thanks to automated louvres of western red cedar. A triangular atrium floods the building's core with natural light from a glass roof supported on engineered glass beams, a pioneering innovation. The curved corner contains an open resource zone and administration. Lecture theatres, skills training and support facilities are off the atrium.

This was the first significant architectural work at the university for 15 years. It set a standard for excellence, reflecting that of the medical school it houses.

333
The University Café
87 Byres Road
1918

Classic Italian café. Art Deco typography outside and a wood-panelled herit-

334
Queen's Gate
Dowanhill Street and Highburgh Road
David Barclay 1901

Bourgeois grandeur, Glasgow style, solid with Dumfriesshire red sandstone, which was introduced in the late 19th century as a substitute for the traditional blonde sandstone whose quarries were being worked out.

Tenement blocks like this in the city's affluent areas were designed for apartments of up to five rooms or more, in contrast to room-and-kitchen workers' housing. High quality stone and woodwork, wally closes, stained glass, decorative plasterwork, carved mantelpieces, and Glasgow Style furniture from Wylie & Lochhead (see 206) distinguished these upmarket tenements. Queen's Gate was part of a four-block development of uniform design but varied height, from the met-

ropolitan scale on Highburgh Road to two-storey terraces at Dowanhill Street and Dowanside Road.

335
Notre Dame Primary School
30 Havelock Street
Glasgow City Council, Gareth Hoskins Architects 2013

Originally Dowanhill Public School *(Steele & Balfour 1894)*, a typical school board design with classrooms around a skylit atrium. A glazed link joins it to a striking, contextual new block built to accommodate assembly and gym halls, a library and kindergarten. Cladding is a terracotta rainscreen which mimics local sandstone. Ground source heat reduces energy costs.

336
Cottiers
93 Hyndland Street
William Leiper 1866
Leiper, early in his career, made his mark with this tremendous Normandy Gothic steeple, once part of Dowanhill United Presbyterian Church, later Dowanhill Church of Scotland. The building was decaying and the décor faded when it was sold in 1984 for a token £1 to Four Acres Charitable Trust for adaptive reuse, and conservation which continues.

The church was a *tour de force* of Victorian aestheticism. The sanctuary, lit by stained glass, feels mystical, medieval under a hammer beam roof. The pulpit is recessed in a Gothic canopy below a rose window. Fragments of stencilled wall and ceiling decoration are visible. This interior was stunning, created by Glasgow-born designer Daniel Cottier, a prominent personality in the Aesthetic Movement. He worked with Alexander 'Greek'

Thomson on the décor at **Holmwood House** (see 445) and exhibited at the 1867 Paris International Exposition. He established a stained glass and interior design business in London, with productive off-shoots in New York, Montreal, Sydney and Melbourne. He ought to be as well known in his home town as Mackintosh. Four Acres named Cottiers theatre, bar and restaurant in his memory. (See also **Lansdowne Church**, 364.)

337

Gardner Street

c. 1895

San Francisco with tenements, on one of the steepest streets in Glasgow. It plunges off the edge of Partickhill all the way to Dumbarton Road. The hill was developed in the mid 19th century with villas set in gardens with panoramic views. One of the oldest is a Jacobean-gabled mansion, formerly **Wellpark House** (10 Partickhill Road; 1843), later a Catholic seminary,

rehabilitated as flats. Others survive, generally Italianate, around the western slopes of the hill along with period terraces.

Directly north is the Edwardian suburb of Hyndland, its streets lined with solidly built, corner-turreted tenements well preserved.

338
Westdel and Royston
2 Queen's Place, 10 Crown Road North
George Washington Browne 1889; Alexander Nisbet Paterson 1896

Arts and Crafts double villa with two homes under the hipped roof. Westdel has the witch's hat turret; Royston has a baroque porch added by Paterson.

Royston was the home of Archibald Barr, professor of civil engineering at Glasgow University and co-founder of the optical engineering company Barr & Stroud. Westdel was owned by publisher and printer to the university, Robert MacLehose. In 1898 he hired Charles Rennie Mackintosh for an interior design, said to have been the architect's first 'white room'. In 1975 the items from it were transferred to the Hunterian. Another publisher, Walter Blackie, commissioned CRM to

design Hill House (1904), Helensburgh, the architect's finest domestic work.

339
Crown Circus
Crown Road
James Thomson 1858
Thomson (no relation to Alexander 'Greek' Thomson) designed several terraces in the West End of which this is the most delicate. The elevation is restrained, Renaissance with a parade of Tuscan columns taking the curve of the street. It was one of the earliest developments on Dowanhill and set the tone for the neighbourhood. Later terraces, like the adjacent **Crown Terrace** (1873–1880; also by Thomson), were more elaborate and boasted fashionable bay windows.

Dowanhill, laid out by Thomson in 1858, is a well preserved, architecturally eclectic mix of Victorian and Edwardian villas and terraces. The neighbourhood extends to the north and is featured in Tour 8, *Woodside, Maryhill & Great Western Road*.

'Eve', Kibble Palace, Botanic Gardens

8

Woodside, Maryhill & Great Western Road

THIS TOUR follows the arrow-straight Great Western Road through the northern part of the West End from St. George's Cross to Anniesland, a distance of nearly five kilometres. There are perambulations either side, starting in Woodside and continuing up Maryhill Road by the Forth & Clyde Canal. Woodside, on the north side of Great Western Road as far as Kelvinbridge, is an inner-city residential and former industrial district. I knew it well as a child, having been raised in a tenement at 6 Napiershall Street where the bay window was filled with the Gothic cliff face of St. Mary's Cathedral. I was often taken by my mother to Kelvingrove Park by way of Woodlands, now a conservation area with streets of 19th-century tenements saved from redevelopment by local action in the 1970s. Further west is salubrious Dowanhill, a well-preserved Victorian neighbourhood and conservation area, as is most of the West End. And there is Botanic Gardens, notable not only for the diversity of its flora and fauna but also for the Kibble Palace, the most spectacular Victorian glasshouse in Scotland.

The heart of Woodside was St. George's Cross, where Maryhill and Great Western roads meet. Its beat is weak now. It was a five-way intersection clamorous with street corner newspaper vendors, crowds of shoppers, and trams crossing the busy junction, trolley poles sparking. The first tramcar in Glasgow, open-top, pulled by two horses, started here at a ceremony in 1872, en route to Eglinton Toll. The tramways were electrified around 1900 and eventually covered over 160 kilometres of routes. It is tempting to speculate how the city would have evolved and looked had the network, one of the most extensive in Europe, been modernised instead of scrapped in 1962. Around 250,000 people turned out to watch the Last Tram procession, the majority not happy to see the 'caurs', as the trams were called affectionately, go.

St. George's Cross is almost unrecognisable now because in 1970 the M8 interchange at Great Western Road destroyed most of it. Woodside was a comprehensive redevelopment area and much of its heritage is gone as well. Woodside Library survives; so too St. George's in the Fields church and Woodside Baths, a Victorian swimming pool restored recently. Surrounding the baths is part of the 1970s housing scheme which replaced the neighbourhood's tenements. As Glasgow schemes go it is better than most, designed with place-making in mind as much as it was a statistic in the city's slum clearance and mass housing project.

Maryhill was a separate burgh from 1856 until 1891 when it was absorbed by Glasgow. It grew rapidly with trade and industry along the Forth & Clyde Canal. Iron foundries, sawmills, glassworks, distilleries and breweries were built. In 1878 the *Glasgow Herald* noted, 'Though the Burgh of Maryhill presents few attractions to the rambler in search of the picturesque its development and dimensions exhibit many pleasing signs of progress.' Among the signs was the brand new Maryhill Burgh Halls. The complex, latterly abandoned, was restored and reopened in 2012. The adaptive reuse reinstated historic stained glass panels illustrating local trades and their workers. The polluted canal has been revived as an amenity, the clean-up attracting new housing. The 1960s high-rise flats on Wyndford Estate have been retrofitted, bucking the tear-down trend, a more eco-friendly solution than new-builds.

Great Western Road was authorised by Act of Parliament in 1836. In the early 19th century the land was open country with estates owned by

Glasgow merchants and industrialists. They lobbied for the road antici-
pating profit from property speculation, which started in Hillhead in
the mid 19th century. Hillhead became a burgh in 1869 and was incorporated into Glasgow in 1891. The River Kelvin was the boundary. The
armorial crest of Hillhead and the heraldry of Glasgow and Lanarkshire
adorn the spandrels and inner parapets of Great Western Bridge, opened
the year the burgh was gobbled up. The Glasgow District Subway, opened
in 1896, sparked more densification.

Some landowners and investors didn't think the city would extend
beyond Kelvinbridge and proposed the road should be reduced from 60
feet wide to a suburban 40 from that point. Others thought it should be
60 for its entire length and they won the argument. Great Western Road
(c. 1840) has an urban grandeur unique in Glasgow. It is punctuated with
Gothic Revival church spires and residential development responsive to
its scale, especially west of Botanic Gardens where it is lined with handsome terraces designed by leading architects, among them Alexander
'Greek' Thomson. By 1900 a tram line to Anniesland and urban railways
had encouraged more development and commuting. Trains connected
outer suburbs too, on a regional network that is the second largest in
Britain. Anniesland retains its train station and there are subway stops
at Hillhead, Kelvinbridge and St. George's Cross.

Great Western Road, officially the A82, became a dual carriageway
on the approach to Anniesland and beyond in the 1920s. The Kilpatrick
Hills are in the distance, and the allure of the west coast, Loch Lomond
and the Highlands. An outrageous plan by the city's obsessive traffic
engineers in the late 1960s to make the historic section from St. George's
Cross to Anniesland an expressway was dropped in 1975 after residents
and heritage groups fought it. Thanks to them, and official concern
about the cost of the plan, Great Western Road remains much as the
Victorians saw it.

340

St. George and the Dragon
St. George's Cross

Charles Grassby sculptor 1897

Only fragments of the townscape here remained after the M8 motorway cut off the cross from the city centre. St. George and the Dragon was high on the corner of the four-storey St. George Cooperative Society store, demolished in 1985. The statue was dismantled, donated to the city by the society and in 1988 reassembled on a plaza across from St. George's Road and Gladstone Street, where the building was. The cast iron railings were recycled from the entrance and steps to the now buried St. George's Cross public lavatory.

341

Clarendon Place
St. George's Cross

Alexander Taylor c. 1840

A gushet tenement with an immense

classical portico above a retail podium. It was known as Massey's Corner, named for the pre-supermarket, locally owned grocery chain store once here. The urban design had a twin portico never built which would have framed Great Western Road, as Waterloo Place (1820) does Calton Hill in Edinburgh.

342

Woodside Public Library
343 St. George's Road

James R. Rhind 1905

An elegant Carnegie library, the first in the city, with an Ionic colonnade

and prominent entrance in Beaux-Arts style. In the pediment above the door are eroded figures (after Michelangelo) reclining on books and, on a plinth, the figure of Wisdom with a book and two boys *(William Kellock Brown sculptor)*. The interior is Renaissance with Corinthian columns and a domed skylight. Another Beaux-Arts gem by Rhind and Brown is **Maryhill Library** (1905), across from the Burgh Halls (see 356).

Next door is **The Mansionhouse**, a Greek Revival villa built in 1830s when Woodside had woods and was rural.

343
North Woodside Pool
10 Braid Square
John Carrick, City Architect 1882
Originally North Woodside Baths and Washhouse, the oldest public baths still open in Scotland. There were wash stalls in the 'steamie' (public laundry), bathtubs and two swimming pools, the

smaller now overlaid with hardwood for a gym. The larger (former men's) pool was designed like a Roman atrium, similar to Bath Spa. The building was refurbished c.1990 as a leisure centre, and again after the timber-trussed roof was damaged by a storm in 2012. Columns are cast iron. The exterior is neoclassical, the entrance pedimented.

344
Woodside Development Area A
St. George's Road and Raglan Street
Boswell, Mitchell & Johnson
1970–1974

Brick-faced blocks with bay windows and attached access towers. The architecture is robust like Glasgow's tenement vernacular, to which the bay windows refer. Around Braid Square, the top-floor flats have pod-shaped extrusions for extra floor space. The urban design evokes traditional streets and terraces, to create a sense of place.

Across St. George's Road is the conventional (1966) urban renewal template—multistorey slab blocks and walk-ups on a rectilinear plan, each block isolated in open space.

345

St. George's in the Fields
485 St. George's Road
Hugh & David Barclay 1886

A dignified Greek Revival church raised on a podium. The portico, with fluted Ionic columns, has finely cut Roman lettering on the entablature. The tympanum has a wonderful carved tableau: *Christ Feeding the Multitude,* the parable of the loaves and fishes *(William Birnie Rhind sculptor).*

'Fields' refers to the land when the first church was built in 1824. It burned down in 1884 and was replaced by this temple, vacated in 1979 and converted to flats in 1988 by Queen's Cross Housing Association. The association also acquired the tenement next door, formerly **North Fire Station** (1889, closed 1984). Relief panels (helmets, hoses and axes) indicate its former function.

346

Applecross Basin, Forth & Clyde Canal
1 Applecross Street

Applecross Basin (1777) was the original canal dock in Glasgow. The whitewashed former warehouses and workshops are thought to be the oldest canal buildings in Scotland. The **Old Basin House** (1790s) was lived in by the Resident Engineer. The bascule bridge is of a type once common, with winding gears intact. On its south side was the Old Basin Tavern, for thirsty workers, boat crews and passengers before railways took the canal's trade.

The waterway, now managed by Scottish Canals, was closed to naviga-

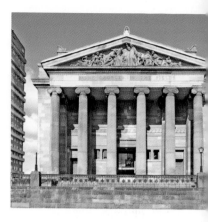

tion in 1963. It reopened in 2001 for recreation after many years of restoration. Among the new facilities for boat owners are **Applecross Wharf Storage Huts** *(rankinfraser landscape architecture 2014),* one of several similar groups at moorings along the canal.

347

The Whisky Bond
2 Dawson Street
1957; Network Five Architecture 2012–2014

A colossal bonded warehouse built for Highland Distillers. It was later known as the 'mushroom factory', an urban farm. Rehabbed as an arts and co-working centre, the largest studio complex in Scotland. Big neutral spaces not too gussied up are perfect for creativity and collaboration. Diverse tenants include designers, Glasgow

Sculpture Studios and, temporarily since the fire at the Art School (see 281), the GSA Archives and Collections.

348
National Theatre of Scotland
125 Craighall Road
Hoskins Architects 2016

Former cash-and-carry warehouse reclad and transformed internally to house departments of the National Theatre of Scotland for the first time under one roof. The rehab is a multi-functional facility, not for public performances but for rehearsals and production resources; also for community outreach to promote talent in 'people of all ages and abilities'.

The design aesthetic is industrial, as the canal-side setting was. The official

name is Rockvilla, revived after being found on an 1860 Ordnance Survey map of the district and thought to derive from a local stone quarry.

349
St. Columba's Church
74 Hopehill Road
Gillespie, Kidd & Coia 1938–1941

One of several unorthodox 1930s designs by Jack Coia. Gigantic west front in brick massed like an Art Deco cinema but in spirit and detail Romanesque. Saint Columba and angels are carved at the entrance. The glass cross on the façade glows like neon inside. Behind the altar is a life-size carved crucifix *(Benno Schotz sculptor)*. The nave, more Scandinavian than Scottish, is ribbed with neo-Gothic concrete arches. The roof is pantiled. The walls were paid for by members of the congregation buying bricks at six pence a time. In the garden is a matching brick clergy house.

Outside, the stone tracks in the granite setts were laid to ease the progress of horse-drawn carts up the hill.

350

Queen's Cross Church

870 Garscube Road

Honeyman & Keppie; Charles Rennie Mackintosh 1899

The Charles Rennie Mackintosh Society was founded in 1973 to preserve this and other works by Mackintosh and to raise his public profile. It has been based here since 1977.

Queen's Cross is the only church Mackintosh designed that was built. It was commissioned by the Free Church of Scotland, known for austerity rather than avant-garde architecture. The building is superficially Gothic with buttresses and window tracery, but not Victorian Gothic Revival. Mackintosh didn't do revivals but probed at the past: the tower is a variation on a medieval one he sketched in Somerset in 1895. There are Art Nouveau birds and leaves in stone; stained-glass windows have heart, tree and leaf motifs, all unconventional and a delight.

The roof is timber, vaulted, ribbed like a boat and crossed with steel tie beams, riveted and exposed. Original drawings show them to have been clad in timber; cost might have been why

they were not. The adjoining church hall has timber trusses. They look Japanese, a characteristic of Mackintosh's way with wood. Other sources he drew on were Scottish fortified tower houses, Celtic mysticism and the Arts and Crafts movement. Recent restoration (*Simpson & Brown Architects 2007*).

351

Timber Basin Project

Panmure Street

MAST Architects 2015

One of several housing developments which have revitalised derelict land by the Forth & Clyde Canal. Boxy is their default setting but here are gables, for Queens Cross Housing Association. Firhill Basin was where timber for Western Sawmills was stored in log booms to prevent the wood drying out. Below the canal is **Firhill Stadium**, home of Partick Thistle Football Club, formed in Partick in 1876 and at Firhill Road since 1909.

352

Ruchill Hospital Water Tower

520 Bilsland Drive

Alexander Beith McDonald, City Engineer 1895–1900

Comparable to the water tower at Stobhill (see 140) this Jacobean-style

Kelvinside-based Westbourne Free Church commissioned this Art Nouveau mission hall. Mackintosh created a skylit timber-trussed and wood-panelled hall and an asymmetric façade more fortified than ecclesiastical. The mission soon needed a church next door *(Neil Campbell Duff 1905)*, built in Gothic Revival style which ignored Mackintosh. There is no record to explain why he was not invited to design it.

campanile was the centrepiece of an extensive hospital built for patients with infectious diseases. The site was remote and salubrious on a hill above the smog in the city.

The land was bought by Glasgow Corporation in 1892 from East India merchant W. J. Davidson and subdivided for the hospital, a golf course and **Ruchill Park**. The panoramic viewpoint at the flagpole in the park is a mound made with rubble dug out for the hospital foundations. The facility closed in 1998. The buildings were demolished recently, the land having been rezoned for housing. The tower is A-listed and has been restored.

353
Ruchill Free Church Hall
15 Shakespeare Street
Honeyman & Keppie; Charles Rennie Mackintosh 1899

354
Craigen Court
Shakespeare Street
Ken MacRae; McGurn, Logan, Duncan & Opfer 1989
Greek Thomson meets postmodernism in this pastiche of Salisbury Quadrant (see 481). The building was more serious than it looks. It was the result of a Tenement for Tomorrow competition in 1984, organised by Maryhill Hous-

ing Association, the Royal Incorporation of Architects in Scotland (RIAS)
and Glasgow District Council. The
exercise showed the much-maligned
typology had a future (see 167).

355
Wyndford Estate
Maryhill Road
Scottish Special Housing Association
(SSHA) 1961–1969

Maryhill's concrete Utopia was better
than the run-down tenements from
which people were rehoused. The point
towers, a slab block and walk-ups
(around 2,000 units) won a Saltire
design award in 1968. The scheme was
nicknamed 'the Barracks' because
it was built on the site of Maryhill
Barracks (1872), the regimental depot
of the Highland Light Infantry. The
gatehouse, iron bollards and perimeter
wall on Maryhill Road remain.

'Barracks' also came to mean soul-
less, a prison. In 2012 Cube Housing
Association started to retrofit the run-
down scheme. The buildings were over-
clad and windows renewed to improve
thermal performance. A combined
heat and power (CHP) district heating
system was installed. The energy savings cut fuel poverty.

356
Maryhill Burgh Halls
10–24 Gairbraid Avenue
Duncan McNaughton 1878; JM
Architects, Buro Happold engineers,
WAVEparticle & rankinfraser land-
scape architecture 2009–2012

French Renaissance-style halls and
adjoining police station, once a symbol
of civic pride and progress. By the end
of the 20th century they were neglected
and closed by city council. Maryhill
Burgh Halls Trust bought them in 2009
and rolled out a plan for an adaptive
reuse, as a multi-purpose venue that
would engage with the community.

Façades and other heritage features
were restored. Spatial sequences were
rethought. Public realm improvements
were made. Access was reoriented from
the porch facing Maryhill Road to
Gairbraid Avenue where there are four
arches. These were the vehicle doors
of Maryhill Fire Station (1892); 'The
Firemen Gates' *(Andy Scott sculptor)*
recall its presence. Its footprint is now
a pocket plaza shared with **Maryhill
Leisure Centre** (2010). The leisure
centre was originally the community
swimming baths and steamie (1898).

Best practice requires additions to

heritage fabric be clear, here with a palette of zinc, granite and wood. The main hall was restored. There is an inner courtyard and café. The rehabilitation is exemplary. A highlight is the 19th-century stained glass.

Nearby, at 51 Gairbraid Avenue, is the boxy but bold **Maryhill Health Centre** (*NORR Consultants 2016*).

357
Stained Glass, Maryhill Burgh Halls
Gairbraid Avenue

Stephen Adam artist 1878

Between 1870 and 1914 some of the finest stained glass in Europe was produced in Glasgow. Maryhill Burgh Halls has an outstanding collection, originally 20 panels, commissioned from the Stephen Adam studio. They illustrate local trades and industries with portraits of working folk; among them blacksmiths, a canal boat builder, calico printers, a glass blower, iron workers, railway men, soldiers at Maryhill Barracks . . . These ordinary people are illustrated with such humanity and their workaday settings so accurately that Adam must have made preliminary sketches from life. Above all they are dignified, not in idealised

pretension of classical robes favoured by the establishment but in working clothes or uniforms.

The panels were removed to the People's Palace in 1963. Ten are back, in the main hall along with new glass *(Alec Galloway artist)*. One of the original panels, *The Canal Boatman* with towpath horse, is in the foyer where there is an interpretative display.

358
Maryhill Locks, Forth & Clyde Canal
Maryhill Road

1787–1790

The canal follows contours to Maryhill Locks, its highest point above sea level. There are five stone-lined, hand-worked locks and connecting basins on a grassy brae. The basins were built to let boats and barges wait for passage at busy times. At the second basin from the top is Kelvin Dock, originally a dry dock where there was a boatyard, Swan & Co., which built 'Clyde puffers', handy coastal steamboats. At the top of the locks is a cottage (c. 1810), once the **White House Inn**, a boatmen's howff and, for a time, Maryhill's first post office.

359

Kelvin Aqueduct, Forth & Clyde Canal

Robert Whitworth engineer 1787–1790

A triumph of engineering, like something the Romans might have built and one of the largest aqueducts since their time. Its arches and buttresses carry the Forth & Clyde Canal across the River Kelvin. When it opened it was described in the *Scots Magazine* as 'that stupendous bridge, the great aqueduct over the Kelvin.' It became a Victorian tourist attraction especially appealing to connoisseurs of the sublime.

360

St. Mary's Cathedral

300 Great Western Road

George Gilbert Scott 1871

The congregation of St. Mary's cashed in on the 19th-century property boom in the city centre and relocated, as others did at the time. The old church at St. Mary's Lane off Renfield Street was sold and demolished. George Gilbert Scott, the architect of Glasgow University, was commissioned to design the new church. The spire was completed by his son John Oldrid Scott in 1893.

The Scottish Episcopal Church designated St. Mary's a cathedral in 1908. In plan it is conventional with a nave, aisles, transepts and chancel. In three dimensions it is a lofty arcaded Gothic Revival space with a ribbed timber roof and a decorated crossing with painted stars. The rood screen (1894) is wrought iron, seemingly light as lace. The altarpiece *(Phoebe Traquair artist)* was part of 1920s refit of the chancel *(Robert Lorimer architect)*.

The glazed porch (2002) completed a repair and restoration programme begun in the 1980s. The interior was altered to accommodate arts events as well as worship, and contemporary murals *(Gwyneth Leech artist)* installed.

361

The Ballet School

261 West Princes Street

Elder & Cannon Architects 2013

Student housing in a heritage building

with minimalist infill blocks in the back court. The site, surrounded by tenements, was previously occupied by Scottish Ballet (see 420). There has been a boom recently in student accommodation, much of it bottom line. The digs here are upmarket, well designed with spatial sequences and landscaping choreographed gracefully.

362
Woodlands Tenements
West Princes Street

Woodlands is a late 19th-century tenement neighbourhood of 20 city blocks either side of West Princes Street. The buildings are handsome. Many retain original features—corner turrets, wally closes and coloured glass.

In 1974 city council planned to 'improve' the then down-at-heel area, claiming the buildings wouldn't last seven years. The great storm of 1968 had damaged many tenements city-wide. Around 70,000 properties of all types were affected and 2000 people left homeless. Emergency repairs reprieved many tenements which were on council's demolition list.

Those here are still standing because Woodlands Residents' Association was formed to save them. The Housing (Scotland) Act 1974 authorised grants for repairs and Woodlands' residents got some. Block by block, the buildings were stone-cleaned and upgraded. Roofs and chimneys were made safe. Entry doors were fitted to closes and back courts tidied up.

The transformation was startling. The streets of formerly soot-black fa-çades gleamed with the original blonde sandstone. Thousands of tenements across the city got the same treatment. The official default of demolition and clearance was discredited. Refurbishment became the new orthodoxy because the people of Woodlands, and those at **Taransay Street** (see 12), showed how to do it.

363
Boys' Brigade Building
North Woodside Road
John Honeyman 1879
Gothic Revival-style mission built for the Free Church College (see 301). It was where the 1st Glasgow Company of the Boys' Brigade, the world's first

such organisation, was formed in 1883. The founder was Free Church elder William Alexander Smith, a member of the 1st Lanarkshire Rifle Volunteers. He taught Sunday school to local boys and thought an army style regime of drill, discipline and exercise would deal with their mischief. It did.

364
Lansdowne Church
416 Great Western Road
John Honeyman 1863
Perched on a bluff where Great Western Road crosses the River Kelvin, a Gothic Revival landmark with a needle spire, the slimmest in the city, perhaps even in Europe. The tower is offset in plan exaggerating its presence on the street. **St.Mary's Cathedral** (see 360) does this too. Together they form a memorable urban vista.

Lansdowne Church was formed by wealthy members of Cambridge Street United Presbyterian Church fleeing industrialisation in Cowcaddens. The poor were left behind. Its Gothic style influenced the decorative scheme for **Great Western Bridge** *(Bell & Miller engineers 1891)*. The high-level, steel-arched bridge replaced a stone bridge of 1838. Previously there was a low bridge (1825) where the river had been forded for centuries.

By 2005 Lansdowne was deteriorating. Four Acres Charitable Trust took over the building in 2013 for rehabilitation as an arts and community events venue modelled on **Cottiers** (see 336). Repair and conservation are part of the adaptive reuse, aided by grants and crowdfunding.

It is now **Websters Theatre**, named after Alfred Alexander Webster, whose emotionally charged and imaginative stained glass was fitted in the transepts in 1914. The south window was removed for conservation in 2008. In the apse is the War Memorial with a frieze *(Evelyn Beale sculptor 1923)* showing Christ receiving historical figures and a kilted soldier who could be Alf Webster. In 1915 he was a 2nd Lieutenant in the Gordon Highlanders in France where he was wounded leading a patrol and died. His passing and the glorious glass he left here mark the end of Glasgow's prewar bohemian culture and in a broader sense an era.

365
Caledonian Mansions
445–459 Great Western Road
James Miller 1897
A picturesque Arts and Crafts mansion block with flats above ground floor retail, still functioning as intended. It was commissioned by the Caledonian Railway whose carved crest and monogram appear at the east corner. The restless array of chimneys and dormers is stabilised by twin corners, each crowned with a turret.

The Caley's Kelvinbridge station (1896) was by the river below. The line was closed in 1964. It was part of the Glasgow Central Railway tunnelled between Dalmarnock and Maryhill.

366
Belmont Street Housing
Great Western Road
Elder & Cannon Architects 1997
A mix of flats and townhouses with shops on Great Western Road. The three sides enclose an inner courtyard like a 19th-century tenement back court. The Belmont Street townhouses have French style bull's eye windows on a mansard roof, a variation on the street's Victorian terraces. The scale

and urbanism fit the heritage context. The saucer-shaped bunnet engages across the generation gap with the turrets on Caledonian Mansions.

On Colebrook Street is the neoclassical **Glasgow Academy** *(Hugh Barclay 1878)* and its **Saunders Centre** *(Page\ Park Architects 2015)*, winner of the Andrew Doolan Award 2016. The school's **War Memorial** *(Alexander Nisbet Paterson 1924)* is at Great Western Road. On Belmont Street is the crown steeple of **Kelvinbridge Parish Church** *(John James Stevenson 1902)*, originally Stevenson Memorial Church, at **Belmont Bridge** (c. 1870). The bridge was built across the Kelvin for development of the City of Glasgow Bank's North Woodside estate.

367
Cooper's Building
499 Great Western Road
Robert Duncan 1886
Built for Cooper & Co., Grocery and Provision Merchants founded by tea and coffee importer Thomas Bishop in 1871 at St. Enoch Square. The style is commercial French Renaissance unrestrained by modesty. Coopers opened a chain of stores in competition with

those of tea mogul Thomas Lipton. The interior here was palatial with Corinthian columns, carved woodwork, a decorated plaster ceiling and a polychrome tiled floor. The clock tower is one of several Victorian landmarks which punctuate Great Western Road.

368
Coach House Trust
84 Belmont Lane
1875

Former coach house in one of the West End's many cobbled lanes. The gable-walled building, on an unexpected gushet, was repurposed in 2001 by the Trust, a voluntary enterprise set up to help socially disadvantaged people gain skills, self-esteem and better their life chances. There is a community garden,

and nearby gap sites have been land-scaped informally. Patinated original brickwork and funky new metalwork.

369
Buckingham Terrace
Great Western Road
John Thomas Rochead c. 1856

An elegant Italianate row of 14 town-houses with palazzo-size pavilions as bookends. It was the first terrace on Great Western Road to be completely stone-cleaned. The cast iron railings and balconies were also restored. The 1975 project, led by the residents and supported by the city and the Historic Buildings Council, was commended at the European Architectural Heritage Awards, a boost for heritage advocacy in Glasgow at the time.

370
The Sixty Steps
Queen Margaret Road
1872
In 1870 an iron bridge was built across the River Kelvin to link Great Western Road to North Kelvinside, an estate being developed by John Ewing Walker. Steps to it rise beside a massive retaining wall, an intriguing feature attributed to 'Greek' Thomson. The

Sixty Steps Preservation Trust installed interpretative panels in 2014, and a plaque marks the site on the Alexander Thomson Heritage Trail.

All that survives of Walker's bridge are stone abutments and the base of the central pier. It was abandoned after construction of **Queen Margaret Bridge** (*Thomas Somers city engineer 1929*) and dismantled in 1971.

371

Queen Margaret College Medical School

70 Hamilton Drive

Honeyman & Keppie, Charles Rennie Mackintosh 1895

The site was the garden of **Northpark House** (*John Thomas Rochead, John Honeyman 1874*), a Renaissance villa built for John and Matthew Bell, owners of Glasgow Pottery, Townhead. The house was sold to the college in 1883, the purchase funded by Isabella

Elder whose philanthropy also created Elder Park (see 2) and endowed the Elder Chair of Naval Architecture at Glasgow University. The college was named after the 11th-century Queen Margaret. It was the first for women in Scotland and subsequently merged with the university.

The baronial form and romanticism of the Medical School building owe much to Mackintosh. After the BBC acquired Northpark in 1935 the medical building was absorbed and hidden by BBC Scotland's studios. They were demolished after the broadcaster relocated to **Pacific Quay** (see 31) in 2007. The medical building and the villa have since been incorporated in a redevelopment by G1 Group, for its head office.

372

Botanic Gardens

730 Great Western Road

The gardens evolved from a medicinal garden at the Old College. They were established in 1817 by the Royal Botanical Institution of Glasgow, in association with the university, and located at Sandyford, west of Charing Cross. Urban development forced a move to Great Western Road in 1839. There was public access for a small fee on Saturdays until 1891, when Glasgow Corporation annexed the Burgh of Hillhead and the Botanics became publicly owned. They have a surprising diversity of architecture.

The curator's house, now the **Tearoom**, is Italianate (*Charles Wilson 1841*); the **Gate Houses** are Tudor Revival (*Alexander Beith McDonald, City*

Kibble was an eccentric inventor and
engineer. He built a conservatory at
his home, Coulport House on the
shore of Loch Long. In 1871 he offered
to re-erect it at Queen's Park but the
city fathers hesitated. Glasgow's Royal
Botanic Institution made Botanic
Gardens available and the glasshouse
was dismantled and barged up the
Clyde in 1873.

Engineer c. 1900). There was a railway
station *(James Miller 1896)*—an onion-
domed fantasy at the park entrance,
torn down after fire damage in 1970
(spooky platforms and a tunnel under
the park remain). Victorian glass-
houses are a delight. On a wide *allée* is
the **Main Range** (1883). It is outshone
by the dazzling **Kibble Palace**.

The entrance to Kibble's conservatory
is a conventional iron and glass, domed
pavilion. It leads to a triple-tier rotunda on iron ring beams held up by cast
iron columns with filigree brackets, all
made at the Saracen Foundry. Kibble
promoted the structure as a 'pleasure
dome' for exhibitions, public meetings
and concerts. Profits were to be shared
equally with the Royal Botanic Institution, but the enterprise did not thrive.
Kibble's folly was taken over by the city
in 1891 and rehabilitated as a winter

373
The Kibble Palace, Botanic Gardens
730 Great Western Road
John Kibble engineer c. 1865

garden. In 1964 the *Architects' Journal* described it 'one of the most astonishing buildings in Glasgow . . . light as a spider's web.'

In 2003 it closed for restoration, was surveyed digitally, dismantled and its components refurbished *(Shepley Engineers, Yorkshire)*. It was reassembled and reopened in 2006. The Victorian-style tree fern forest was replanted. Cast iron 'squirrel' benches and marble classical statues, among them 'Eve' *(Scipione Tadolini sculptor c. 1880)*, were reinstated and interpretative panels introduced. Suspended mirrors bounce light around the space which continues to be a captivating spectacle.

374
Òran Mór
731 Great Western Road
John James Stevenson 1862; Peter McGurn, ZM Architecture 2004
Originally Kelvinside Parish Church, north Italian Gothic style, now theatre and music venue Òran Mór (Gaelic for great music). The change of use—the vision of entrepreneur Colin Beattie—is advertised with a neon halo on the steeple. The bells *(Whitechapel Foundry)* were dedicated in 1918 as a First World War memorial.

The church was derelict. A bid for residential use which would have gutted it was rejected by the city in favour of Òran Mór which promised public access and cultural benefit. A new floor was inserted in the nave to create an events hall and to enclose bars and eateries below. The nave lost one-third of its height and volume but, having

been lofty, remains a big space. Eleven portraits *(William Mossman sculptor)* of famous theologians stare from the arches of the former aisles. The ceiling was transformed into a celestial mural by Alasdair Gray.

Also by Alasdair Gray, with Nichol Wheatley, is a ceramic mural, *All Kinds of Folk*, commissioned for the refurbished **Hillhead Subway Station** *(1896; AHR Architects 2012)* on Byres Road. Next door is **The Curler's Rest**, an 18th-century cottage much altered (the name is from a curling pond once nearby).

Back near Òran Mór are the silent movie-era former **Hillhead Picture Salon** *(Brand & Lithgow 1913)* and the tiled frontage of **Botanic Gardens Garage** *(David Valentine Wyllie 1912)*, the oldest auto services building in Scotland, both on Vinicombe Street. At 12 Cranworth Street is **Western Baths** *(Clarke & Bell c. 1880)*; Turkish-Italianate exterior and Gothic inside, like swimming in a flooded church.

375
Grosvenor Terrace
Great Western Road
John Thomas Rochead c.1855

Spectacular terrace of three-storey townhouses modelled on the 16th-century façades on Piazza San Marco, Venice. It brought sophistication and status to Great Western Road, which was planned here as a tree-lined continental boulevard. The three main classical orders appear, one on each level: Doric on the main floor, Ionic above and Corinthian at the top.

In 1938 the Grosvenor Hotel opened in the eastern part of the terrace. It was gutted by fire in 1978 and the unstable shell demolished. Such was the loss to the streetscape that when the hotel was rebuilt *(T. M. Miller & Partners c.1980)* the lost façade was reproduced with glass-reinforced concrete panels made from moulds taken from the undamaged part of the terrace.

376
Kelvinside Hillhead Parish Church
Saltoun Street
James Sellars 1876

Inspired by the 13th-century Saint Chapelle, Paris, complete with flèche, buttresses and a west front with gargoyles and bas-relief angels flanking a rose window. All well maintained, a result of repair and restoration over the

past decade *(Page\Park Architects)*. As at Saint Chapelle, there is a breathtaking array of stained glass, a wall of coloured light. The windows (1893–1909) are diverse in style by leading designers Daniel Cottier and Edward Burne-Jones, and Sadie McLellan (1958).

377
Windows in the West
Saltoun Street
1898

This tenement was shown in a painting, *Windows in the West (Avril Paton 1993)*, a winter scene of the façade on Saltoun Street and folk at the windows. The artist's intimate and affectionate glimpse of urban life in the West End was bought by Glasgow Museums and became one of the most popular exhibits. The four storeys turn the corner

into Roxburgh Street where bow windows continue and there are cast iron railings beside steps to wally closes.

378
Notre Dame High School
160 Observatory Road

Thomas S. Cordiner 1953
Dowanhill housed Glasgow University Observatory from 1840 until 1936. The clean air attracted the Sisters of Notre Dame de Namur who opened a convent in 1894, followed by a teachers' training college for women and a school. The Sisters bought the observatory site for the present school, designed c.1938, completed after the Second World War.

The building is stuck in a time warp between Arts and Crafts and Scandinavian modernism. Roofs are pantiled; the entrance has wide eaves and stone mullions but windows were metal-framed. Bas-relief panels representing religion and learning are in social realist style; above them is an Art Deco

plinth with a cross. To the south, on Victoria Crescent Road, are **Notre Dame Chapel** and **Primary School**, now part of an upmarket residential adaptive reuse *(Smith Findlay Architects 2015)*.

379
Elstow
5 Victoria Circus

1857; Alexander Nisbet Paterson 1899

Villas on Dowanhill were classical until the Victorian fetish for fantasy homes took hold. Elstow too was Italianate, had a mid-life crisis and emerged with a baronial facelift.

The makeover was the whim of William Tillie of Tillie & Henderson, shirt and collar makers. Their Venetian-style warehouse *(Alexander Kirkland 1856)* on Miller Street was one of the finest in Glasgow until torn down in 1969. Their factory in Londonderry, Northern Ireland was the largest of its type in the world and was mentioned by Karl Marx in *Das Kapital*. Marx should have visited Elstow to see how the profits were spent.

380
Benvue
4 Sydenham Road
Boucher & Cousland 1859
Victorian villa of James Smith, foundry owner in Scotland and friend of Jefferson Davis, President of the Confederate States of America. Smith had been to America to establish an ironworks. His younger brother, Robert, was a Confederate colonel killed in 1862 during the American Civil War.

In Glasgow there was sympathy for the Confederacy, a residue from the days of the tobacco lords. Merchants and manufacturers, especially shipbuilders, put profit over principle. Clyde-built ships were used as blockade runners to supply the slave-owning Confederate states. Jefferson Davis visited James Smith at Benvue in 1869.

381
Kensington Gate
David Barclay 1902
Serpentine terrace of townhouses facing private gardens. Arched doorways, miniature Ionic columns and bow windows crowned with Arts and Crafts dormers are uniformly well preserved. There are wood panelled halls and stained glass by Oscar Paterson.

Above the gardens is **St. Luke's Greek Orthodox Church**, since 1960. It was originally Belhaven Church *(James Sellars 1877)*, designed in Normandy Gothic style.

382
Kirklee Terrace
Great Western Road
Charles Wilson 1845–1864
The first of the grand terraces on Great Western Road, an assertive composition with finely modelled classical features. The three-storey centrepiece is flanked by two-storey rows slightly recessed extending to pavilions, all in Roman palazzo style. Period mews cottages in the back lane.

383
Lowther Terrace
Great Western Road
James Miller (Nos. 8 and 10) and
Sidney Mitchell (No. 9) 1904

Jacobean and Scottish Renaissance
townhouses, formerly a Church of
Scotland care home rehabilitated
(Smith Findlay Architects 2017) as
upscale apartments. Number 10 has a
splendid Renaissance-style interior. It
was built for John Traill Cargill, chairman of the Glasgow-owned Burmah
Oil Company, Rangoon.

384
Kirklee Bridge
Kirklee Road
Foreman & McCall engineers 1900
Exceptionally grand masonry bridge
built by Glasgow Corporation. The
central arch spans the River Kelvin

and two others the Kelvin Walkway.
Beaux-Arts style with pairs of Ionic
granite columns, balustraded parapets,
cast iron lamp fittings and, in the spandrels, majestic medallions with city's
coat of arms.

At Kirklee and Bellshaugh roads is
the equally grand **Kelvinside Academy**
(James Sellars 1878), its Greek Revival
style scholarly. The Ionic-columned
porch features a cameo of Minerva,
goddess of wisdom.

385
Great Western Terrace
Great Western Road
Alexander Thomson 1869–1877

The most dignified and austere Victorian terrace in Glasgow. The composition
is unconventional—a long, two-storey
and basement row with three-storey
palazzo-style pavilions like mantel-
piece ornaments rather than bookends.
Ionic porches flattered buyers, a who's
who of Glasgow's commercial and
professional aristocracy.

There were eleven townhouses. Number 4, the home of tobacco merchant
James W. MacGregor, was restored

(Page\Park Architects 1994) as a complete unit; others had been subdivided as flats. Its double-height skylit classical hallway shows how Thomson would have fitted out the whole terrace had he not died in 1875. He did decorate No. 7 for publisher Robert Blackie. Number 8 was transformed by shipowner and art collector William Burrell who lived here from 1902 to 1927. Robert Lorimer gave the 18-room townhouse a baronial makeover, decorated with Burrell's artworks which included medieval tapestries.

The Burrell House was latterly a local authority care home. Planners and conservationists wanted it restored as a single property, which proved an unrealistic expectation. Eventually it was rehabilitated as four apartments *(Jewitt & Wilkie Architects 2012)*. A staircase by Lorimer remains.

Outside, the cast iron railings are Thomson's original design. The 19th-century carriage access remains but the steps at each end of the terrace were reoriented in the 1970s when planners proposed widening Great Western Road. Nearby **Westbourne Terrace** (1871), 21–39 Hyndland Road, is also by Thomson. At 52 Westbourne Gardens is the former **Westbourne Free Church** *(John Honeyman 1881)*. Roman grandeur, suburban scale.

386
Carlston
998 Great Western Road
James Boucher 1877
Renaissance villa built for James Marshall, co-owner of Macfarlane's

Saracen Foundry. A cast iron and glass conservatory, one of the firm's products, was attached to the west side of the house. The main façade is opulent. The original stable yard remains, its buildings converted as mews style dwellings.

387
Glen Tower
1000 Great Western Road
1882
Paired Corinthian columns and a tower distinguish this Italianate villa. The tower was originally a 'gentleman's smoking room'. The gentleman was James M. Thomson, whose father was James Thomson of J. & G. Thomson, pioneering engineers and shipbuilders.

388

Stoneleigh

48 Cleveden Drive

Henry Edward Clifford 1901

Numerous villas were built when Kelvinside estate was developed in the late 19th century. Stoneleigh is one of the finest, an Elizabethan-style mansion for a broker at Glasgow Stock Exchange. Like many homes of this type it has been converted as apartments with period features retained. Across the road is the well maintained **Cleveden Crescent** *(John Burnet 1876)*.

389

St. John's Renfield Church

22 Beaconsfield Road

James Taylor Thomson 1927–1931

A monolithic neo-Gothic landmark above Great Western Road. It was built for the congregations of St. John's and Renfield churches in the city centre which merged in 1923. It survived the blast of a *Luftwaffe* parachute mine during the Second World War.

The interior is luminous with traceried windows, stained glass *(Douglas Strachan & Gordon Webster)* and Art Deco pendant lighting. A flèche rises from the roof ridge. Architect James Taylor Thomson had worked in New York and was evidently influenced by

the vigour and freedom of the early 20th-century Gothic he found there. Restored in 2009 *(ARPL Architects)*.

At the top of Beaconsfield Road is **Kelvinside House** (1874), Italianate with a baronial addition *(James Thomson c. 1894)*. It was built for J. B. Montgomerie Fleming whose father had, with business partners in 1839, bought Kelvinside estate and subdivided the land for villas and terraces.

390

Kelvinside Station

1051 Great Western Road

J. J. Burnet 1897

Looks like an Italianate villa, actually a station master's house and ticket hall built by the Caledonian Railway. The building was dressed up to match the mansions on Great Western Road. It sits on steel beams at the portal of

a tunnel to Maryhill. The platforms were reached by stairs to a cutting now filled by housing. The line closed in 1966. The abandoned station building was reopened as a restaurant in 1980. In 1995 a fire gutted the interior, since reconstructed.

391
Gartnavel Hospital
1055 Great Western Road
Charles Wilson 1843

Gartnavel was picturesque above parkland, like a stately home rather than Glasgow Royal Asylum for Lunatics. The previous asylum *(William Stark 1814)* was a classical domed building on Dobbie's Loan, where Glasgow Caledonian University is now. Industrialisation forced a move west. The new hilltop site, previously small farms on Kelvinside estate, was thought therapeutic. There were recreation grounds. A farm supplied the hospital kitchen.

Two blocks were built, 'divested of all gloom and appearance of confinement'. The style is Tudor Gothic. West House was for the haves; East House a charity block. The latter is a derelict spooky pile awaiting rehabilitation, perhaps as flats for buyers able to ignore ghosts. West House is currently used as offices

by NHS Greater Glasgow and Clyde.

Gartnavel was absorbed by the National Health Service in 1948. The parkland has since been much diminished, notably by the brutalist **Gartnavel General Hospital** *(Keppie Henderson & Partners 1968–1972).*

392
The Calman Cancer Centre
75 Shelley Road
J. J. Burnet 1904; Austin-Smith: Lord 2012

In 1980 oncology professor Kenneth Calman founded the charity Tak Tent (old Scots 'take care') to advance holistic care. This Cancer Support Scotland centre is a realisation of that ideal.

The outpatient facility is a repurposed chapel built originally for the Royal Lunatic Asylum. The style is Arts and Crafts, the structure timber framed with brick walls harled. The bell tower is a picturesque gable, the entrance a rustic porch.

The exterior was restored and the sanctuary opened up, partly skylit. A wood floor was laid to complement Burnet's barn-like timber roof. Stained-glass windows *(Robert Anning Bell 1904)* were conserved but the reconditioned space feels secular, is coloured warmly and welcoming. A discreet low-level extension on the east side respects the original design. A Glasgow Building Preservation Trust project.

393
Maggie's Centre, Gartnavel
1055 Great Western Road
OMA (Office for Metropolitan Architecture), Lily Jencks & Harrison Stevens landscape design 2011

Maggie's Centres, founded in Scotland, offer support to people with cancer, their families and friends. They are designed by top talent. This is the second in Glasgow. The first *(Page\Park Architects, Charles Jencks landscape design 2002)* converted a gatehouse *(John Burnet 1881)* at the Dumbarton Road entrance to Glasgow University.

The OMA-designed centre won the Andrew Doolan Award 2012. It sits in an elevated patch of woodland above the fluorescent world of Gartnavel General Hospital. The single-storey, seven-sided pavilion is irregular in plan and volume. Sliding timber screens allow flexible spaces, contemplative or group-oriented, around a courtyard garden. Full-height windows meld with the landscape. A woodchip path leads to a glade with sculpted tree seats. All very Zen: landscape design is an essential part of Maggie's Centres, the therapeutic powers of Nature being as important as the architecture.

394
11 Whittingehame Drive
John Ednie 1908

Romantic Scottish Arts and Crafts villa with tall chimney stacks, crow step gables, and rusticated stone interspersed with ashlar. Cast iron gates are interlaced with an ivy design in wrought iron. The natural theme is repeated at the front door in stained glass *(Oscar Paterson)* and on a tripartite carved relief. The gravel path is in keeping with the house and its garden setting.

The villa was built for A. MacKellar of Finnieston Engineering Co., engineers and ship furnishers, a client of Wylie & Lochhead (see 206) for whom Ednie was an interior and furniture designer. The back garden overlooks the Victorian Bingham's Boating Pond, now a wildlife refuge.

395

Kelvin Court

Great Western Road

James Newton Fatkin 1938

The prospectus gushed, 'London has nothing to excel these imposing blocks of luxury flats.' They were fully serviced and furnished with all mod cons including central heating and constant hot water, taken for granted now but not then. Styling is moderne, with facing brick on a reinforced concrete frame. Stair towers have glass block windows and period lettering. Construction coincided with the Empire Exhibition at Bellahouston Park. It was the largest apartment development in Scotland until exceeded by the housing schemes of the postwar era.

396

Ascot Cinema

1544 Great Western Road

McNair & Elder 1939; Holmes Partnership 2003

Hollywood Art Deco with a wide marquee, vertical fins, and glass illu-

minating a double-height foyer, framed with streamline moderne stair towers clad in faience. Fabulous, as was the vast auditorium, latterly a bingo hall. Renamed the Gaumont c.1950 and Odeon in 1964. Only the front survived demolition for flats.

397

Anniesland Court

843 Crow Road, Anniesland Cross

Jack Holmes & Partners 1968

A wafer-thin, 22-storey reinforced concrete tower, the only A-listed residential high-rise in the city and the tallest listed building in Scotland. Also the country's tallest example of Brutalism, the style softened here during recent refurbishment by Glasgow

Housing Association. Originally there were 42 single flats and 84 three-room apartments in an unconventional configuration, accessed by covered gangways from an external stair and elevator shaft.

There are seven main levels where the lift stops. Each level has three floors connected by stairs, each floor built to accommodate six units. The stairs were said by the architects at the time to be like closes in the tenements from which tenants were rehoused. Balconies on the north face were for clothes drying.

The tower is impressive, pure modernism. It rises from a podium, for council offices, retail and parking. The retail part was not a success, its deck oriented perversely to the prevailing wind and rain. A four-storey block of flats, originally flat-roofed, was sited

perpendicular to the tower, to engage with Anniesland's tenement urbanism. Its ground-level space has been revitalised by Anniesland Public Library.

398
Anniesland Mansions
Anniesland Cross
Hugh Campbell 1913
Edwardian mansion block, 'mansion' meaning high class, with Ionic columns, balustrades and pediments on its domed corner—a gateway to the city (Anniesland Cross was originally called Anniesland Toll).

It was one of the last traditional tenements built in Glasgow following the Finance Act of 1909 which increased tax on construction. After the First World War suburban housing became more profitable for private builders and attractive to buyers. In the 1920s, Glasgow Corporation shifted its focus from tenements to garden city-style housing estates in the suburbs, notably Knightswood west of Anniesland Cross, Mosspark on the Southside and Riddrie in the East End.

'The Gatekeeper' New Gorbals

9

New Gorbals to Cathcart

AT THE CORNER of Malta and Kidston terraces on the southwest edge of New Gorbals is *The Gatekeeper*, a bronze figure suspended above a surreal photomural. The figure recalls *The Floating Angel*, a symbol of loss and eternity by sculptor Ernst Barlach created in Germany in the aftermath of the First World War. In New Gorbals *The Gatekeeper* evokes the memory of the old and the rise of the new community.

The Gorbals was a village on a feudal estate on the south bank of the Clyde. Weaving was the local trade. The lands were bought and subdivided on a map of 1804, by Glasgow Town Council, Hutchesons' Hospital and the Trades House. 'Tradeston', to the west, was developed as an industrial and warehouse zone. The other two subdivisions, Laurieston and Hutchesontown in the Gorbals were residential. No one anticipated how dense they would be.

Glasgow's economy and population grew rapidly between 1800 and 1914. Fortunes were made. There was shocking inequality. Merchants' mansions were a world away from overcrowded tenements of which those in the Gorbals became the most notorious. They housed unskilled workers from the Highlands and Ireland who arrived in Glasgow, lured by the chance of a better life; Jewish people too, from Eastern Europe. In the 1870s, the City Improvement Trust built decent housing but speculators added more tenements and rents were cheap. By 1948 *Picture Post* reported, 'Nearly 40,000 people live in the Gorbals. They live four, six, eight to a room, often 30 to a lavatory, 40 to a tap. They live in Britain's most abandoned slum.' The area became the default for media looking for lurid stories. Comprehensive redevelopment transformed it in the 1960s. The Gorbals and neighbouring Laurieston were razed and replaced with high- and low-rise flats. Most of the population was rehoused on council estates on the outskirts and in new towns.

Laurieston had been promoted as a classy suburb by James and David Laurie who built the elegant Carlton Place (1802–1818). It was where, with Hutchesontown, the classic Glasgow street grid of tenements with back courts first appeared. Façades evolved from Georgian precedents, unless you were Alexander 'Greek' Thomson. He lived in Laurieston for a time. His Caledonia Road Church is one of the few structures from the 19th century remaining in the vicinity. In the 1870s a web of railways was built with ruthless enterprise. Folk who could afford to leave did and Laurieston went from desirable to decay in a generation.

Redevelopment of Laurieston and the Gorbals in the 1960s produced a modernist townscape in the Le Corbusier mode, the orthodoxy of the time. In 1954 a delegation from Glasgow visited Marseilles to see *Unité d'Habitation*, a modernist slab block, designed by Le Corbusier, which energised a generation of architects. Among them was Basil Spence who designed the only masterpiece to rise from Glasgow's postwar housing programme—Queen Elizabeth Square, two monolithic, reinforced concrete slab blocks, the most adventurous, thoughtfully configured and sculptural in the city. These 'gardens in the sky'—a vertical village with balconies and modular units for singles, couples and families stacked up to 20 storeys—were ahead of their time, too far ahead. The city failed to maintain the blocks and the social structure for which they were intended. Rainscreen technology was deficient. The concrete deteriorated. The Mediterranean-inspired design was said to be unsuitable for Glasgow's climate. The blocks became uninhabitable and were dynamited in 1993.

The architect was an easier target for blame than the client, Glasgow Corporation, which wanted the new look, but quick and cheap. Spence's blocks combined the aesthetic and political ambitions of modernism but became a symbol of everything that went wrong with the city's high-rise housing, which is why few people thought them worth saving. Le Corbusier's *Unité d'Habitation* remains a landmark in Marseilles.

The Gorbals was revived in the 1990s by the multi-agency Crown Street Regeneration Project. A design competition was held for the masterplan *(czwg Architects)*. The 'back to the future' scheme reinstated lost streets and lined them with postmodern tenements and terraces designed with community input and managed by New Gorbals Housing Association. Seven design teams of architect and developer were appointed. The buildings are a mix of rental and owner-occupied properties. To foster a sense of community there is no distinction between them or their quality. There is a neighbourhood park and public art. Landscape design ensures the streets are as much for people as traffic. The 'urban village', as it was promoted, accommodates singles, couples and families as Basil Spence's slab blocks did, but it is much more popular. The New Gorbals experiment continues in the Laurieston Transformational Area.

Laurieston is separated from the Southside by the M74 motorway viaduct, impressive to fans of steel girders. To the south are Govanhill, Queen's Park, Langside, Shawlands and Cathcart which were developed in the 19th and early 20th centuries. Suburban rail lines from Central Station encouraged development in these communities, which tend to be overlooked unfairly compared to the West End. There is variety: a monument to the Battle of Langside, mosaics in Byzantine style at St. Margaret's Newlands Church, a Sikh temple, and Holmwood House designed by 'Greek' Thomson.

399

Gorbals New Park

Alexander Crescent

c. 1998

An urban park in the Victorian tradition, within a hoop of new tenements. There are gates decorated with flora and fauna of the Four Seasons and a gazebo *(Jack Sloan artist, Hector McGarva metalwork)*, an echo of old-style bandstands. It is crowned with a phoenix symbolising the neighbourhood's revival. Paths are aligned to the street plan. Caledonia Road Church is visible. The public realm was integrated in the masterplan *(CZWG Architects 1990)* to regenerate the Gorbals and contributes to its success.

400

Caledonia Road Church

1 Caledonia Road

Alexander Thomson 1856

In 1968 Andor Gomme, in the book *Architecture of Glasgow*, wrote of this ruin: 'It is one of Glasgow's greatest buildings—indeed one of the greatest 19th-century buildings anywhere;

yet in a way only too characteristic of Glasgow, the church, after years of ill-treatment amounting to dereliction, has been gutted by fire [1965] . . . In almost any other country than our own, so great a work of art would call out enthusiastic and complete restoration as a matter of course.'

Greek Thomson designed it for the United Free Church. He repeated the composition—detached tower, podium and raised Ionic porch—at St. Vincent Street Church (see 239), to more dramatic effect on a hill. Caledonia Church commands a gushet site on what was Caledonia Road. Like most of the old Gorbals street plan the road has been overlaid; Gorbals New Park is where it was.

At the back of the church were tenements designed by Thomson, demolished after the fire. Decades of decay have not diminished the building's dignity. Numerous plans to reuse it have come and gone. The hollow shell has been tested as an arts and performance space. It could have been part of Gorbals New Park had traffic engineering not got in the way. The ruin is isolated by a main road and a sure way to heaven is to try to cross it.

401
Malta Terrace
Hypostyle Architects 2001
New tenements with drum-shaped towers like a castle gateway, the entrance to the block's inner courtyard. The buildings demarcate the southwest perimeter of New Gorbals, at Malta and Kidston terraces. They reinterpret

Glasgow's 19th-century housing— walk-up access, elevations flush to the street, back court, here landscaped.

Malta Terrace became a pin-up for the Crown Street Regeneration Project thanks to its public art *(Heisenberg artists)*—a mysterious photomural and the meditative, angelic *Gatekeeper* and *Attendants*, the latter above the closes on Malta and Kidston terraces.

402
Southern Necropolis Gate Lodge
Caledonia Road
Charles Wilson 1848

An entrance to paradise in the style of a Norman castle thought to have been the cemetery company's office, gardeners' bothy and waiting room for mourners. The cemetery replaced Gorbals village burial ground which was full, having been used for mass burials during an outbreak of cholera in 1832.

There are memorials to Alexander

Thomson and Gorbals-born Thomas
Lipton, tea and grocery mogul.
Thomson's black granite marker was
commissioned by Glasgow Institute
of Architects in 2006. Charles Wilson
who designed the Lodge is here too.

403
St. Francis Centre
405 Cumberland Street
Peter Paul Pugin 1881

One of several churches in Glasgow
designed by Pugin, youngest son of
Augustus Welby Pugin, the high priest
of the Gothic Revival. It was built as St.
Francis Church next to a friary *(Gilbert
Robert Blount 1869)* occupied by
Franciscan Greyfriars. Above the door
of the church are the dates 1476 and
1868: the former when the Greyfriars
founded a monastery near the Old College on High Street; the latter when the
order eventually returned, having been
banished during the Reformation. The
church was converted as a community
centre *(Page\Park Architects 1996)*
and the friary, also Gothic Revival, as
sheltered housing.

404
Friary Court
Queen Elizabeth Gardens
Page\Park Architects 2002

A deconstruction of the traditional
tenement block. The plan is semi-
circular from which seven segmental
buildings rise. Their circumference
forms elevations to the street; their
narrow ends project into a landscaped
back court. Between each segment is an
open-air passage from the street to the
courtyard. The passage accesses glazed
stairways which cut each segment
transversely in two. Sounds complex
but on the ground is simple and smart.

At Cumberland Street is a **Gorbals
Arts Project** installation, one of
many. They were part of the Gorbals
Percentage for Art scheme by which
developers agreed to fund artworks
in the public realm. This one, *Gorbals
Boys* (three wee boys in their mothers'
high heels), is a sculptural recreation of
a popular photo *(Oscar Marzaroli 1963;
Liz Peden artist 2008)*.

405
Paragon
Queen Elizabeth Gardens
CZWG Architects 2004
Brick-clad steel-framed apartment and
townhouse development named after

a long-gone Gorbals cinema. Heights vary from two to seven storeys around a courtyard. The project replaced the notoriously leaky Queen Elizabeth Square, aka Hutchie C (Hutchesontown Area C, Gorbals Comprehensive Redevelopment Area).

Queen Elizabeth Square *(Basil Spence & Partners 1960–1965)* had two colossal 20-storey concrete slab blocks with 400 modular units, some split-level, and garden decks. Initially, the blocks were called 'the hanging gardens of the Gorbals' but became high-rise slums. They were dynamited in 1993. Had they been kept they could have been retrofitted and festooned with plants, eco-friendly and sustainable. Paragon's cantilevered balconies and dummy *pilotis* recall their side elevations.

406
Hutchesontown Public Library
192 McNeil Street
James R. Rhind c. 1905
Former library with eclectic northern

Renaissance styling. Carvings by architect Rhind's favoured sculptor William Kellock Brown. The bas-relief above the entrance is a masterly Renaissance-style tableau of St. Mungo flanked by female figures holding the symbols of the city: the salmon, the tree, the bird and the bell, and a ship. There are baroque domes and a tower with griffins and an angel with an open book.

407
The Villa
McNeil Street
Elder & Cannon Architects 2003
A variety of housing types for New Gorbals Housing Association was built at Moffat Gardens in the Gorbals East zone of the masterplan. On the southeast edge of its pocket park are rental units in this look-at-me elliptical block with a flamboyant copper roof and an adjoining Bauhaus-style cube.

Throughout New Gorbals the public realm *(Ian White Associates landscape design)* is enhanced with street trees and paving with a mix of materials to

The plume of smoke on the chimney is a glass fibre kinetic sculpture *(Rita McGurn artist, Adrian Lamb sculptor 1994).* It revolves like a weathervane, a memory of the industry once here.

409
Gorbals Parish Church of Scotland
1 Errol Gardens
ADF *Architects 2011*

All-in-one church, conference centre and café. Copper sheeting on a curved form gave it instant presence, like a gateway on the edge of New Gorbals. A wall-mounted cross is the only obvious religious symbol. The rest of the structure is boxy but warm and inviting. The copper curve contains the sanctuary and meeting hall.

defines uses. Stones here are laid out in the fan-shaped continental manner, to mark a drive-slow zone (no signs required). The pine cones—a marriage of public art and traffic calming—are practical and a delight.

408
Twomax Business Centre
187 Old Rutherglen Road
c.1816

The oldest iron-framed industrial building in Glasgow, originally a cotton mill, latterly the Twomax garment factory. For a time the building was owned by clothing makers and retailers Stewart & McDonald (see 205). The serrated roof is not original.

410
Citizens Theatre
119 Gorbals Street
Campbell Douglas 1878
The 'Citz', founded in 1943, originally at the **Athenaeum Theatre** (see 191), has been in the Gorbals since 1945, in the former Her Majesty's Theatre (1878). The Victorian auditorium has its original proscenium, ornate plasterwork, cast iron columns supporting balconies and the oldest stage machinery still in place in Britain.

The façade had six Doric columns salvaged from the Union Bank (see 90) on Ingram Street, and a balustrade with six statues—four ancient Greek muses (Music, Dance, Comedy and Tragedy) and Shakespeare and Burns. This fantastic frontage, centre stage in a streetscape of tenements since demolished, was shared with the Palace Theatre, also Victorian, torn down in 1977. The statues were rescued by staff at the Citz and stored.

Shakespeare and Burns reappeared looking out of place in a suburban style entrance built in the 1980s. A comprehensive upgrade to the facilities should see it replaced with a foyer fit for the future *(Bennetts Associates)*. The plan is for a skylit atrium to reveal fully the auditorium's stone gable; and for the historically resonant statues to be displayed within a glazed façade to better identify the theatre and see its street presence restored.

Rendering courtesy of Bennetts Associates

411
The Glasgow House
Norfolk Street
PRP Architects 2010
An experiment by Glasgow Housing Association and City Building Glasgow

to test energy use and reduce fuel poverty. The brief was to demonstrate that social housing can deliver energy savings at low cost, with contemporary design and eco-friendly strategies to reduce annual fuel bills to £100. Two types were built: one an engineered timber prefab; the other with thermal-rated clay blocks. Skills training was part of the initiative.

412
O2 Academy
121 Eglinton Street
Lennox & McMath 1932

Originally the New Bedford Cinema with a Spanish-Moroccan, Art Deco façade. Like most of its type it became a bingo hall. It was refurbished in 2002 as a live music venue. A similar makeover in 2005 revived the **Regal Cinema** *(Charles McNair 1929)* at 330 Sauchiehall Street.

413
British Linen Bank
162 Gorbals Street
James Salmon (junior) c. 1900

The only tenement in Laurieston to survive slum clearance in the 1970s. There was nothing slummy here. The building is A-listed. The banking hall had wood panelling and a marble floor. The interior is long gone but the entrance retains a baroque cartouche with the bank's name, a royal shield and Britannia framed by four cherub

masks. In 2015 Historic Environment Scotland announced funding toward repair and adaptive reuse by Southside Housing Association and Glasgow Building Preservation Trust.

414
Laurieston Phase 1A
Cumberland Street
Page\Park Architects, Elder & Cannon Architects, Ian White Associates landscape design 2015

A design-led initiative by Glasgow City Council, the Scottish Government, New Gorbals Housing Association and developer Urban Union.

Laurieston Transformational Area is essentially an extension of New Gorbals but with a more formal plan and less mannered architecture. It reverses the planning mistakes of the 1960s by reinterpreting the place-making of the 19th century. The street grid has been

reinstated, lined with blocks of flats. There are row houses and, on wider streets, walk-ups inspired by the urbanism of old Laurieston's tenements. The built forms encourage sociability while allowing privacy. There is green space, landscaping being integral to the plan.

Laurieston won Saltire Society landscaping and housing design awards in 2015. In 2016 it was the most recent project to make the Royal Incorporation of Architects in Scotland's (RIAS) list of the top 100 buildings in the country since 1916.

415
Cumberland Street Station
William Melville engineer 1900

Abandoned grandeur with a Roman Doric entrance and French *oeil-de-boeuf* windows. Bridges and arches carried an elevated section of the Glasgow & South Western Railway to St. Enoch Viaduct (see 57) and into the city centre. The line dates from the 1870s. It follows the alignment of Paisley Canal which was filled in for it. This station was closed in 1966. Trains still run, freight only. A 'crossrail' link between the electrified lines north and south of the river could see it reopened.

416
Abbotsford School
Abbotsford Place
Hugh & David Barclay 1879
Germanic neoclassicism, could be Berlin, like Glasgow a 19th-century tenement city with civic architecture of high quality. Most of Berlin was bombed during the Second World War. Glasgow managed to destroy much of its fabric without enemy help. Abbotsford School was spared during the comprehensive redevelopment of the 1960s. It was the first to use the standard school board plan, with classrooms around a galleried atrium.

H. & D. Barclay also designed the baroque **Chalmers Free Church** (1898), nearby on Pollokshaws Road.

417
St. Andrew's Cross Electricity Works
197 Pollokshaws Road
Andrew Myles 1894–1900
Originally a coal-fired power station with steam turbines, built by Glasgow Corporation to generate electricity for street lighting and tramways. It was one of two mammoth plants of the time, the other being Pinkston at Port Dundas. Both had twin chimneys which belched smoke across the city. After the First World War a new

curved prow parted a sea of traffic on the cross which was laced with tram tracks. There was an ornate cast iron shelter for passengers. The gushet site attracted a publican—the ground floor is a long-established bar which provided refreshment to industrial workers and patrons of the nearby Plaza Ballroom.

power plant at Dalmarnock increased capacity. St. Andrew's was relegated in 1937 as Glasgow Corporation Printing Works. The building appears derelict behind its monumental arcaded brick façade. The Pinkston and Dalmarnock plants were demolished c. 1980.

418
The Star Bar
St. Andrews Cross
537–539 Eglinton Street
c. 1879

Eglinton Street and Pollokshaws and Victoria roads meet at Eglinton Toll, originally a star-shaped intersection also known as St. Andrew's Cross, as inscribed on this tenement. Its

419
YMCA Building
Pollokshaws Road at Maxwell Road
Robert Miller 1896

Horror movie gothic—actually Tudor Gothic and not horrible. The spiky gabled corner has an eroded pictorial panel, probably biblical, with Gothic lettering in the style of a medieval manuscript above the entrance. The building has been rehabilitated as flats.

Horrible is the block of flats (2006) directly east on Victoria Road, built on the site of the **Plaza Ballroom** (1922) whose body parts were kept and stuck on. By far the worst example of façadism in the city.

420
Scottish Ballet
Albert Drive at Pollokshaws Road
Malcolm Fraser Architects 2009

A big industrial shed repainted and retrofitted as an arts space? Not quite. It's a new big shed with, according to Scottish Ballet, 'the largest dedicated dance rehearsal studio in Europe', ventilated with fresh air and skylit to reduce costs and carbon emissions.

The industrial look—serrated roofline, precast concrete panels, aluminium and glass—is in step with the site which was part of Coplawhill Tram Works (see next entry). Only letters spelling 'Scottish Ballet' on Pollokshaws Road hint at what the shed is for, and there is no obvious entrance because access is by stair from inside the Tramway on Albert Drive. No matter. The clever thing is the building looks as if it's always been here.

Transport which opened here in 1964. The museum was moved to Kelvin Hall in 1987 and subsequently to **Riverside** (see 27).

In 1988 the old depot was repurposed as a theatre and arts centre. A subsequent upgrade kept brick walls distressed and timber-trussed roofs, cast iron columns and steel I-beams, respecting the hard-graft workplace this was. Trams entered through arches on Albert Drive. A section of track is preserved on the polished concrete floor inside. Also preserved is the ramp, and exterior walkway at the rear, which accessed stables when trams were horse-drawn.

421

Tramway

25 Albert Drive

William Clark engineer 1894–1899;
ZM Architecture 2000

This was Coplawhill Tram Works where around 1,000 people were employed to build and service Glasgow's fleet of 1,200 trams until the last one ran in 1962. The sheds were a perfect contextual location for the Museum of

The intervention included a café which opens to the biodiverse **Hidden Gardens** *(NVA environmental arts, City Design Co-op 2003)*. A workspace, the aluminium-clad **Boilerhouse** *(Collective Architecture 2006)*, fits with the industrial heritage. It is beside the freestanding brick chimney which was part of the tram works foundry.

422
Glasgow Gurdwara
37 Albert Drive
CRGP Architects 2013

The old gurdwara was a villa on Nithsdale Road. A search for a new site found this empty lot, formerly part of Coplawhill Tram Works, bypassed by developers because of old mine workings below. The Sikhs were undaunted and erected the first purpose-built gurdwara in Scotland. The largest spaces are a multi-purpose room on the ground floor and prayer hall upstairs. The building, decorated typically with onion domes, functions as a religious and community centre.

423
Glasgow Samaritan Hospital for Women
Coplaw Street
Macwhannell & Rogerson c.1905
A free-form fantasy in rusticated stone

with drum towers, turrets and dormers, built as a residence for nurses. The Scottish Renaissance-influenced Arts and Crafts design was part of Samaritan Hospital, between Victoria Road and Ardbeg Street, closed in 1991. The buildings were rehabilitated (2002) for Govanhill Housing Association and its Development Trust.

At 70 Coplaw Street is **The Ark**, an eco-friendly adaptive reuse *(Lee Ivett architect 2017)* of a heritage church. An upper floor fitted in the nave created a community hall above a meeting room, studios and offices, for charitable group Noah's Ark and Radio Ramadan.

424
Millennium Hut, Larkfield Centre
39 Inglefield Street
Studio KAP Architects, Clare Barclay artist 1999

A Millennium Space project for Glasgow City of Architecture and Design, this solar powered timber workshop was built with new and recycled materials to promote an eco-friendly economy. Low-impact and environmentally sustainable, it was used to teach local kids to grow plants from seed. Its form was inspired by the self-build corrugated iron doocots assembled by pigeon-fanciers to keep their birds. One of those doocots stands nearby.

425
Govanhill Baths
99 Calder Street
   Alexander Beith McDonald, City Engineer 1914–1917

In 2001 city council declared the baths surplus to requirements despite protests from the community to keep them open. They were the last built by Glasgow Corporation to serve densely populated tenement districts where many flats had no bathrooms, lavatories were shared and clothes washed at the steamie.

Govanhill Baths had a steamie, Turkish baths and three pools (men, women and children). The building was structurally advanced with concrete arches spanning skylit swimmers.

The structure and its heritage features remain thanks to a five-month sit-in and the formation in 2005 of Govanhill Baths Community Trust. A phased conservation and rehabilitation *(NORD Architecture 2012)* is being taken forward *(Hall Black Douglas Architects and Alastair Coey Architects)* to create a community wellness, recreation and swim centre.

On the façade is a plaque with the city's coat of arms and a portrait of the Lord Provost who laid the foundation stone. Glasgow's tenement communities were well served at the time. Govanhill, which escaped redevelopment in the 1960s, is an example. **Govanhill Public Library** *(James R. Rhind 1906)* brought Beaux-Arts style to Calder Street and there is an Italianate school (next entry).

426
Annette Street Primary School
27 Annette Street
   Hugh & David Barclay 1886
Superb palazzo designed to dignify the Victorian school board's mission. Typical utilitarian square plan with an atrium. Exceptionally well proportioned and detailed front elevation with a rusticated stone base, pilas-

tered main doorway and window pediments. The top floor is composed like an eaves gallery with a parade of columns and confident cornice. The school is surrounded by streets lined with tenements. One of them, **265–289 Allison Street**, was designed by 'Greek' Thomson (1875).

427
Bankhall Court
17 Bankhall Street
John Gilbert Architects 2010

A care home for people with dementia, designed for Govanhill Housing Association. Accommodation is south-facing with sunspaces (glazed recessed balconies overlooking the street). There are stained-glass panels in the stairwells *(John K. Clark)*. Staff facilities, a dining room and lounge are on the ground floor. Circulation corridors are at the rear and there is a communal roof garden. The garden and sunspaces met the regulation 50 percent open space required for care home developments, the physical environment being

beneficial if well designed, as it is here. Solar panels for water and underfloor heating, and other measures, gave the building a BREEAM Very Good rating. Its contemporary style is a comfortable fit mid-block in a traditional Govanhill streetscape. It is run by the Mungo Foundation.

428
Dixon Halls
Dixon Avenue at Cathcart Road
Frank Stirrat 1879

Scots Baronial style, built originally as Crosshill and Govanhill Burgh Halls. The boundary between the two burghs bisected the building so there were separate entrances, courtrooms and offices. When the districts became part of Glasgow in 1891 the building was renamed Dixon Halls in honour of its benefactors, the Dixon family.

The Dixons were iron-founders. Their foundry was nicknamed 'Dixon's Blazes' because, from the 1830s until 1958, the furious flames from the furnaces lit the sky day and night. The Dixons developed Govanhill and Crosshill with tenements for their workers, and to profit from real estate.

Dixon Halls is now a senior citizens' community and care centre, the Dixon Community, which started as a lunch club for pensioners in 1972.

429
Crosshill Avenue Cottages
Queen's Drive
Ronald Bradbury, Glasgow Corporation 1949

Picturesque cottages in a small estate influenced by the garden city movement of the early 20th century. The built forms and materials recall Arts and Crafts style. The hamlet received a Festival of Britain award of merit in 1951. Now sheltered housing managed by Glasgow Housing Association.

The steeple nearby (40 Queen's Drive) belongs to **Queens's Park Church** *(Campbell Douglas & Sellars 1873)*, French Gothic, now flats.

430
Balmoral Crescent
78–118 Queens Drive
William McNicol Whyte 1886
Opulent French Renaissance tenements with a statue of Liberty high on the east corner. New York's Statue of Liberty was completed in 1886; Glasgow City Chambers, which also has a figure of Liberty, was being built at the time.

Either might have inspired this copy. The story is that it was intended for the roof at Victoria Road, across from the gate to Queen's Park, but officials said 'No'. The architect got his revenge by putting carved caricatures of them on the façade.

Whyte designed another notable tenement block, the Scots Baronial **Inverclyde Gardens** (c. 1905), 137–159 Broomhill Drive in the West End.

431
Queen's Park
Joseph Paxton 1857–1862
The long perspective of Victoria Road is closed by the main gate and *allée* of Queen's Park, a formal piece of urban design. The rest of the park rolls across a hill, with woods and grassland like a country estate. Designer Joseph Paxton, who planned Birkenhead Park (1847), the first municipally funded park in Britain, also provided plans for Glasgow's Alexandra and Kelvingrove parks.

Classic Victorian features survive, notably a domed glasshouse, bowling greens, a boating pond, and an amphitheatre which has a new canopy *(zm Architecture 2014)* on its stage. Also in the park is a neoclassical villa, **Camphill House** *(David Hamilton c. 1810)*, rehabilitated as flats (1995). The

'camp' is thought to refer to an ancient fort on the hill, where a flagpole marks a viewpoint from where there is a panorama across the city. The park was named not for Queen Victoria but after Mary, Queen of Scots, whose army was defeated nearby at the Battle of Langside (see 438).

432
Camphill Queen's Park Church
20 Balvicar Drive
William Leiper 1876
Powerfully composed in Normandy Gothic style on a corner site which it commands with a dramatic tower and

octagonal spire (1883). Fine medallion *(McCulloch & Co., London)* with a trio of lyre-playing angels above the door, and an outstanding life-size angel with outspread wings *(John Mossman sculptor)*.

433
Langside Hall
Langside Avenue at Pollokshaws Road
John Gibson 1847; Alexander Beith McDonald, City Engineer 1903
Originally built for the National Bank (see 95) and relocated here, stone by stone (over 70,000 of them). The foyer was refitted with Art Nouveau tiles, and rooms opened for public use.

The palazzo façade is frothy with Renaissance decoration *(John Thomas sculptor)*. The entrance arch features Glasgow's heraldry in a cornucopia of thistles. Father Clyde stares from the keystone. Figures of Peace and Plenty

flank the royal coat of arms above the cornice. In 2013 the community-based Langside Hall Trust was formed to take over the building from the city. Refurbishment and public realm improvements are planned.

Across Pollokshaws Road is **Camphill Gate** *(John Nisbet 1906)*, said to be the first tenement of 'fireproof' construction in the city. The developer/builder was Mactaggart & Co.

434
Savings Bank of Glasgow
Shawlands Cross
Neil Campbell Duff 1906

Shawlands Cross, typical of Glasgow's 19th-century urbanism, is a four-way intersection defined by character buildings. Chief among them is the former Savings Bank swaggering like a cavalier. The style is northern Renaissance with baroque features and gables

jumping out from the mansard roof. There is a dome at the corner and lion and unicorn heraldry at the entrance.

On Pollokshaws Road is **Shawlands Kirk** *(John Archibald Campbell 1889)*, spiky Gothic, and a gushet tenement defining the intersection. On Moss-Side Road is the baroque corner-domed former **Waverley Cinema** *(Watson, Salmond & Gray 1922).*

435
St. Margaret's Newlands Church
353 Kilmarnock Road
Peter Macgregor Chalmers 1908–1935

Monumental Episcopal church in 12th-century German Romanesque style. The hall was built in 1908, the barrel-vaulted nave and base of the tower in 1912 and the chancel in 1923. The tower (originally to have been a spire) was completed in 1935. The basilica plan has an apse at each end. There are carved oak fittings in the chancel and stained-glass windows, most by William Morris & Co. and Gordon

Webster. Wonderful Byzantine-style mosaic, *Christ in Glory (Powell & Sons Whitefriars Glass Co. 1927),* in the east apse half-dome, influenced by the early Christian mosaics in the Romanesque basilicas of Ravenna.

436
Rawcliffe House
29 Mansionhouse Road
John Burnet 1862

Victorian mock chateau, formerly Rawcliffe Lodge built for Alexander Bannatyne Stewart of Stewart & McDonald (see 205) clothing manufactures and merchants. Stewart acquired the symbols of success—a steam yacht, a country house on the Isle of Bute and artworks which were displayed in a gallery here.

From 1918 until recently the mansion was a Carmelite monastery. The front is French Renaissance. The rear elevation which overlooked extensive gardens is Scots Baronial with crow-step gables and conical turrets. Original features, notably stained glass *(W. & J. Keir),* were retained during residential conversion as Rawcliffe Gardens (2012), with infill flats in the grounds.

At 25 Mansionhouse Road is **Maria Villa** *(Alexander Thomson 1857),*

two houses composed to look as one. Detailing is Greek and Egyptian, and there is an innovative colonnade and glass curtain wall.

437
Langside Hill Free Church
122 Langside Avenue
Alexander Skirving 1896

The last classical church built in Glasgow, where Greek Revival lingered longer than elsewhere—longer than in Edinburgh, the so-called 'Athens of the North'. Dramatically posed Ionic porch and entrance podium influenced by 'Greek' Thomson for whom Skirving worked as senior draughtsman. Cast iron railings are in Thomson's style. The building was vacated in 1979 and refurbished in the 1990s as a bar and restaurant.

438
Langside Battlefield Monument
Battle Place
Alexander Skirving architect, James Young sculptor 1887
A Scottish Trajan's Column decorated with carved thistles which spiral up to a Corinthian-style capital, also with thistles, on which sits the Lion of Scotland, paw on a cannon ball. Around

the base are thistle, rose and *fleur-de-lis* motifs, a knight's helmet, bagpipes, cannon, swords and shields. The column rises from a Thomsonesque plinth with four eagles. A plaque is inscribed: 'The Battle of Langside was fought on this ground on 13 May 1568 between the forces of Mary Queen of Scots and the Regent Moray, and marked the Queen's final defeat in Scotland.' The monument was erected for the 300th anniversary of her execution.

439
Victoria Infirmary
517 Langside Road
Campbell Douglas & Sellars 1890
The original administration building, Renaissance-style with baroque belvederes, pairs of Ionic columns and the heraldry of Glasgow and Renfrewshire. On the gable the royal arms of Queen Victoria who laid the foundation stone in 1888. In the gable's curved pediment

is a puma representing, according to legend, medical care. The infirmary closed in 2015. Services were relocated to **New Victoria Hospital** (*HLM Architects 2009*) on Grange Road nearby and Govan (see 7). Some of the old buildings, including this one, are to be converted to flats.

Down Battlefield Road is **Battlefield Rest** (*Frank Burnet & Boston 1915*), 'the most exotic tram shelter in Scotland', like something escaped from a fairground. It is clad with tiles in the old Corporation colours, had a newsstand, washrooms and waiting room. In 1990 the then derelict building was spared demolition after a campaign to save it. The waiting room was rebuilt and reopened as an Italian restaurant in 1994. The corner with the clock is original.

At 2 Sinclair Drive is the Edwardian baroque **Langside Public Library** (*George Simpson 1915*), the last of 11 Carnegie libraries built in Glasgow. It was the first public library in the city to allow open access—users could browse for books rather than requesting them first from a librarian. The boundary wall has a plaque noting the Battle of Langside, the subject of a painting (1919) inside.

440
Hampden Park
Aikenhead Road
Scotland's National Stadium is home to Queen's Park Football Club, founded in 1867. The arena (1903) was for a time the biggest in the world, a super bowl with space for more than 100,000 spectators (150,000 at a Scotland v England game in 1937). New stands were built (1994, 1999) and the old South Stand rebuilt to create a 52,000 all-seat venue. There is a Museum and Hall of Fame. The North Stand was extended with a concourse (*Holmes Miller 2013*) and the stadium adapted temporarily with an artificial surface for athletics and the closing ceremony of the 2014 Commonwealth Games.

441
Wallace Scott & Co. Tailoring Institute
42 Spean Street
J. J. Burnet 1913–1916
Once a model factory with offices and workshops and a labour force of 800 mostly female workers employed to make clothing. It was built for Robert Wallace Forsyth of department store

chain R.W. Forsyth (see 220). Architecturally and socially it was a progressive project, in a garden city-style setting. Facilities for the staff included dining and concert halls, and recreation grounds by the White Cart Water.

The building is kin to early 20th-century factories in Germany and America, and to Burnet's steel-framed Kodak House (c. 1911), London. The concept was modernist, with classical proportions. Floors are open-plan with luminous windows; walls are brick with snappy decorative panels.

In 1957 the property was acquired by the South of Scotland Electricity Board, now Scottish Power which moved out in 2017 (see 244). Housing is planned for the site, with Burnet's building retained.

Nearby is SPX ClydeUnion Pumps, 149 Newlands Road, formerly **G. & J. Weir Engineering Works** (1886). Its 1912 office block was an American design *(Albert Kahn architect)* licensed from the Trussed Concrete Steel Company. An Art Deco amenity building is next door *(Wylie Shanks & Wylie 1937)*.

442
Cathcart Old Parish Church
Kilmailing Road
  c. 1830

Atmospheric Gothic ruin and graveyard with historic stones. A notable slab is inscribed with the names of three Covenanters captured by government dragoons at Polmadie in 1685, and that they were shot by the 'bloody murderers'; a typically mordant memorial to the 'killing times' of the 17th century. The church tower was left after the nave was torn down around the time a new church *(Henry Edward Clifford 1914)* was completed nearby on Carmunnock Road in 1929.

443
Castlemilk Stables
59 Machrie Road
  David Hamilton c. 1790; Elder &
  Cannon Architects 2007
An exemplary, multi-award-winning rehabilitation of a Georgian steading by Glasgow Building Preservation Trust and Cassiltoun Housing Association. The building, attributed to architect David Hamilton, was part of the Stuart family's Castlemilk Estate which was bought by Glasgow Corporation in 1938. The former landowner's

historic Castlemilk House was torn down in 1969. The steading was used by Glasgow Parks Department. In the 1990s it was abandoned, a roost for pigeons and prey to vandals. It was damaged by fire and the distinctive onion dome on the octagonal clock tower lost.

Castlemilk, one of the city's sprawling postwar housing schemes, didn't have much heritage apart from Carmunnock Village, a conservation area formerly part of Castlemilk Estate. The stables had potential as a community asset. The rehab, which followed a 10-year campaign to save the building, created a mixed-use facility. Historic fabric was repaired and the dome rebuilt. A luminous steel and glass cloister was built in the courtyard behind the dome. The intervention was needed to increase floor space, to make the adaptive reuse viable financially. As for the aesthetics, the distinction between old and new is clear, preserving the steading's historic character.

444
Cathkin Braes Wind Farm
Cathkin Road, Carmunnock
2013
A stand-alone 125-metre-high wind turbine at Cathkin Braes Country Park, the highest point in Glasgow. It

was promoted by the Castlemilk and Carmunnock Community Windpark Trust following a 2001 feasibility study by students of Glasgow Caledonian University. The project was delivered by Glasgow City Council and Scottish and Southern Electricity (SSE). It is the most visible product of Sustainable Glasgow, a council-led partnership set up in 2010 to make the city one of the greenest in Europe.

On the horizon to the south is Scottish Power Renewables **Whitelee Windfarm**, the largest onshore wind farm in the UK. Its 215 turbines on Eaglesham Moor have become an eco-tourism attraction. Sustainable design is a feature of its Visitor Centre *(Hypostyle Architects 2009)*.

445
Holmwood House
61–63 Netherlee Road
Alexander Thomson 1858
Just outside the city limits, above the valley of the White Cart, is the finest

example of 'Greek' Thomson's domestic work. In the early 1990s the site was saved from development: planning permission for infill housing was refused after heritage groups intervened. The National Trust for Scotland bought the property in 1994. An architectural survey *(Page\Park Architects)* was commissioned to guide restoration.

The style is Greek Revival of exceptional originality. Spatial sequences are unconventional with variations in scale and appointment in every room; technically innovative too—the parlour has a semi-circular plate glass window detached from the outer colonnade. Pundits have suggested that the built form of this and other villas by Thomson might have influenced Frank Lloyd Wright's Prairie Style.

Alterations by a convent school and other previous occupants have been reversed. Conservation is revealing and reinstating richly coloured décor which was inspired by classical themes. There are Greek-patterned stencilled walls, a dining room with a frieze of illustrations from the *Iliad*, and a staircase skylit from a cupola supported by chimeras of Greek mythology. The coach house is in the same style. There is a walled kitchen garden with herbs and vegetables that would have been cultivated at the time.

Holmwood House was built for James Couper, co-owner, with his elder brother Robert, of Millholm Paper Mills on the river below. Their name lives on at the **Couper Institute** *(James Sellars 1887)*, Scottish Renaissance style, at 84–86 Clarkston Road. There were mills along the White Cart in the 19th century. One remains here, now residential, below **Old Cathcart Bridge** (1624; rebuilt in the 18th century). The tenement by the bridge (1863) housed the mill owner and his workers. The bridge is on the White Cart Walkway, north of Holmwood.

The Trust also owns Charles Rennie Mackintosh's most complete domestic design, Hill House (1904) at Helensburgh west of Glasgow on the north bank of the Clyde.

House for an Art Lover

10

Paisley Road West to Pollokshields

FROM MAY TO OCTOBER 1938 the Empire Exhibition was held in Bellahouston Park. King George VI made the opening address to over 100,000 people in Ibrox Stadium and toured the expo site. During its six-month run more than 12.5 million visitors (including season ticket holders) were counted through the turnstiles despite the weather, which was dreich. Though the sun rarely shone, the buildings did. Imperial avenues gleamed with Art Deco and streamline moderne pavilions as good as anything built around the world at the time.

The festive architecture was in the tradition of the Glasgow International Exhibitions of 1888 and 1901 held in Kelvingrove Park, and for the same purpose—for pleasure and to promote the great city and its products. Among them were streamlined 'Coronation' trams which ran by the park gates on Paisley Road West and Mosspark Boulevard. The trams were named for the King's coronation in 1937 but designed and built for the expo. The imperial theme was driven by captains of industry keen to speed the city and its export trade out of a recession. The initiative was supported by the British Government and the Scottish Office. The logo was a Lion Rampant criss-crossed like tartan; the United Kingdom and Scotland had separate pavilions.

Architect Thomas Tait, a leading Scottish modernist and partner in J. J. Burnet's London practice, was appointed to lead the project and recruited its design team. Around 100 structures were prefabricated and erected for 700 exhibitors who showcased everything from arts and crafts to heavy industries. Landscape design featured water cascades and fountains. A restaurant shaped like a ship steamed out of Bellahouston Hill. On the summit was Tait's Tower of Empire, a futuristic 90-metre-high pinnacle with a viewing platform above the expo's fantastic white city. Illuminated at night, the tower shone like a beacon visible for miles around. It was symbolic. The British Empire had been built, administered and defended by significant numbers of Scots, and Glasgow had grown from trade with it. Bellahouston Park in 1938 seemed briefly the centre of it.

It took only ten months to build the expo and it vanished as quickly, like the empire after the Second World War and with it Glasgow's global prominence. The park was re-landscaped. One building from the exhibition survives here, the Palace of Art which was designed to be permanent. On the hill above it, near where the Tower of Empire stood, is a stone pillar commemorating the laying of the event's foundation stone by the King.

To mark the 70th anniversary of the expo, Glasgow School of Art's Digital Design Studio created a 3D model of the site and buildings. This was unveiled at another remarkable architectural project in the park—the construction from drawings of an unbuilt masterwork by Charles Rennie Mackintosh. The original design, by Mackintosh and Margaret Macdonald, was submitted in 1901 to a competition, organised by a German design magazine, for a *Haus eines Kunstfreundes* (House for an Art Lover). The replica was completed in 1996, in time for Glasgow's year as UK City of Architecture & Design 1999.

Bellahouston would have been a suitable site for the Burrell Collection, gifted to the city in 1944, but donor William Burrell stipulated his artworks be housed further away from urban air pollution. Burrell was an entrepreneurial shipowner who made his money from cargo ships which traded around the empire. He ordered new ships cheap during economic slumps, steamed them into boom times and sold them at a profit. He made a fortune. His art collection is one of the finest and most diverse in the world assembled by one person. A truly world-class museum for it opened in Pollok Country Park in 1983. The park is the largest in Glasgow. It was part of Pollok Estate, the ancestral home of the Maxwell family since the 13th century. In 1966 it was given to the city along with Pollok House, the family's Georgian stately home.

The nearby village of Pollokshaws was part of the Maxwell realm. Water power from the White Cart attracted industry, mainly cotton spinning and weaving. It became a burgh in 1812 and was annexed by Glasgow a century later. Comprehensive redevelopment in the 1960s left the townscape ravaged by a high-rise scheme, cleared by 2014 to make way for a development similar to the new tenements at Laurieston. The Maxwells also planned neighbouring Pollokshields, as a garden sub-urb. By 1910 it had evolved as two districts bisected by Shields Road. The east side is a grid of flat streets lined with handsome tenements and some shops. West Pollokshields (commerce banned from the start) is all leafy, rolling avenues with Victorian and Edwardian villas each with its own garden, often a large one. A public park (Maxwell Park) was laid out on land gifted by the Maxwells, and Pollokshields Burgh Halls built in Scottish Renaissance style. The suburb was self-consciously pic-turesque—no two houses were to be built to the same plan. There is a medley of styles: Italianate, Arts and Crafts, Tudor and Scots Baronial.

Pollokshields East and West were designated as conservation areas in 1973, among the earliest of more than 25 citywide. This appreciation of the city's Victorian architecture was a turning point after decades of neglect and demolitions. The phenomenal revival of Glasgow as an international centre of culture owes much to the city's wonderful archi-tectural heritage and those who campaigned to save it.

446
Angel Building
Paisley Road Toll
Bruce & Hay 1889

Attention-seeking commercial block on the gushet at Paisley Road West and Govan Road, built for mail order retailers Ogg Brothers as a clothing and drapery warehouse. Loose-fitting Renaissance style with a showy *chapeau*. The angel with a star on its head represents Commerce and Industry *(James Alexander Ewing sculptor)*.

447
The Old Toll Bar
1–3 Paisley Road West
1892

One of Glasgow's finest Victorian pub interiors. The long bar has a wooden gantry with whisky casks flanking an antique clock in a pediment decorated with scrollwork, all reflected in gilded advertising mirrors by Forest & Son

of Glasgow. The bar, sited typically on the ground floor corner of a tenement (c. 1860), takes its name from Paisley Road Toll, the intersection outside.

Also here is the **Grand Ole Opry**, a country and western club in a former cinema (1921) by William Beresford Inglis, owner of the Beresford Hotel (see 287). Auditorium and stage now with Wild West murals and props.

448
Kingston Halls
344 Paisley Road West
Alexander Beith McDonald, City Engineer 1904

An Edwardian baroque edifice ma-
rooned in a desolate setting, deprived
of the community that gave it purpose.
A common sight in Glasgow after
the wrecking balls of comprehensive
redevelopment hit neighbourhoods in
the 1960s. Kingston and, to the west,
Kinning Park were devastated by the
m8 motorway. The building contained
public halls, a police station and a
Carnegie library, all behind a façade of
decorative rhetoric *(McGilvray & Ferris
sculptors)*: St. Mungo, cameos of local
worthies, and a statue of Learning
above the library door.

449
Kinning Park Pumping Station
100 Seaward Street
 *Glasgow Corporation, D. & A. Home
 Morton engineers 1910*
Monumental brick façade, white-
glazed inside, windows arched with
Roman grandeur. Brickwork very
finely laid. Rippling parapet on
Milnpark Street. The partly skylit
full-height machinery hall housed two
marine steam engines and pumps, later
electrified. Single-storey brick office on
Seaward Street. The complex was built
by Glasgow Corporation as a substa-

tion for Shieldhall Sewage Works, both
now operated by Scottish Water.

450
Walmer Crescent
 Alexander Thomson 1862
Built as an upmarket three-storey and
basement terrace but essentially tenements in a curved elevation with two
wings. Recessed doorways, rectilinear
two-storey bays, a continuous hood
moulding and a top-floor colonnade
emphasise the play of light and shade,
a typical Thomson quality. Cast iron
railings remain in situ.

Originally there was a segment-
shaped garden between the crescent
and Paisley Road West. In 1908 a
single-storey parade of shops was

inserted. The entrance to Cessnock Subway Station (1896) burrows into the crescent's east wing.

451
Bellahouston Academy
423 Paisley Road West
Robert Baldie 1876

Scots Baronial meets Loire château— the Auld Alliance in architecture. The composition, with its Frenchified roof-line, bartizans, crow-step gables, and clock tower above a Gothic doorway, owes much to George Gilbert Scott's Glasgow University (see 313).

The school was private but not profitable. It was bought in 1885 by Govan School Board which added a swimming pool, one of the first in Scotland, now derelict. The baronial block became an annex after the academy relocated in 1962. Declared surplus in 2008, it was rehabilitated in 2015 as Bellahouston Business Centre. Typical school board skylit atrium refurbished as the centre's reception area.

452
GalGael Trust
15 Fairley Street

GalGael was launched in Govan in 1997 to break the cycle of unemployment and the depression and addiction it can cause. And what better way to revive skills, self-esteem and a sense of purpose in a community with a shipbuilding heritage than building and sailing boats? Beautiful, traditional Scottish hand-crafted wooden boats. The workshop is a no-frills shed. The office is on the ground floor of a sail loft (1896) which has a wooden hammer beam roof, in section visible on the gable end, part of Govan's early industrial architecture preserved.

453
Ibroxholm Oval
Edmiston Drive
Glasgow Corporation 1962; 3D Reid Architects 2013

An energy-efficient retrofit saved this concrete tower block, one of a trio that was to be demolished (the other two were). Glasgow Housing Association, aided by the Scottish Government's Innovation and Investment Fund, refurbished it for mid-market rent to key workers, notably staff at Queen Elizabeth University Hospital (see 7).

The building envelope was reconfigured and reclad with rainscreen and thermal-performance technology. A combined heat and power (CHP) system was fitted. GHA's estimate that the project would be 'fifteen times more carbon efficient than producing a like number of new-build properties' supports the notion that the most sustainable building is the one you already have.

454
Glasgow Climbing Centre
534 Paisley Road West
Angus Kennedy 1868; 1994

Former Ibrox United Presbyterian Church repurposed with mountainous practice walls as high as the Gothic wood-beamed roof. The original stained-glass window remains in place. The nave had no aisles which made the unconventional adaptive reuse doable.

455
Ibrox Park
100–170 Edmiston Drive
Archibald Leitch & Partners 1928

Rangers Football Club played its first game on Glasgow Green in 1872 and was founded officially the following year. It moved to Ibrox in 1887 and to this site in 1899. The stadium was a bowl of terraces, now all-seat stands. Brick and glass-block stair wings were added in the 1980s, and a steel-trussed top deck to the old stand. The 1928 brick façade is energetic with arches. Ibrox has historical presence, rare in the modern game where stadia get makeovers and sponsors' names. It is one of the few in the UK to be heritage-listed. Original letters 'Rangers F.C.' shout above the entrance.

456

Moss Heights

Moss Heights Avenue

Ronald Bradbury & Archibald
George Jury, Glasgow Corporation
F. A. Macdonald & Partners engineers
1950–1953

457

Palace of Art

Bellahouston Park

Thomas Tait & Launcelot Ross 1938
Built for the Empire Exhibition of
1938 and the only one of the expo's
pavilions intended to be permanent.

The city's first high-rise scheme and
the first to be built for families. The
reinforced concrete slab blocks stand
on a windy ridge but were oriented to
avoid the worst of the weather prevailing from the west (windows face north
and south).

In 1983 the scheme stood in for a
grim, high density Soviet suburb in
the BBC spy drama *An Englishman
Abroad*. In reality Moss Heights
featured spacious 'modern luxury flats'
with 'all modern amenities', including
fitted kitchens and central heating.
The elevations were animated above
each entrance with concave balconies,
removed during an upgrade by Glasgow Housing Association (2011–2013)
and replaced with glazed sunspaces.
The flat roofs had been altered previously with gratuitous postmodern
pods. The project was and remains a
symbol of postwar hope and progress.

The others were scrapped after the
event (the Palace of Engineering
survived, relocated to Prestwick
Airport and is still there). Most were
Art Deco or streamline moderne. The
Palace of Art is essentially classical,
with a glazed portico to the foyer and
galleries around a courtyard garden.
The horizontal emphasis and glazing
are modernist. The building was to
have been a gallery for artworks in the
municipal collection but was converted
in 1951 as a community sports and
recreation centre.

Architect Tait designed the masterplan for the event and its most famous
and visible structure. This was the
Tower of Empire, better known as
Tait's Tower, a slim, steel-framed skyscraper with an observation deck. After
the expo it was torn down, said to be a
likely landmark for German bombers,
an urban myth.

458
House for an Art Lover
Bellahouston Park

Charles Rennie Mackintosh 1901;
Andy MacMillan, GSA School of
Architecture 1989–1996

After Mackintosh and Margaret
Macdonald visited the Vienna Secession Exhibition of 1900 they entered a
competition, *Haus eines Kunstfreundes*
(House for an Art Lover), organised by
a German publisher. Their submission
was incomplete and disqualified but its
14 Art Nouveau design drawings were
given a special prize.

Almost a century later the drawings,
in the archive at the Hunterian Gallery
(see 325), inspired engineer Graham
Roxburgh to build this revival. Details,
like the Tree of Life bas-relief on the
south elevation, and massing reflect the
original concept; some of the interiors
too, notably the Music Room.

The house is a popular events venue
and was a catalyst for improvements
to the setting, which was landscaped

and decorated with public art. An art
centre opened recently (next entry).

459
Art Park Pavilion
Bellahouston Park

ZM Architecture 2014

The Art Park is an arts and heritage
centre in the former Ibroxhill House
stables and dovecot buildings next to
the House for an Art Lover. The Art
Pavilion abuts the masonry of the
Victorian Walled Garden. Modern it
may be but its materials complement
the setting. The dome is a prominent
feature, angled and skylit for north
light, and there is a picture window
inserted in the garden wall.

460

Ibroxhill House Portico

Bellahouston Park

Ibroxhill estate was bought by the city in 1903 to augment the park which had been established in 1895. This classical portico is a fragment of Ibroxhill House (c. 1800; demolished 1914). It is now a gateway to the sculpture garden at the House for an Art Lover.

461

Garden for a Plant Collector

Gross Max landscape design 2008

By an old bothy at the southwest door of the Victorian Walled Garden is this minimalist, ethereal glass box. Its ferns and carnivorous plants are cultivated with fibre optics which provide ultra-violet light to encourage growth.

462

Dumbreck Court

20 and 40 Dumbreck Court

Archibald George Jury city architect 1968–1972

Sudden high-rise drama on the

southeast edge of Bellahouston Park. Several walk-up blocks were built as part of the scheme which is typical of the 1960s. It contrasts with **Mosspark**, an interwar council housing estate on the other side of Mosspark Boulevard. Mosspark's two-storey, semi-detached, gabled houses with gardens were laid out on tree-lined streets in the pictur-esque garden city manner.

North of the towers is **Hazelwood Conservation Area**, with Arts and Crafts bungalows designed c. 1914. Some retain wood-bracketed porches, stained glass and other period details. They were completed in the early 1920s on the grounds of **Hazelwood House** *(James Milne Munro 1882)*, a Jacobean-style villa which remains the neigh-bourhood's focal point.

463

Hazelwood School

50 Dumbreck Court

Alan Dunlop Architect, Buro Happold engineers, City Design Co-op land-scape design 2007

A serpentine design with classrooms and a corridor for circulation, all on ground level weaving around the landscape to preserve existing trees. Natural materials were sourced, sympathetic to the setting and a sustainable agenda. The learning environment created is both soothing and stimulating for students and staff.

Hazelwood replaced two special needs schools run by city council. Consultation between the client, architect, teachers, parents and health professionals produced a building completely responsive to the children and young people with visual, hearing or physical impairments who use it.

The structure is a glulam (glue-laminated) timber frame. Larch siding and reclaimed slate were used for cladding. The eco-friendly and energy-saving measures are simple—energy-efficient heating, natural ventilation, daylighting with timber louvres to reduce solar glare and heat gain. The roof is zinc which allowed a low pitch and the building to nestle in the landscape, which includes play areas. Tactile natural materials help children who rely on their sense of touch to navigate.

Hazelwood has been recognised as an exemplar and won national and international awards. The architect, chosen

by competition, had not designed a school before. The project shows there is no substitute for open minds, good clients, talent and teamwork—and that there is no reason why the less fortunate in society do not deserve the best. In the architecture here they have it.

464
Craigholme School Sports Facility
97 Haggs Road
SMC Davis Duncan Architects 2007

A sports hall wrapped with a clear span of curved glulam beams supporting an aluminium roof. The timber beams are anchored internally on the north side of the wood-floored hall and supported on an exterior colonnade of steel struts to the south. There is natural light. Walls are clad with larch, contextual to the setting on the edge of Pollok Country Park. The structural display is a delight.

'Engineered timber' is a sustainable alternative to steel or concrete. To date, the tallest timber structure planned for Glasgow (and Scotland) is a seven-storey cross laminated timber (CLT) block of flats *(MAST Architects, CCG Scotland 2017)* for Sanctuary Scotland Housing Association.

465

Haggs Gate

Haggs Road

ZM Architecture 2010

The name of the road and this apartment development recall Haggs Castle (see 472). The architecture is enhanced by an art installation inspired by the adjacent Pollok Country Park. Tree patterns are rendered on four large glass panels *(Patricia Cain, Alec Galloway artists)* integrated with the rectilinear façades.

466

Pollok House

Pollok Country Park, 2060 Pollokshaws Road

William Adam, John Adam 1747–1752; Robert Rowand Anderson 1892–1908

A gracefully-proportioned Georgian country house attributed to Adam *père et fils*. The setting, only five kilometres from the city centre, is bucolic. The White Cart Water flows past the front lawn. The single-track carriage way from Pollokshaws Road passes through woodland, and fields with Highland cattle.

The mansion was refurbished in Edwardian country house style for John Stirling Maxwell, whose architect, Robert Rowand Anderson, added an entrance hall to the north façade, twin Palladian pavilions and electric lighting. The property was donated to the city in 1966. The plush salons where

the Maxwells relaxed and the servants' quarters and kitchen have been restored since 1998 by the National Trust for Scotland, to recall upstairs/downstairs life as it was around 1930.

Other notable features on the former Maxwell estate include **Pollok Steading** (18th century; Renaissance gateway 17th); the water-powered **Pollok Sawmill** (mid 19th century) and **Pollok Bridge** (1757), an elegant span crossing the river. In the 20th century the sawmill generated electricity for Pollok House. The **Gatehouse** (*R. R. Anderson 1891*) is at Pollokshaws Road.

467

The Burrell Collection
Pollok Country Park, 2060 Pollokshaws Road

Barry Gasson, Brit Andresen, John Meunier architects, F. J. Samuely & Partners engineers 1978–1983

For 40 years visitors to the Art Galleries at Kelvingrove saw a selection of beguiling items labelled 'Burrell Collection'. It was a mysterious hoard—everything from Chinese antiquities to French Impressionist paintings—not well known until this gallery for it was built.

William Burrell was a Glasgow shipowner and collector who bequeathed around 9,000 artworks to the city in 1944. He required they be displayed away from the urban smog of the time. In 1966 Pollok Park became available thanks to the generosity of the Maxwell family whose estate it was. Postwar clean air regulations fixed the pollution problem. In 1971 a design competition was held. The winning entry accommodated the diverse collection sympathetically and responded intelligently to the site, a meadow with woodland on two sides.

The original entrance pavilion is stone clad, vernacular, perpendicular to an atrium in the style of a Victorian sculpture court, a surprise as the spatial sequence is throughout. Circulation is focussed around the building envelope, with cross-corridors for orientation and access to areas where conservation requires low light. Along the north edge, floor to ceiling glass dissolves the conventional indoor/outdoor relationship, the woods outside like a mural as if part of the collection. The structure's materials—laminated timber, steel and stone—are a comfortable fit with Burrell's medieval stone

doorways which were integrated into the building's fabric. You walk through them, their history alive.

In 2016 the Burrell was closed until

2020 for an extensive makeover *(John McAslan + Partners, Event Communications, Gardiner & Theobald LLP).* The renewal is needed to fix a leaky roof, replace glazing, modernise systems and reduce the building's carbon footprint. Spatial interventions will allow more of the collection to be shown than the 20 percent displayed at any one time previously, and accommodate 21st-century interpretation of it.

The original architecture still seems contemporary, free of stylistic polemics. It was A-listed by Historic Scotland in 2013. Unlike the 'iconic' museums of recent times the Burrell was a model of restraint and tranquillity created to serve the collection and the setting, not the egos of the architects.

468

Pollokshaws West Station

2092 Pollokshaws Road

1848; Richard Shorter architect 2013

The oldest railway station in Glasgow still in passenger use. It was refurbished by Glasgow Building Preservation Trust with South West Community Cycles as a cycling resource centre and bike repair workshop. The project was part of ScotRail's Adopt a Station initiative, as was the community space at Maxwell Park Station (see 478).

469

The Round Toll

1 Barrhead Road

c. 1750

Trapped on a traffic circle about 300 metres south of Pollokshaws West Station is this perfectly circular stone tollhouse. Until the 1830s drovers, horsemen, farm and other vehicles (except stagecoaches) were charged by the tollkeeper a fee to proceed.

470

Pollokshaws Burgh Halls

2025 Pollokshaws Road

Robert Rowand Anderson 1898
Hybrid historicism, mainly 17th-century Scottish Renaissance inspired by the Old College on High Street, which had been sold by Glasgow University and demolished. Architect Anderson was moved to commemorate it by replicating some of its features here, notably the clock tower, and carvings around the Palladian window in the crow-step gable.

Construction and upkeep of the halls were funded by the philanthropic John Stirling Maxwell, laird of Pollok House. He gave the building to Glasgow in 1912, when the Burgh of Pollokshaws was annexed by the city (as was Pollokshields).

He was jailed for sedition, having campaigned against the First World War, which cost him his job as a teacher in Pollokshaws. The cairn, erected on the 50th anniversary of his death, is engraved: 'In memory of John Maclean . . . Famous pioneer of working-class education. He forged the Scottish link in the golden chain of world socialism.'

Standing like a classical folly on the plaza is the **Clock Tower** (1803) of Pollokshaws Town House, the only part saved from demolition in 1931.

In 2000 Pollokshaws Burgh Hall Trust rescued the building for public use again after it had been derelict for a decade.

471
John Maclean Monument
McArthur Street
1973
A granite cairn, the only monument in Glasgow to Pollokshaws-born John MacLean, a graduate of Glasgow University, republican and Red Clydesider.

472
Haggs Castle
100 St. Andrew's Drive
c. 1585

A 16th-century tower house much altered, originally built by the Maxwells, who abandoned it after Pollok House opened. The ground floor was used in the mid 19th century as a smithy for a nearby coal mine. Around 1850 it was restored as a lodge for Pollok Estate's factor. The military occupied it during the Second World War. It was bought by the city in 1972 and housed the Museum of Childhood until sold in 1998 and returned to residential use, privately owned.

271

473
Marlaw
130 Springkell Avenue
Gareth Hoskins Architects 2012

A steel-framed modernist house on the edge of West Pollokshields Conservation Area, with a striking, cantilevered room above the entrance. The intent was to match the *fin-de-siècle* villas of Pollokshields but not look like them. It occupies part of the old orchard garden of **Beneffrey** *(Leiper & McNab 1910)*, 124 Springkell Avenue, a baronial mansion, one of the last built in the area. At 110 Springkell Avenue is the Arts and Crafts style **Kelmscott** *(John Nisbet 1903)*. The client was property developer and house builder J. A. Mactaggart. The name was chosen for its association with Kelmscott Manor, the Cotswold house of William Morris.

474
Dunholme
112 Hamilton Avenue
James Miller 1909

Picturesque English-style Arts and Crafts manor house influenced by the inventive revivalism of Edwin Lutyens. Asymmetrical arrangement of gables and axial chimney stacks on steeply pitched roofs, and deep eaves, casement windows and a superb Renaissance doorway. The house was built for surgeon Duncan McCorkindale of the Royal Infirmary.

475
Corrieston
23 Sherbrooke Avenue
1893

Italianate villa with a characteristic tower and original cast iron finial. The wrought iron main gate flanked by stone pillars, the gravel driveway and garden preserve the 19th-century ambiance. Built for timber merchant Alexander Bruce and bought in 1923 by J. W. Whyte, proprietor of the Horse Shoe Bar (see 211). Later the home of John Ritchie Richmond, art collector and a deputy chairman of G. & J. Weir Engineering Works, Cathcart.

Next door at 21 Sherbrooke Avenue is **Balmory** *(William James Anderson c. 1893)*, an Arts and Crafts villa with a distinctive drum tower. At 17 Sherbrooke Avenue is **Sherbrooke House** (c. 1892), Scots Baronial with a French tower, part of Pollokshield's delightful domestic architectural mélange.

476
Sherbrooke Castle Hotel
11 Sherbrooke Avenue
Thomson & Sandilands 1896
Architect John Thomson was a son of

'Greek' Thomson. Nothing could be further astray from the father's classicism than this nouveau-riche dream of aristocracy. The baronial pile was built for John Morrison of Morrison & Mason, contractors whose projects ranged from docks on the Clyde to the City Chambers. His business partner, Thomas Mason, owned the Italianate **Craigie Hall** *(John Honeyman 1872)* at 6 Rowan Road (off Dumbreck Road). In the 1930s Morrison's mansion became a hotel. During the Second World War it was a Royal Navy training centre.

477
Ardtornish
30 Sutherland Avenue
James Miller 1892

Tudor Revival villa with stucco gables, each half-timbered with a different pattern. Pitched roofs, typically tall chimney stacks, and an open loggia with the front door facing a mature garden. Subdivided as flats, a market-led intervention approved by planners here and elsewhere to preserve former single-family heritage homes.

478
Maxwell Park Station
Terregles Avenue, Fotheringay Road
1894

Chalet-style station, one of ten built by the Caledonian Railway on the Cathcart Circle. The line promoted real estate development on the Southside in the late 19th century. The station here departed from the single-storey template, being two storeys with a pedestrian bridge through the upper level, which was the ticket office and station master's house. The bridge connects the station to residential streets on both sides of the railway, electrified in 1962. The stations were subsequently de-staffed and demolished, bar a few. The ticket office here was rehabilitated by Pollokshields Heritage as a community rendezvous and exhibition space.

At Fotheringay and Beaton roads is the **Fotheringay Centre**, a refurbishment of Pollokshields United Reformed Church *(Steele & Balfour 1903)* for the congregation and Hutchesons' Grammar School. An extension *(Davis Duncan Architects 2003)* for the school quotes from the old church with clarity and respect.

479
Pollokshields Burgh Hall
70 Glencairn Drive, Maxwell Park
Henry Edward Clifford 1890

A Scottish Renaissance castle to warm the heart of any patriot. The land for it and the park were donated by John Stirling Maxwell, one of the founding members of The National Trust for Scotland.

A turreted mock tower house rises behind the entrance which has the Maxwell coat of arms, the date of construction and lions above the door. There are period interiors, notably the main hall which has a Palladian window with stained glass *(Oscar Paterson artist)* commissioned by Maxwell. The building was variously the burgh hall, a Masonic hall, a court room, council offices, and rehearsal rooms for the Glasgow Orpheus Club. In 1982 it was sold by the city for £1 to Pollokshields Burgh Hall Trust which restored it as a multi-use venue in 1997.

Nearby, also by architect Clifford, is **Somersby** (1902) at 31 Dalziel Drive, a gabled and turreted Arts and Crafts villa, one of the finest in Pollokshields.

480
Moray Place
Alexander Thomson c. 1860

The architectural jewel of Strathbungo, which was a village on Pollokshaws Road absorbed by Glasgow in 1891. The two-storey terrace has a full-length

colonnade on the upper level with delicately carved anthemion and Greek key patterns. All scholarly, as 'Greek' Thomson was, yet there is delight in the way the decoration, and lotus-shaped chimney pots, are applied.

Pedimented pavilions balanced the elevation until an extension was added in 1900 to 1 Moray Place, originally Thomson's family home. Few architects live and work in buildings they design. Thomson did—he was the designer and developer and this was his first speculative project.

481
Salisbury Quadrant
Nithsdale Drive
c. 1880

Greek Revival tenement with a continuous hood moulding which could be by

'Greek' Thomson. Attributed to Robert Turnbull, who was taken into partnership by Thomson in 1874. Thomson died the following year. The design was probably completed by Turnbull.

Also enjoyably Thomsonesque is **Pollokshields West Free Church** (*McKissack & Rowan 1879*), an Ionic-columned temple with an eccentric baroque tower commanding the corner of Shields and Nithsdale roads.

482
The Knowe
301 Albert Drive
Alexander Thomson 1853

An Italianate Romanesque villa by Thomson as if on a journey through time to the Mediterranean and classical world which became his obsession. The garden was altered in the 1970s when apartments were built, and the villa subdivided as flats in 1996. The driveway curves up from a gateway and lodge also designed by Thomson.

483

Pollokshields Church of Scotland
525 Shields Road

Robert Baldie 1878

Gothic Revival with a clock tower
and spire at Albert Drive and Shields
Road. Conventional interior plan
with arcaded side aisles to the nave.
Outstanding medieval, Renaissance
and Pre-Raphaelite-style stained glass
*(Stephen Adam, Robert Anning Bell and
W. & J. Keir).* Outside is the congregation's War Memorial *(Peter Macgregor
Chalmers 1921)*, a granite cross with
biblical carvings.

484

Millar & Lang Art Publishing House
48 Darnley Street

Gordon & Dobson 1902

A mermaid and cherub decorate the
façade; a dragon drinks from a drain
pipe; a nymph scans the sky. There is
a decorative panel with Neptune and
a sailing ship, and a wonderful wally
close. Halfway up the stair is an oculus
with a stained-glass Venus on a swan,
after Botticelli. Seagulls, flying fish
and whales decorate the glass screen
(William Gibson Morton artist) to
Millar & Lang's former office. The
company specialised in art and post-
card publishing but nothing rolled out
on their printing presses matched the
weird, marine-themed Art Nouveau
décor here.

Nearby, at 80 McCulloch Street, is
a new healthcare facility, **The Shields
Centre** *(Anderson Bell + Christie 2015)*.
It enhances the streetscape with a
classical colonnade and Corten steel

privacy screens *(Alex Hamilton artist)*
perforated with patterns of plants
chosen by local people.

485

Scotland Street School
225 Scotland Street

Charles Rennie Mackintosh;
Honeyman, Keppie & Mackintosh
1903–1906

Mackintosh's most inventive interpretation of Scots Baronial style. The

who would use his buildings. The play-ground's iron fence swoops between shallow-arched stone gateways. Like the gateways, the infants' entrance and aspects of the interior respond sensitively to young people's stature. The janitor's house (with a gable in the Voysey manner) looks like a child's drawing.

The Dumfriesshire stone applied to the school was not Mackintosh's choice (his presentation drawing, in the Hunterian collection, shows a paler finish). But the building is more or less as he intended, despite a cost-conscious client and a dispute over plans and details. Decorative stonework *(McGilvray & Ferris sculptors),* thought to symbolise the Tree of Knowledge, survived the board's scrutiny.

Scotland Street School was designed for 1,200 pupils; when it closed in 1979 there were 89 on the roll. It was threatened with demolition after its tenement community was bulldozed to make way for the M8 motorway. Mackintosh was not then the architectural pin-up he is now, except to the *cognoscenti.* After they protested city council mothballed the building. It is now **Scotland Street School Museum**. There is a Mackintosh room where visitors can see how the building evolved.

front elevation is a *tour de force*—big windows to the assembly hall on the ground floor and to classrooms, semi-circular stair towers with leaded glass and conical caps, a top floor like a loggia and ventilation stacks with spider finials on the roof.

There are separate entrances and stairs for boys and girls and a door for infants, customary school board features. No traditional galleried light well though, simply corridors for circulation. The stair towers are exceptional, their transparency seeming to anticipate modernism almost two decades before it happened. However, the source was probably Falkland Palace (16th century) which Mackintosh had sketched . . . drawing and memory stimulating subsequent work.

Mackintosh was empathetic to those

Maps

Each tour 1–10 has its own map, shown above; maps 1 & 3 are in two sections.
Buildings are indicated by their entry numbers on the maps.
Pictograms mark subway 🚇 *and train* 🚆 *stations.*

3.1

Springburn Road

M80

n & Clyde
l

M8

6

3

Glasgow

5

4

Edinburgh Road

2

Gallowgate

M74

London Road

Dalmarnock Road

kshaws
Road

Cathcart Road

White Cart
Water

N

1 km

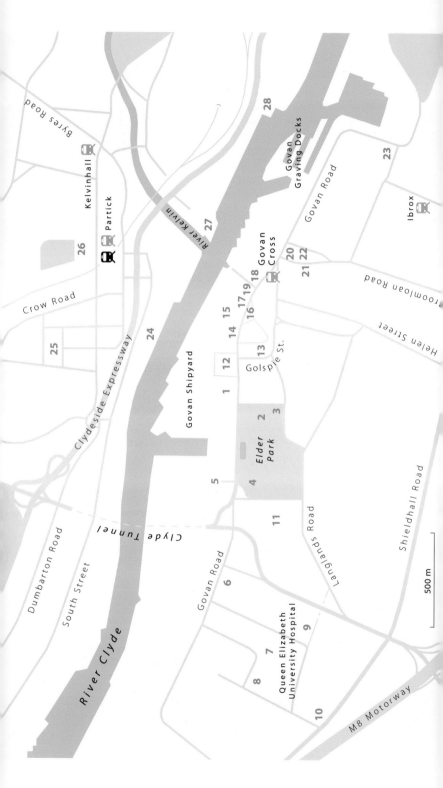

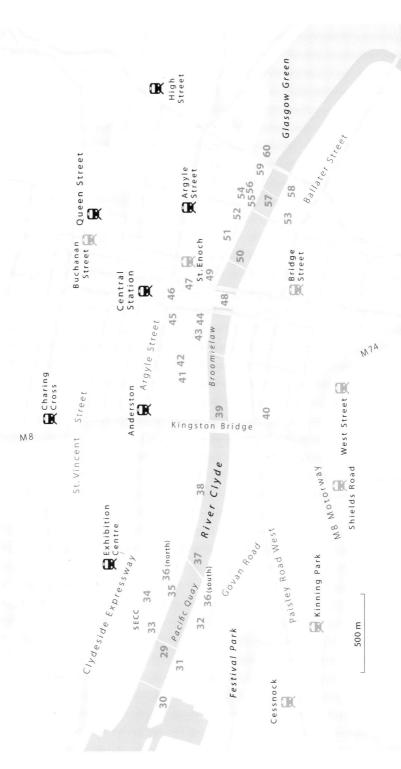

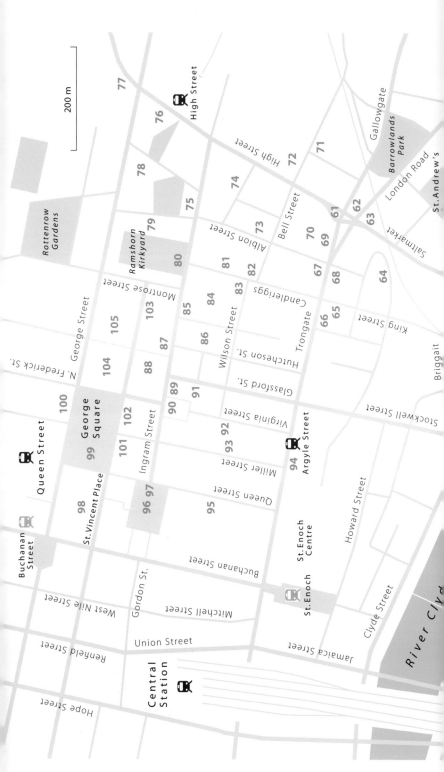

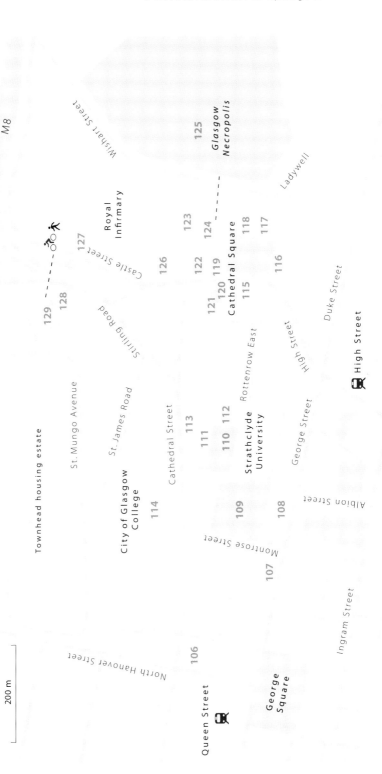

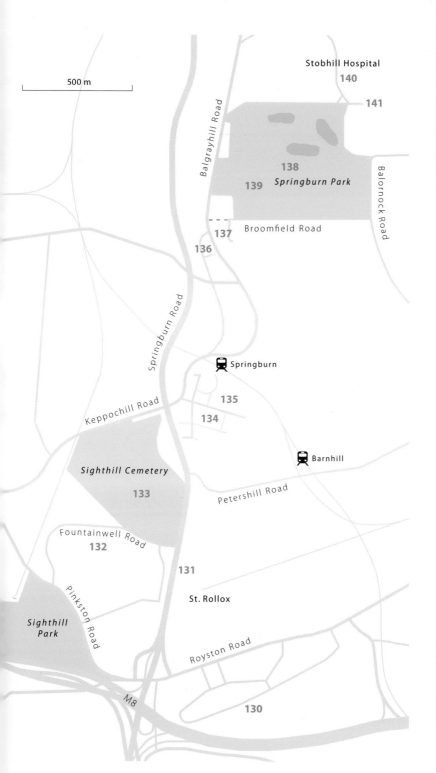

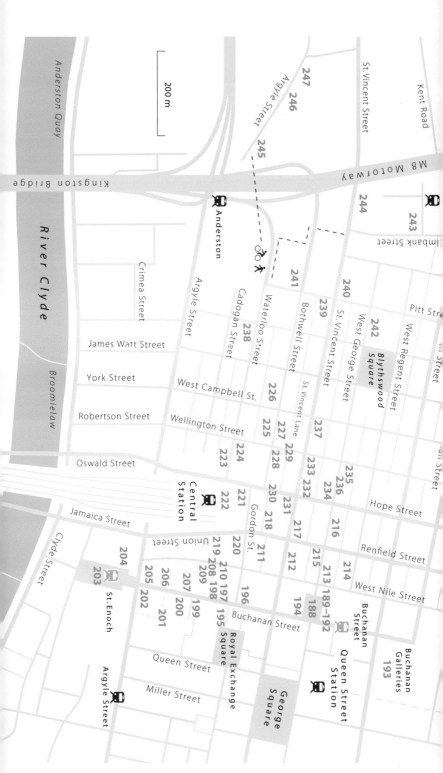

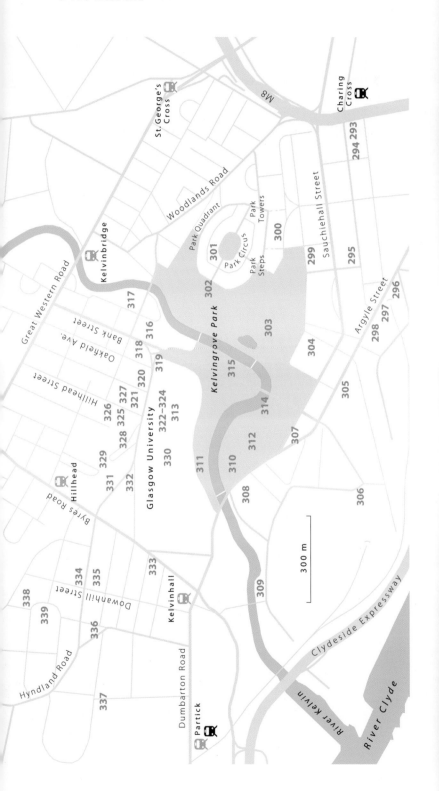

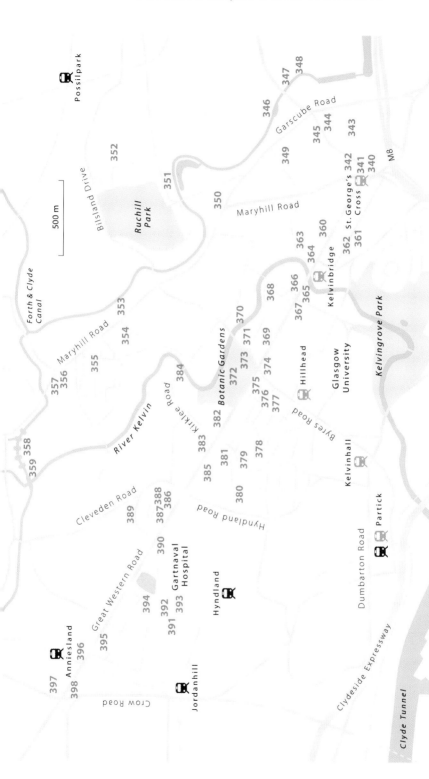

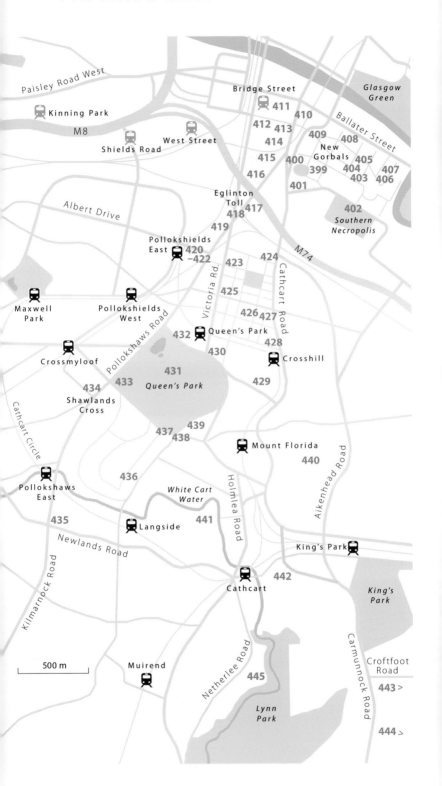

Further reading & references

For a glossary see **www.lookingatbuildings.org.uk**; for biographies see the *Dictionary of Scottish Architects* **www.scottisharchitects.org.uk** and architects' websites.

Charles Rennie Mackintosh Society **www.crmsociety.com**

Fairfield Heritage Centre **www.fairfieldgovan.co.uk**

www.glasgowarchitecture.co.uk

Glasgow Building Preservation Trust **www.gbpt.org**

Glasgow City Heritage Trust **www.glasgowheritage.org.uk**

www.glasgow.gov.uk walking/heritage trails

Glasgow Institute of Architects **www.gia.org.uk**

Glasgow Museums **www.glasgowlife.org.uk/museums**

www.glasgowsculpture.com

www.theglasgowstory.com

Glasgow Women's Library **www.womenslibrary.org.uk**

Historic Environment Scotland **www.historicenvironment.scot**

Mackintosh Architecture: Context, Making and Meaning
    www.mackintosh-architecture.gla.ac.uk

The Mitchell Library **www.glasgowlife.org.uk/libraries/the-mitchell-library**

The National Trust for Scotland **www.nts.org.uk**

Royal Incorporation of Architects in Scotland **www.rias.org.uk**

www.saltiresociety.org.uk

www.scottishcivictrust.org.uk

www.urbanrealm.com

Buchanan, William. *Mackintosh's Masterwork: The Glasgow School of Art.* London: A. & C. Black/Glasgow School of Art Press 2004

Donnelly, Michael. *Glasgow Stained Glass: a preliminary study.* Glasgow: Glasgow Museums and Art Galleries 1981

Glendinning, Miles, Ranald MacInnes & Aonghus MacKechnie. *A History of Scottish Architecture: From the Renaissance to the Present Day.* Edinburgh: Edinburgh University Press 1996

Gomme, Andor, & David Walker. *Architecture of Glasgow.* London: Lund Humphries 1968; revised edition Lund Humphries/John Smith & Sons 1987

Hayes, Nick. *Building Knowledge: An Architectural History of the University of Glasgow.* Edinburgh: Historic Scotland/University of Glasgow 2013

Macaulay, James. *Charles Rennie Mackintosh.* New York: W. W. Norton & Co. 2010

McKenzie, Ray, with Gary Nisbet. *Public Sculpture of Glasgow.* Liverpool: Liverpool University Press 2002

Molleson, Kate ed. *Dear Green Sounds: Glasgow's music through time and buildings.* Glasgow: Waverley Books/Glasgow UNESCO City of Music 2015

Stamp, Gavin. *Alexander Thomson: The Unknown Genius.* London: Laurence King 1999

Williamson, Elizabeth, Anne Riches & Malcolm Higgs. *The Buildings of Scotland: Glasgow.* London: Penguin Books 1990

Index

Designers and buildings are indexed with the **entry numbers** (not page numbers) where they appear. Main entries are **highlighted**.